LAUGHTER, PAIN, AND WONDER

LAUGHTER, PAIN, AND WONDER

*Shakespeare's Comedies
and the Audience in the Theater*

David Richman

DELAWARE

Newark: University of Delaware Press
London and Toronto: Associated University Presses

Associated University Presses
440 Forsgate Drive
Cranbury, NJ 08512

Associated University Presses
25 Sicilian Avenue
London WC1A 2QH, England

Associated University Presses
P.O. Box 488, Port Credit
Mississauga, Ontario
Canada L5G 4M2

The paper used in this publication meets the requirements of the American National Standard for Permanence of Paper for Printed Library Materials Z39.48-1984.

Library of Congress Cataloging-in-Publication Data

Richman, David. 1951–
    Laughter, pain, and wonder : Shakespeare's comedies and the audience in the theater / David Richman.
        p.   cm.
    Includes bibliographical references (p.   ).
    ISBN 0-87413-388-2 (alk. paper)
    1. Shakespeare, William, 1564–1616—Comedies.   2. Shakespeare, William, 1564–1616—Stage history—1950–   3. Shakespeare, William, 1564–1616—Dramatic production.   4. Theater audiences.   5. Comic, The.   I. Title.
PR2981.R47   1990
822.3'3—dc20   89-40413
                                                            CIP

PRINTED IN THE UNITED STATES OF AMERICA

For Susan, Sam, and Beatrice

Assuredly the Englishman who without reverence, who without a proud and affectionate reverence, can utter the name of Shakespeare stands disqualified for the office. He wants one, at least, of the very senses, the language of which he is to employ, and will discourse, at best, but as a blind man, while the whole, harmonious creation of light and shade, with all its subtle interchange of deepening and dissolving colours rises in silence to the silent fiat of the uprising Apollo. However inferior in ability to some who have followed me, I am proud that I was the first in time who publicly demonstrated to the full extent of the position that the supposed irregularity and extravagances of Shakespeare were the mere dreams of a pedantry that arraigned the eagle because it had not the dimensions of a swan. . . . It has been and it still remains my object to prove that in all points from the most important to the most minute, the judgment of Shakespeare is commensurate with his genius: nay, that his genius reveals itself in his judgment as in its most exalted form.

—Samuel Taylor Coleridge, 1817

CONTENTS

ACKNOWLEDGMENTS

THEATER IS A COLLABORATIVE ART. IT IS A PLEASURE to acknowledge my continuing obligation to the scores of actors, designers and other theater artists, student and professional, with whom I collaborate in productions of Shakespeare and other dramatists.

I would like to thank Jay Halio and Elizabeth Reynolds of the University of Delaware Press and Lauren Lepow, Michael Koy, and Leslie Foley of Associated University Presses. Grateful thanks are also due to Jennifer Gilkie and Kim Bond, and especially to Nandita Batra, for assistance with the reading and research.

The research was funded in part by a grant from the American Philosophical Society, to which I am pleased to express my gratitude.

Professors Jarold Ramsey, David G. Riede, Joseph H. Summers, James Symons, and Steven Urkowitz read this book in manuscript and offered invaluable suggestions for its improvement. I am greatly in their debt. Whatever errors of fact, judgment or taste remain in these pages are solely mine.

I am grateful to my colleague Gilbert B. Davenport for the sketch that graces the cover, and my gratitude extends to all my colleagues in the Theater and Dance Department at the University of New Hampshire for creating an environment in which it is a joy to work.

My parents, Sylvia Dickter and the late Sam Richman, gave me life and life's opportunities. In an ultimate sense, they made possible the writing of this book.

Among the book's sources of inspiration, I must mention my children, Sam and Beatrice, who daily demonstrate the fusion of tragedy and comedy.

My greatest debt is to my wife, Susan, whose acting has taught me much about Beatrice and Titania, and whose exacting critical and editorial standards have made this a better written and more useful book.

LAUGHTER, PAIN, AND WONDER

INTRODUCTION

Writing about Gustav Mahler's careers as composer, conductor, and operatic stage director, Bruno Walter offers a concise statement of the stage director's fundamental obligation:

> Dramatic interpretation demands a wider imaginative scope than pure music, for the theater has developed no technique of written instructions which could be compared with the accuracy of a musical score. . . . This very fact imposes on a stage director's conscience an obligation to select among the possibilities open to his imagination those essential to the work as a whole, underlining them at the expense of what is inessential so as to preserve continuity of style.[1]

The theater's inability to offer precise written instructions to performers creates the director's greatest challenge and most dangerous trap. Many modern and contemporary playwrights attempt to save their scripts from inappropriate interpretations in performance by including extensive stage directions and notes.[2] But older plays, with their paucity of stage directions, bring directors to an exhilarating and terrifying condition in which everything is possible and all is permitted. As Walter's comment implies, directors of such plays must select what is essential from among infinite possibilities.

Working in concert with actors, directors must find or make the essential answers to numerous questions before they can fill with living art the empty spaces in which they work. Where and how are characters positioned on the stage? When, how, and why do they move and gesture? From where do they enter, and whither do they exit? What compels them to utter the lines the playwright has given them? At what tempo and volume, with which emphases, and with what degrees of duration and qualities of diction do they deliver those lines? Answering such questions imposes grave responsibilities, for the act of delivering a line or executing a gesture requires the performer to choose among endless possibilities. To speak the speech a certain way necessarily eliminates, or at least subordinates, other interpretations that had also been possible. Essential implications, overtones, and undertones are illuminated, while what is deemed inessential may be cast into deeper darkness.

Working in concert with designers as well as actors, directors must find or make theatrical images that give their productions coherence and guide their spectators to an immediate, sensuous apprehension of the plays they are mounting. Such images often create a production's overall style and may even define the nature of the actors' performances. Theatrical imaginations may range from a bare stage to the most elaborate scenic and lighting devices, but finally, theater artists must select among the possibilities and make choices. Their responsibility to the work as a whole requires the fashioning of stage environments that give life and form to their visions and within which actors can speak and move most effectively.

Contributing to directorial freedom is the inescapable fact that producing the plays of any dramatist not of our own time involves an act of temporal translation. No effort of historical imagination, however rigorous or bold, can make a contemporary audience think, feel, and observe like an Elizabethan or ancient Athenian audience. Performance rarely lays claim to historical accuracy or objectivity. As Anthony Dawson points out, it is almost always "disdainful of history, concerned mainly with making texts speak directly to contemporary audiences."[3] In his searching analysis of the antithetical relations between new historicism as a mode of interpretation and current theatrical practice, Dawson calls attention to the necessary subjectivity of theater artists' choices. "The actor's premise is that character counts, that meaning is embedded in subjectivity. This is also the premise of a good deal of performance criticism, making dialogue difficult between itself and historicism or deconstruction." But Dawson goes on to praise the theater's ability "to insist on the inescapability of subjectivity and to suggest its limits."[4] The following pages will perforce offer much evidence of theatrical subjectivity. But this book's burden is to suggest that a careful look at the plans for theatrical action encoded in plays' texts can impose necessary limits on that subjectivity.[5]

In order to breathe fresh life into what they take to be the plays' driving ideas or commanding images, directors frequently transplant their productions to milieus that they deem more familiar or more suggestive to their audiences. In productions of Shakespeare, the need for fresh life is intensified by the dramatist's very overfamiliarity. His plays are more frequently staged than any others, and directors and designers continually labor to strip away "that scaly accretion of time called a classic's performing tradition."[6] Douglas Seale's 1958 production of *Much Ado About Nothing* set in the 1850s, and Trevor Nunn's 1981 production of *All's Well That Ends Well*, set in the age of "Upstairs, Downstairs," surprised their audiences into a state of full wakefulness and invigorated attention. In his production of *A Midsummer Night's Dream*, Peter Brook

> forced one to forget not, let me emphasize, the play itself, but anything one had seen done with it or imagined being done with it in the theater. He swept the mind of the spectator as clear as he had swept his stage, allowing the text of the play, beautifully and deliberately spoken, to play upon you with a freshness of words seen for the first time upon the printed page. He persuaded you to forget a century of theatrical tradition with its conventions and its cliches, and he commanded you into a frame of mind where the very notion of magic or of supernatural agency had to be created afresh.[7]

But for every success of this sort, there are countless failures. From Lamb's pronouncement about the inability of any merely human actor satisfactorily to play King Lear, to Peter Saccio's denunciation of Michael Moriarty's 1980 Stratford, Connecticut, *Richard III*,[8] the history of Shakespeare in performance is rife with fulminations against actors and directors who manhandle their texts.[9] Many theater people hold that a play cannot truly be said to exist until it is performed. This doctrine seems to grant a license to disregard the ways in which plays' texts can give shape and definition to the limitless imaginings of directors, designers, and performers. Yet as Bruno Walter insists, directors have an obligation to select, from among infinite imaginative possibilities, those essential to the work as a whole.

How do directors determine the essential possibilities? They do so by using the same tools other critics use to similar ends of increasing and communicating their understanding of the play. But as I suggested at the outset, directors ponder questions that other critics do not need and often do not choose to consider. In seeking solutions to pragmatic problems of staging and acting, they give sustained and detailed thought to the relations that the performances they guide into being will have with their audiences. These are kinetic relations, unfolding and accumulating over the time of performance, and they draw for sustenance on the spectators' minds, emotions, and imaginations.

In the following pages, I will be arguing that an understanding of Shakespeare's ways of evoking and manipulating imaginative and emotional responses in the theater can inform what directors communicate to designers and actors, and can help determine the nature and quality of what is put on the stage. Drawing on my own and others' productions of Shakespeare's comedies, I will try to show that laughter, pain, and wonder are the primary responses the comedies in performance invite in their audiences. Shakespeare's comedies differ greatly from each other, but laughter, pain, and wonder, differently mixed and in different proportions, are present in all of them.

My discussion of laughter in the comedies is based on the premise that while reading is usually a solitary activity, laughter most frequently occurs when people are in groups. Indeed, a necessary condition for sustained laughter is the presence of a group of other laughers.[10] A solitary reader may indulge in the occasional smile or chuckle, or may even let loose a rare guffaw. But Shakespeare's comedies do not usually evoke in the study such quantity and quality of laughter as they evoke in the theater. These plays are every one of them among the world's funniest shows, and the most penetrating readers may be surprised when productions remind them how much laughter the comedies and even some of the tragedies can generate.

The comedies achieve peculiar emotional effects because they make their audiences experience pain in the midst of laughter. Many of Shakespeare's comic characters suffer, and so profound is the sympathy between characters and spectators that the audience shares the suffering. I do not refer so much to bodily pain—although even that is present in some of the comedies—but rather to agonies of the mind and spirit that may spring from fear or danger, from a consciousness of wrongdoing, or from a sudden ineluctable apprehension of death. I will try to demonstrate that in the comedies, such agonies can seem more intense, and serious truths can appear more somber, because they are set off by light wit.

But these plays are not unique in their mixing of laughter and pain. Comedies of several other great playwrights—Jonson, Molière, and Chekhov—achieve similar effects. I will try to show that what makes Shakespeare's comedies truly unique is their power to excite wonder, an emotion that most theorists associate with tragedy. I refer to the amazed hush in the audience when Rosalind gives herself to her father and her lover, when Viola and Sebastian meet and recognize each other, or when Hermione's seeming statue descends from its pedestal.

Since my productions of Shakespeare's comedies constitute the laboratory in which I have discovered most of what I set forth in the following pages, I will from time to time draw on these productions to illustrate my discussion. I will also draw on directors' comments and reviewers' accounts of many other productions of the past forty years. In the main, I limit these latter illustrations to the Royal Shakespeare Company and the festivals at Stratford, Ontario, and Stratford, Connecticut, because these companies tend to elicit the most informative comments from reviewers. For my purposes, I am less interested in the largely undeveloped assertions of newspaper reviewers or in the relatively brief accounts of individual productions in comprehensive stage histories than in detailed descriptions of the staging and acting of specific sequences.

That Shakespeare deliberately excites and manipulates complex and seemingly contradictory responses in his audience is hardly a novel idea. Maynard Mack, E. A. J. Honigmann, and Jean Howard all explore the dramatist's manipulations of audience response.[11] This book takes as its peculiar territory the ways in which such explorations affect the choices that directors, designers, and actors make in giving stage life to the comedies.

To be sure, such choices are also affected by countless varying conditions, including the strengths, imaginations, and physical characteristics of the actors, and the layout and flexibility of the theater in which the play is produced. Without referring to a particular company and a particular theater, it is impossible to offer a specific solution to any problem of staging or acting. Nevertheless, the director's obligation to give shape and coherence to the production obtains in any theater, with any group of collaborating artists. Sustained and detailed thought about the relations between play and audience helps the director to select among possibilities open to the imagination those essential to the work as a whole.

For example, it is attractively possible to portray the madly used Malvolio as naked and chained in a visible prison, as did Jonathan Miller's 1972 Oxford-Cambridge production, or to show the Duke of Vienna as a capricious and sadistic tyrant, as did Keith Hacker's 1974 R.S.C. production. But, as I hope to demonstrate in my discussions of *Twelfth Night* and *Measure for Measure,* these directorial interpretations may run counter to the blueprints for theatrical action and the codes for revealing dramatic character that can be found in those plays' texts. To examine the relations between play and audience encoded in the texts is to set limits on the imaginations of directors, designers, and actors, and within those limits to offer great challenges and opportunities.

My exploration of the connections between the playwright's manipulations of audience response and the choices a director makes in the theater is based on two controversial assumptions. First, I postulate that it is possible to gauge with reasonable accuracy an audience's probable reactions to given situations and events. I grant that no two individuals will respond in precisely the same way to any scene, and that different audiences may respond differently to the same production. A line or a bit of business that gets a laugh and an ovation one night may fall flat the next afternoon. Even so, it is necessary that directors, designers, and actors formulate hypotheses about their audiences' probable responses. An ability to predict the collective reactions of the spectators is no small measure of theatrical talent. In the following pages, I offer frequent observations about probable audience response, and much of this book's usefulness will rest on the perceived accuracy of those observations.

Whenever I direct a play of Shakespeare, I adopt the working hypothesis that there is usually a discernible purpose behind each scene, speech, line, and word. If I cannot make something work on the stage, I must reluctantly employ what Margaret Webster used to call the blue pencil. It is generally agreed that Shakespeare did many things right, but that he also made more than a few blunders—that like Horace's Homer, he was wont to nod from time to time. But there is almost no agreement about what those blunders are. What for one interpreter is an error is for someone else a glory. I find it safer and wiser to assume that the playwright knew what he was doing most of the time. When I encounter in rehearsal a passage that my actors and I do not immediately understand or approve, we make every effort to penetrate it and make it work on the stage. Only as a last resort do we cut or alter. Thus, the Shakespeare who emerges in these pages may seem an unbelievable superman, forever conjuring laughter, pain, and wonder. But I would rather err in that direction than too readily dismiss and jettison passages to which I have not given sufficient attention.

What do Shakespeare's laughter, pain, and wonder add up to? Sir Philip Sidney, adumbrating the great age of English drama that he would not live to see, writes, "the whole tract of a Comedy should be full of delight."[12] Throughout *An Apology for Poetry* he describes delight with unsurpassed eloquence. He writes of Amphion moving stones, of Orpheus listened to by beasts, and he describes the power of poets "to drawe with their charming sweetness the wild untamed wits to an admiration of knowledge."[13] Sidney's delight is such that readers or hearers quite lose themselves in the joy of the thing contemplated.[14] Shakespeare knew Sidney's work well, and in his comedies he so mixes laughter, pain, and wonder as to bring his spectators to a Sidneyan rapture.

Yet reading Sidney with the hindsight that a knowledge of Shakespeare must bring is also a peculiarly frustrating experience. Although the great courtier poet foreshadows Shakespearean delight, he falls far short of Shakespearean laughter:

> But our Comedians thinke there is no delight without laughter; which is very wrong, for though laughter may come with delight, yet commeth it not of delight, as though delight should be the cause of laughter; . . . nay, rather in themselves they have, as it were, a kind of contrarietie: for delight we scarcely doe but in things that have a conveniencie to our selves or to the generall nature: laughter almost ever commeth of things most disproportioned to our selves and nature. Delight hath a joy in it, either permanent or present. Laughter hath onely a scornful tickling. . . . Wee shall, contrarily, laugh sometimes to finde a matter quite mistaken and goe down the hill agaynst the byas in the mouth of some such men, as for the respect of them one shall be heartily sorry, yet he cannot chuse but laugh; and so is rather pained than delighted with laughter.[15]

In this last sentence, Sidney approaches an important comic principle that is illustrated copiously in the works of Shakespeare and many other comic playwrights—namely, the nearness of laughter to pain. But for Sidney, as for so many literary theorists down to our own time, laughter is usually scornful, aggressive, derisive, the contrary of delight. I will suggest in the following chapter what audiences at Shakespeare's comedies come to know, that Shakespeare can elicit laughter that inspires and is inspired by delight. For Shakespeare, laughter is seldom the "scornful tickling" that Sidney describes. The laughter that his comedies provoke in their audiences far outruns almost all theoretical assertions made about it. It is a fact of considerable interest that this includes assertions made by his own comic characters. The people in Shakespeare's comedies often laugh and are often objects of laughter; yet this laughter is almost always Sidney's scornful tickling. To explain this seeming contradiction, I begin my discussion of Shakespeare's laughter by examining the differences between the sorts of laughter in which his characters engage and those they excite in their audiences.

1
LAUGHTER

Mᴏsᴛ ᴏғ Sʜᴀᴋᴇsᴘᴇᴀʀᴇ's ᴄᴏᴍɪᴄ ᴄʜᴀʀᴀᴄᴛᴇʀs ᴀʀᴇ ᴠɪᴄ-
tims of scornful laughter, and the derision often approaches or becomes
violence. When Kate makes her first entrance in *The Taming of the
Shrew*, she suffers many jokes at her expense, and a kind of jeering
undersong accompanies her throughout the play. Launce and Speed,
the two servants in *The Two Gentlemen of Verona*, are constantly
baiting each other; indeed, Launce deliberately brings about a whipping
for Speed so that he can "rejoice in the boy's correction."[1] Although
Navarre and his bookmen in *Love's Labour's Lost* deny themselves
most pleasures, they make it their chief recreation to laugh at Don
Armado's linguistic extravagance. The mocking lords are mocked by
the French ladies, and the young men savagely excoriate the pageant
of the nine worthies. In *The Merchant of Venice* all the Venetian
boys hoot about Shylock's ducats and his daughter, and Salarino and
Salanio make themselves sport out of the Jew's misery. The language
of mockery comes even nearer to the language of violence in *Much
Ado About Nothing*. Beatrice quips that Benedick "pleases men and
angers them, and then they laugh at him and beat him" (2.1.120–26).
Benedick later describes himself under her tongue's lash as standing
"like a man at a mark, with a whole army shooting at me" (2.1.221–23).
As You Like It is a gentler play than *Much Ado About Nothing*,
but even here Jaques mocks almost everyone. Rosalind treats Phebe
with scorn, and Touchstone terrorizes William. The derision in *As
You Like It* is as nothing compared to what Sir Toby and his accomplices
do to Malvolio in *Twelfth Night*, and Malvolio is not his play's only
butt.

It is commonly held that Shakespeare's comic vision darkens after
Twelfth Night. Certainly none of his characters is more thoroughly
shamed than Parolles in *All's Well That Ends Well*. In *Measure for
Measure* Lucio takes pleasure in Pompey's imprisonment and mali-
ciously mocks the duke and Angelo. In *Cymbeline* Shakespeare comes

near to Jonson or Middleton in his creation of Cloten, "a comic character drawn with a savagely serious pen."[2] Imogen compares him unfavor-
ably to her husband's meanest garment, his attendant lords alternately
flatter and scoff at him, and he is scorned by the man who kills
him—a fate that Richard III, Edmund, and Macbeth are spared. In
The Winter's Tale Autolycus is better natured than Jonson's or Middleton's rogues, but he takes a Jonsonian pleasure in gulling his victims
as he swindles them. In *The Tempest* Trinculo remarks, "I shall laugh
myself to death at this puppy-headed monster" (2.2.145–46), and Caliban laughs when Trinculo is beaten.

The foregoing catalog is by no means exhaustive. My purpose is
to suggest how frequently such incidents occur in the comedies. In
many of them, notably *Love's Labour's Lost, Much Ado About Nothing, Twelfth Night,* and *All's Well That Ends Well,* important parts
of the action are driven forward by the spirits of scorn and malice.
Derisive laughter is notably present in most of the comedies and is
wholly absent from none of them.

I set this fact against the critical commonplace that Shakespeare's
comedies are kindly, tolerant, genial, and thus different from the work
of other comic writers. Most English comedies purvey the austere,
fervent spirit of social and moral correction. Spectators are invited
either to participate in the whipping that these plays administer to
vice and folly, or to have their own follies and vices taxed by the
whippers. A similar corrective impulse informs such incidents as I
have been recounting in Shakespeare's comedies. These incidents give
his comedies an enriching stringency.

Yet the presence of such incidents in Shakespeare's comedies does
not wholly contradict the notion of their geniality. In his comedies
the audience rarely participates in the scornful laughter that it frequently
observes. Playgoers are almost never permitted to relish an absolute,
unsympathetic superiority to the characters. The playwright develops
numerous ways to mitigate the audience's scorn, many of them involving intense emotional reactions that modify or suppress the laughter.
In subsequent chapters, I will be discussing such reactions. Later in
this chapter, I hope to demonstrate that Shakespeare can reduce or
eliminate potential derision in his audience by exciting other less malicious kinds of mirth. The laughter in admiration of the trickster often
overrides laughter in scorn of the victim.

Simple laughter always occurs in the absence of sympathy and frequently in the presence of malice.[3] Although Shakespeare rarely moves

his audience to malicious mirth, he yet proves himself one of the great masters of scorn when he does choose to excite it. The scenes involving Malvolio comprise his most successful campaign of derision. Yet, as the dramatist develops this best of his butts, the laughter grows more complex.

From Malvolio's first appearance, the audience dislikes him. Shakespeare engenders this dislike by performing a feat of theatrical sleight of hand. He carefully prepares Olivia's entrance, inclining his spectators to disapprove of her affectation and its consequences. Of her steward, the audience hears nothing until he enters with her. Yet within moments, Shakespeare shifts the burden of dislike and disapproval that Olivia has been incurring onto Malvolio.[4]

All that has been said about Olivia prior to her first entrance suggests that when she enters, she will be the picture of aristocratic grief: quite pale, eyes downcast, slow of pace, frugal of gesture. But she does not maintain the tone established by her initial line, "Take the fool away" (1.1.35). Rather, she allows Feste to try to laugh her out of her gloom, and she memorably diagnoses her steward's chief malady. Her initial scene with her retainers suggests an essential generosity of spirit beneath the affectation. In praising Lisa Harrow's performance in John Barton's 1969 R.S.C. production, Robert Speaight warns that if you push Olivia too far in the direction of silliness, you distort the balance of the play.[5] I would add that the balance will be held if the actress shows the generosity and capacity for love behind the mourning mask the character is affecting. A slow smile at Feste and an expression of amused exasperation at the drunken Toby may help reveal that she is capable of growth. Her manner and speech might become increasingly enlivened, although she should not, until the scene's end, wholly abandon her grief. In David Jones's production at Stratford, Ontario, in 1975, Marti Maraden gave Olivia wit and character, inspiring a deepening affection in the audience.[6] Revealing as Maraden did Olivia's generosity and insight clears the character of much of the audience's dislike.

Malvolio's encouragement of Olivia's affectation causes that dislike to focus on him. He supports his mistress's affectation of grief with his own pose of studied and decorous sobriety, but his lines suggest that there is nothing beneath his mask but a monumental capacity for self-approval. Like his mistress, he should be dressed in black. There is no stage direction to this effect, as there is in *All's Well That Ends Well*, but so much has been made of Olivia's mourning that it is inconceivable that she would appear in any other color, and Malvolio would certainly ape her. In Bill Alexander's 1987 production at Stratford-upon-Avon, Antony Sher made his first entrance as a black-clad and ostentatious director of mourning rites.[7] The steward also apes what he deems to be the diction and rhythms of the ruling classes, and the actor's performance will be funniest and most effective if he makes the character overprecise in speech and gesture—vowels a modicum too flat or broad, consonants enunciated with unnecessary clarity—to suggest that the steward is not "to the manner born." Both Paul Scofield on the Caedmon recording and Brian Bedford at Stratford, Ontario, made him sound like Henry Higgins's most eager pupil. In an Old Vic production in 1958, Richard Wordsworth gave the steward a cockney accent, a choice that met with Muriel St. Clare Byrne's disfavor.[8] Such an accent would constantly remind the audience that the steward is falling short in his pretensions to gentility, and it would consequently lessen the effect of his gulling. The tricksters and the audience would take far more malicious pleasure in the discomfiture of an arrogant success than of a pathetic failure. The laughter that Malvolio generates springs in large part from his being thoroughly and seamlessly what the other characters say he is.

Malvolio incurs the audience's dislike so quickly that spectators will probably not notice when reactions that have been gathering about Olivia have shifted to her steward. What they will notice is that they dislike Malvolio and are eager to see him discomfited, while they are coming to care about Olivia in a way that precludes continuous scornful laughter. The play offers much criticism of her before it allows her to find bliss. But the playwright divorces much of this criticism from malice, and Olivia is never made a target for sustained derision.

In diagnosing her steward as "sick of self-love," Olivia pinpoints the source of all the behavior the audience is inclined to dislike in him. Later in the play Maria elaborates on this behavior:

> The devil a Puritan that he is, or anything constantly but a time-pleaser; an affection'd ass that cons state without book and utters it by great swarths; the best persuaded of himself, so cramm'd, as he thinks, with excellencies that it is his grounds of faith that all that look on him love him. . . . (2.3.137–44)

All Malvolio's early appearances are contrived so that Maria's words confirm what the audience has already seen. The steward's most vivid display of mirthless officiousness immediately precedes her descriptive speech. It comes as he rebukes the drunken Sir Toby and the other revelers.[9] The revelry that prompts the rebuke is a theatrical spectacle of misrule, anarchy, and topsy-turvydom, such things that are of the essence in comedy time out of mind.[10] The scene may be most effective in performance if it is played with enormous, unflagging energy, conjuring the festive but potentially dangerous atmosphere of a wild party. One of the primary ways to make an audience laugh is to create a mood in which the laughter will have a cumulative effect, so that things that do not seem funny in themselves will evoke a response of great hilarity when they occur in their proper order and sequence. As the party's putative host, Sir Toby is largely responsible for the saturnalian celebration. The character is a gentleman going to seed, and there is a sour underside to his nature, but if the actor chooses to portray him as too vitiated with drink and other vices, the brisk pace and high energy so necessary to his major scenes may be lost. The actor playing Sir Andrew may best serve the pace and spirit of these scenes if he finds ways to energize his character's silliness. Exemplary in this regard were Barry Ingham, who played the character as a Scotsman trailing his bagpipes in Barton's 1969 R.S.C. production, and Christopher Plummer, falling through the trap door in Tyrone Guthrie's 1957 production at Stratford, Ontario.[11]

The raging Malvolio's invasion of the party, either black-clad or in his nightgown, radically changes the atmosphere. The character's incongruous appearance may get a scornful guffaw, or the spectacle of his anger may command a thundering silence. In either case, Sir Toby quickly puts the steward on the defensive by employing one of the most invariably successful tricks known to comedians. He takes literally a remark that the steward means metaphorically, and like his great lineal descendant in comedy, Groucho Marx, he compounds his deliberate mistake with an insult.

> *Mal.* . . . Is there no respect of place, persons, nor time in you?
> *Sir To.* We did keep time, sir, in our catches. Sneck up! (2.3.88–90)

The revelers evade the killjoy's reprimands till, defused and baffled, he can do no more than punctuate their quips and songs with ineffectual retorts. In my production, Sir Toby hurled cake at the steward's chain of office, giving spectacular emphasis to Maria's injunction that he rub his chain with crumbs.

The rebuke provides the immediate cause of the elaborate practical joke, which bedevils the steward and delights the audience during much of the play's remainder. Malvolio's vanity renders his subsequent conduct perfectly predictable. In the scene in which his imagination and Maria's forged letter blow him to his dream of Count Malvolio, much of the pleasure that the eavesdropping characters and the eavesdropping spectators receive grows out of the satisfaction of seeing in the flesh and hearing enlarged with all the amplitude of the steward's self-love the very things that they had hoped and expected to see and hear. Even before he appears, the audience enters into the spirit of malicious festivity with Maria's announcement that Malvolio has been "practising behaviour to his own shadow" (2.5.14). The steward's fantasy of marriage to Olivia, which precedes his finding of the letter, gives the actor full scope to reveal the character's personal vanity. As he imagines his life as Count Malvolio, the spectators will be delighted, astonished, and not a little appalled by the depth of his self-regard.

Since the speech is one of Shakespeare's best monologues, it remains a popular audition piece. I have heard hundreds of renditions and have observed with surprise that many actors choose to give a mannered performance that systematically satirizes the character. Such was the strategy adopted by Bob Dishy in Gerald Freedman's 1978 production at Stratford, Connecticut. He superimposed posturings and grimaces and did not allow the comedy to spring from his lines.[12] If the actor adopts such a strategy, he joins with the audience in a campaign of derision against the character. Some Shakespearean parts encourage such Brechtian estrangement between actor and role, but the actor playing Malvolio will achieve richer and more memorable results if he remains at one with the character and allows the character to establish a relation with the audience.

Reviewing Brian Bedford's 1975 performance at Stratford, Ontario, Berners W. Jackson describes Bedford as an unlovely and unlovable Malvolio who nonetheless managed to make himself totally agreeable to the audience.

> He affected to be puzzled by their reactions, he asked for their approval, he took them into his confidence. This was an astonishing virtuoso performance with the actor playing upon the audience like a musician upon a cacophonous instrument, directing and manipulating the responses not only of the whole group but also of individuals.[13]

Part of the scene's irony rises from the character's misjudging his relation to the spectators precisely as he misjudges his relation to Olivia. Watching a performance like Bedford's, the playgoers can eagerly participate in the steward's fantasy and at the same time laugh at his preposterous misprision.

Malvolio engages in a continuing dialogue with the letter, and the lines encourage the actor to express genuine and increasing surprise and pleasure as he reads it. His responses to the amorous professions, at first tentative then ever bolder, yield the audience accumulating matter for increasing mirth. Each new discovery tending toward the grand hypothesis that he is Olivia's unknown beloved occasions a new laugh, and each laugh is greater than the one that precedes it. The scene provides a model for the cumulative power of laughter to breed itself out of itself. Malvolio's language, from the hesitant but hopeful "let me see, let me see, let me see" (2.5.102) to the more assured prose rhythms of "Why, she may command me: I serve her; she is my lady. Why, this is evident to any formal capacity" (2.5.105–6) suggests mounting urgency and excitement. Through timing and stress, the actor can communicate a movement from wild surmise to certainty.

In Malvolio's next scene, the incongruity of the mirthless figure's appearance in the ridiculous costume that Maria has prescribed will elicit new laughter. So will the steward's inept attempts to assume the manner of the songster and sonneteer. The laughter here depends on the audience's accepting as preposterous the idea of a match between Malvolio and Olivia. But the continuing stage tradition of casting as Olivia an actress who might credibly play Gertrude or Volumnia can vitiate this scene's effectiveness—can indeed undercut the entire scheme against Malvolio. With Bedford's second Malvolio for Stratford, Ontario, in 1981, Olivia was played as a stately and mature chatelaine by Pat Galloway—for many years the company's grande dame. Bedford's decorous steward seemed well suited to her, and the audience was consequently given less reason to laugh at his scenes of amorous pursuit.[14]

Assuming in performance such a mismatch between steward and mistress as the text strongly suggests, the playgoers will be encouraged during five substantial scenes to dislike Malvolio and to laugh at him. Only Parolles and Cloten among the hundreds of characters in Shakespeare's comedies are made the objects of so strong a dislike and such a sustained campaign of derisive laughter. But as the steward

continues to be "madly used" (5.1.311), an important change occurs
in the attitude that the audience is encouraged to take toward him.
That such a change will come is adumbrated in the midst of the
earlier scenes of scornful laughter. The eavesdroppers in the letter
scene intend to laugh, but they are instead driven to rage by Malvolio's
presumption. Until this moment the playgoers and the tricksters have
been in complete accord. Now Sir Toby and his companions incur
some derisive laughter in their own right, and the playwright lays
groundwork for a separation between audience and tricksters that will
widen toward the play's end.

The laughter alters further when the encounter between the cross-
gartered steward and his confused lady comes to an abrupt end. Olivia,
the passionate Malvolio's object, is called away by a servant in order
that she may passionately pursue her own inappropriate lover. Apart
from the delicious irony, the interruption provides the only way for
the scene to end in a manner that will allow Malvolio's adventures
to remain funny. The scene's brevity and its sudden interruption help
create an impression that, had Malvolio and Olivia been left together
much longer, their encounter might have changed into something very
different from comedy. Olivia's reference to bed and the steward's
eager response (3.4.29–30) suggest urgent sexual pursuit that, if left
to run its course, might culminate in rape. There may be a hint of
terror in Olivia's cry that Malvolio has been seized by "midsummer
madness" (3.4.53). With the servant's abrupt entrance, the dramatist
may be intimating to the audience that he must end this comic scene
quickly before it turns painful or terrible. Great comedy, particularly
the work of Molière and Chekhov, as well as that of Shakespeare,
often creates such an impression.[15] In subtly suggesting the potential
tragedy inherent in Malvolio's comedy, Shakespeare drops an important
hint that the relation between audience and steward is beginning to
change. He deliberately neglects to make clear the change's nature,
but when it comes in Malvolio's encounter with Feste, disguised as
Sir Topas the curate, it should not take the spectators wholly by
surprise.

In this scene the audience is given to understand that the steward
occupies the traditional habitation and posture of madmen, namely,
that he is bound in a dark room. Yet if the audience is encouraged
to perceive or imagine even so detested a creature as Malvolio in
such a position of humiliation and physical torment, its reaction will

in all likelihood include a new element of pain or sympathy. Contributing to such a reaction is the fact that the steward has already been thoroughly shamed. A prediction that Sir Toby has previously made is coming true: "We may carry it thus, for our pleasure and his penance, till our very pastime, tired out of breath, prompt us to have mercy on him" (3.4.132–34).

Events in the scene do indeed prompt both characters and audience to have mercy. The most surprising prompter of this new mercy is the partial transformation that Malvolio's shaming has wrought in his character. The habitual tones of reprimand and command give place to new tones of placation and entreaty. Where the audience had previously heard, "I marvel your ladyship takes delight in such a barren rascal" (1.5.77) it now hears, "Good fool, as ever thou wilt deserve well at my hand, help me to a candle, and pen, ink, and paper; as I am a gentleman, I will live to be thankful to thee for't" (4.2.78–80). He still retains his pretensions, since he claims a title to gentility to which he has no right. But his changes in tone and style suggest a walk of some distance through the valley of humiliation.

Although the playgoers view Malvolio for the first time with some measure of sympathy, his scene with Feste does not move away from comedy or even from laughter. But the laughter is no longer so malicious as it has been. It is called forth chiefly by the several sorts of verbal and theatrical cleverness that Feste exhibits. Throughout the play the fool has shown himself a subtle casuist, and the persona of Sir Topas the curate, which he here adopts, proves an effective vehicle for his peculiar combination of choplogic, scholastic parody, clever and complex wordplay, nonsensical doubletalk, and cutting wit tinged with sorrow. The laughter Feste excites diverts the audience from its former derisive mirth at Malvolio's expense. As so often happens in Shakespeare, the audience is made to concentrate chiefly on the quality of the trick rather than on the humiliation of the victim.

To be sure, Feste's wit in this scene is not unmixed with malice. But much of the derision is divorced from the laughter by the transformation in Malvolio's character and by his position of physical torment. Yet if the playgoers are permitted to look for a long time at a spectacle of torment, if they behold Malvolio caged in a dark place and bound, the necessary balance between laughter and disturbance may be lost. Antony Sher's Malvolio suffered visibly in the 1987 R.S.C. production. He was tied to a stake while Feste tormented him with exploding caps. Driven mad by torment, Sher's Malvolio grew to resemble a baited bear. The performance apparently threatened the play's tension and balance, as well as its humor.[16]

When I staged the play, my actors and I discovered in rehearsal how enormously difficult it was to achieve a satisfactory balance in this scene. The actor playing Feste argued persuasively that the fool would not take pleasure in seeing the imprisoned Malvolio. With the spectacle of the tormented steward constantly before his eyes, he could not bring off Sir Topas with appropriate verve. Even Sir Toby and Maria were uneasy, and I suspected that the audience would share their unease.

I had never been satisfied with this scene in any production of *Twelfth Night* I had attended. Although the quality of the laughter was changing, I suspected that the scene ought to be as funny as Malvolio's previous scenes. Yet I had always observed that the scene in performance created an embarrassed awkwardness, distracting from rather than enriching the play's movement. I judged that the scene would be most effective in performance and would make its proper contribution to the play if we could discover a staging that would allow the spectators to imagine Malvolio's captivity without having him continuously before their eyes.

Studying the scene, I became convinced that the continuous spectacle of a suffering Malvolio would run counter to indications in the text. Although the texts of Shakespeare's plays offer few stage directions, the dialogue itself yields an abundance of strong suggestions about staging.[17] In the present case, both the dialogue and the stage direction in the First Folio suggest that the spectators are intended to see little or none of Malvolio's physical torment. In the Folio, no entrance is listed for Malvolio in this scene. Instead, the stage direction "Malvolio within" appears on the page in a position corresponding to that usually taken by directions of entrance. It is clear from its placement on the page that this direction governs the entire scene. In most modern editions of the play, the direction's intent is blurred. The word "within" is written in parentheses after the speech ascription for Malvolio's first speech. Thus, it appears that only that first speech must be spoken offstage, and the staging for subsequent speeches is left unclear.

The stage direction in the Folio suggests almost to the point of certainty that Malvolio must act the entire scene "within," that is to say, offstage. This notion is reinforced by Maria's remark to Feste, "thou mightst have done this without thy beard and gown: he sees thee not" (4.2.62–63). Even an Elizabethan audience, with its highly developed imaginative powers and its great tolerance of stage convention, would be hard to convince that an onstage Malvolio could not see an onstage Feste, unless Malvolio were blindfolded or totally enclosed in a stage property that could serve as the dark house. On the other hand, it would be the simplest thing in the world to convince any audience that an offstage Malvolio could not see an onstage Feste. More important, it is to the highest degree unlikely that the playwright would waste Feste's wit on the ears of spectators whose eyes are so taken with Malvolio's agony that their ability to pay proper attention to the fool is diminished or eliminated. What instruments we have agree that Malvolio should be unseen by the audience.

Although I was encouraged by these reflections to keep Malvolio offstage, I had to bear in mind that despite Maria's and Toby's eavesdropping, this is essentially a two-character scene. For Malvolio to spend the entire scene offstage would create difficulties for the actor playing Feste and would strain beyond endurance the imaginative powers of any modern audience. Thus, my cast and I were faced with a problem of considerable dimensions. If Malvolio were shown, the scene's effect and its contribution to the play would likely be damaged. If he remained unseen, the scene would place such a strain on the audience's imagination that the dramatic illusion itself would be endangered.

Our solution was to replicate the trap set in the stage floor. In the Globe and other Elizabethan theaters, such a trap gave access to a space under the stage that was used by spirits, devils, and other apparitions, and that was appropriately called Hell.[18] Now Malvolio twice compares his dark house to hell. Taken together with the stage direction in the Folio, this comparison suggests the possibility that the actor be positioned not off the stage but under it. As we staged the scene, Malvolio opened the trap and thrust his head and upper body through the opening. At appropriate moments Feste pushed him down again and slammed the door on him. For example, after the steward declared that he in no way approved Pythagoras's opinion of the transmigration of souls, Feste as Sir Topas thrust him down on "Fare thee well. Remain thou still in darkness" (4.2.55). Malvolio popped back up when he supposed himself to be in conversation with the fool, and Feste in his own person thrust him down on "Advise you what you say: the minister is here" (4.2.91). Thus Malvolio was out of sight, bellowing from beneath the stage, while the mock dialogue between the fool and the curate was carried out. Malvolio popped up again after he supposed Sir Topas to have departed, and Feste pushed him back on "Nay, I'll ne'er believe a madman till I see his brains" (4.2.112). By keeping in constant motion around the open trap, Feste kept Malvolio from getting a clear view of him, while the steward with his flailing arms repeatedly tried to grab the fool's dancing legs.

Evidence in the scene suggests such a staging. In addition to Malvolio's comparisons of the dark house to hell, there is Feste's little song at the scene's end in which he compares himself to the old vice, crying, "Ah, ha!" to the devil (4.2.124). Now if Malvolio is indeed under the stage, he occupies the place where devils go, driven there by the vice, and the analogy in the song takes on peculiar and effective resonance.[19] Certainly Shakespeare, who may recently have used the same trap and the same space under it for the ghosts of Julius Caesar and Hamlet's father, might have taken pleasure in using this traditionally tragic facility for comic purposes.

But my purpose is less to speculate about how Shakespeare's company might originally have staged this scene than to suggest a staging consistent with the play's text and consonant with its ever-shifting moods. Our staging encouraged our audiences to laugh at Feste's wit, to laugh occasionally at Malvolio's expense, and at the same time to recognize and sympathize with the steward's sufferings and the changes in his character. We allowed the spectators to see enough of Malvolio so that their imaginative powers were not strained, but not so much of him that sympathy with his suffering overwhelmed their ability to laugh. If quality and quantity of laughter can serve as evidence, our audiences were delighted with the scene thus staged. It was as funny in performance as I had always believed it ought to be, and it served as the essential bridge between the earlier scenes of derisive laughter and Malvolio's complex final appearance.

Shakespeare's achievement in this scene is to divorce laughter from derision. From the malicious laughter of Malvolio's earlier scenes, the audience moves to the relatively detached laughter proper to farce. As we shall see, diverting the spectators' potential derision with other kinds of mirth is one of Shakespeare's chief means of keeping them from sharing the scorn in which so many of his characters indulge. After the scene between Malvolio and Feste, the audience's response to the steward continues to change. Whether he will draw further laughter is problematic, but his final appearance may elicit pain. I can discuss this scene more profitably when I take up the question of Shakespeare's endings.[20] For the present, I submit that the spectators begin to sympathize with Malvolio as they observe him beginning to slough off the effects of his vanity and self-love.

During his first five scenes, his self-love makes his behavior so thoroughly predictable that it would not be inaccurate to describe him as an automaton. His vanity and resulting automatism make him a striking illustration for the arguments of nearly every comic theorist. He exemplifies with particular vividness the conclusions of Henri Bergson, perhaps the greatest of all theorists of laughter. Bergson finds that laughter is the specific remedy for vanity, and that vanity is an essentially laughable failing.[21] Even more germane to Malvolio is Bergson's central metaphor: "Something mechanical encrusted on the living."[22] This is an apt description of the sickness of self-love that governs Malvolio's behavior during the play's first three acts.

But having recognized this, it is necessary to recognize that Bergson's theories do not account for the Malvolio of the fourth and fifth acts. Bergson famously characterizes laughter as occurring in an "anaesthesia of the heart":

> Here, I would point out as a symptom equally worthy of notice the absence of feeling which usually accompanies laughter. It seems as though the comic could not produce its disturbing effect unless it fell, so to say, on the surface of a soul that is thoroughly calm and unruffled. Indifference is its natural environment, for laughter has no greater foe than emotion. . . . I do not mean that we could not laugh at a person who inspires us with pity, for instance, or even with affection. But in such a case we must, for the moment, put our affection out of court and impose silence upon our pity.[23]

Throughout his treatise, Bergson implies in spite of this pronouncement that laughter often exists in concert with malice. He repeatedly insists that laughter is a corrective whose function is to intimidate by humiliating.[24] He finds "something bitter, self-assertive, even pessimistic in laughter,"[25] and he compares it in the final sentence of his treatise to a froth with a saline base. "It sparkles, it is gaiety itself; but you may find its substance scanty and its aftertaste bitter."[26] That laughter can exist in indifference or in malice follows naturally from Bergson's central metaphor. A living laugher may feel superior to an automaton; indeed, the automaton's characteristics may excite derision as Malvolio's undoubtedly do. But since a living laugher can have no real fellow feeling for an automaton, laughter can never exist simultaneously with sympathy.

As we have seen, the Malvolio of the fourth act has begun to free himself from the effects of his governing affectation. The laughter which the scene with Feste elicits is leavened with sympathy. Even so, my staging of this scene was a concession to Bergson, since it was based on the assumption that the spectators' laughter would be choked off if they were made to concentrate too intensely on the spectacle of Malvolio's physical torment.

Many critics dismiss Bergson because the theorist does not allow for the simultaneous existence of laughter and sympathy.[27] Any discussion that relies on the greatest comic theorist for illumination of the greatest comic dramatist must take into account Bergson's fundamental failure theoretically to comprehend Shakespeare's practice.[28] Bergson cannot describe Shakespeare's ability to excite laughter by automatism's precise opposite, by a spectacle of gloriously unpredictable life.

Falstaff subsumes in his ample person both the causes of laughter that Bergson can illuminate, and those he cannot. As he appears in the first part of *Henry IV*, he is in many ways a butt, a gull. Like Malvolio, he is sufficiently predictable for Prince Hal and Poins to manipulate him with a device in much the same way that Maria and Sir Toby manipulate the predictable steward. In setting up his jest of the double robbery, Poins can predict Falstaff's apparent cowardice, a factor that will make it possible for the prince and himself to overmaster the original thieves. But what will make the jest truly worth executing is not so much Falstaff's cowardice as his capacity for lying:

> The virtue of this jest will be the incomprehensible lies that this same fat rogue will tell us when we meet at supper: how thirty, at least, he fought with; what wards, what blows, what extremities he endured; and in the reproof of this lies the jest. (1.2.176–83)

At first, Poins appears to read Falstaff as accurately as Maria reads Malvolio. Indeed, there is an uncanny similarity between Falstaff's situation and Malvolio's, in spite of the enormous differences between the two characters. Structurally, the jovial knight occupies the same position as the bilious steward, that of chief gull.

But Falstaff leaves this position when the jest against him reaches its climax. The prince catches Falstaff out in his lie and insults him:

What a slave art thou to hack thy sword as thou hast done, and then say it was in fight! What trick, what device, what starting-hole, canst thou now find out to hide thee from this open and apparent shame? (2.4.251–56)

This is the scene's moment of greatest tension. The audience is balanced on a knife edge, knowing that it is about to witness Falstaff shamed or Falstaff triumphant. If Falstaff were wholly like Malvolio, a gull rendered mechanical and predictable by those vices that have excited scorn in tricksters and playgoers alike, the audience would be prepared and eager to take malicious pleasure in his shaming. But open and apparent as Falstaff's vices are, they do not call forth the audience's dislike. During the moment between the prince's and Poins's questions and Falstaff's reply, the audience will hope that he can indeed find some starting-hole as he has been challenged to do. And of course, the fat knight does:

By the lord, I knew ye as well as he that made ye. Why, hear you, my masters: was it for me to kill the heir-apparent? Should I turn upon the true prince? Why, thou knowst I am as valiant as Hercules but beware instinct—the lion will not touch the true prince. (2.4.258–65)

The laughter here will differ as much from the laughter at Malvolio's expense as something mechanical differs from someone living. It rises on waves of unalloyed delight springing from deep sympathy.

Poins's prediction proves precisely wrong. The jest does not lie in the reproof of Falstaff's lies. It lies in his ability to tell an astonishing lie at the very moment when it seemed he would be reproved. Exactly unlike Malvolio, Falstaff surprises both tricksters and spectators, and in his ability to surprise, to evade, to give the lie to prediction, he proves himself the very opposite of mechanical; he proves himself triumphantly human. He turns the laugh back on the tricksters, rejoices at his ability to do so, and the audience rejoices with him. Such laughter is inspired by something quite out of Bergson's theoretical ken. Neither can the French theorist account for Rosalind in her moments of self-irony, Beatrice using her wit finally as a source of joy rather than as weapon or shield, or even Barnardine, who, like Falstaff, vindicates his unpredictable humanity by refusing mechanically to die at any man's persuasion.

Yet when this major shortcoming is acknowledged, it will be found that Bergson's theories give more illumination than the work of any other writer about the causes and effects of laughter in Shakespeare's comedies. In the succession of confusions in *The Comedy of Errors,* in Dogberry's havoc on the English language, in Falstaff's girth, in Malvolio's affectation, one can detect variant manifestations of Bergson's central metaphor, for there is some degree of what he would call automatism inherent in all these. Other comic theorists like George Meredith and Suzanne Langer make up for Bergson's gaps by allowing for the existence in comedy of sympathetic laughter,[29] but no other writer explores with Bergson's precision and thoroughness so many of laughter's other causes.

A considerable amount of Shakespeare's laughter exists on "the surface of a soul that is thoroughly calm and unruffled."[30] Malvolio and Falstaff are exceptional. Most of the laughter in the comedies is actuated neither by deep scorn nor deep sympathy. As we shall see, such emotionally neutral laughter is best suited to guide the audience's emotional response to the plays. And such laughter, as intrinsic to Shakespeare's comedies as the laughter of sympathy, is best accounted for by Bergson.

In his wide-ranging exploration of mechanicality, Bergson calls attention to the frequency with which laughter is occasioned by physical details—words or actions that focus on parts of the body. Particularly effective in exciting laughter is a concentration on the physical when the audience has been led to expect an analysis of a moral or spiritual question.[31] One of the most hilarious scenes of this sort can be found in *The Comedy of Errors,* probably Shakespeare's first comedy. Like most of his early comic scenes, it is a boisterous virtuoso piece that shows off the rough, rude clown. Such a clown is Dromio of Syracuse, here talking about the woman who claims marriage with him:

> *Dro. S.* Marry, sir, she's the kitchen-wench, and all grease; and I know
> not what use to put her to but to make a lamp of her and run
> from her by her own light. I warrant, her rags and the tallow in
> them will burn a Poland winter. If she lives till doomsday, she'll
> burn a week longer than the whole world. . . . For why she sweats,
> a man may go over shoes in the grime of it. . . . No longer from
> head to foot than from hip to hip; she is spherical, like a globe;
> I could find out countries in her. . . .
> *Ant. S.* In what part of her body stands Ireland?
> *Dro. S.* Marry, sir, in her buttocks; I found it out by the bogs. . . .
> *Ant. S.* Where Spain?
> *Dro. S.* Faith, I saw it not, but I felt it hot in her breath.
> *Ant. S.* Where America, the Indies?

Dro. S. O, sir, upon her nose, all o'er embellished with rubies, carbuncles,
    sapphires, declining their rich aspect to the hot breath of Spain. . . .
Ant. S. Where stood Belgia, the Netherlands?
Dro. S. O, sir, I did not look so low. (3.2.93–137)

The laughter here is frankly bawdy and aggressive, but the derision
is not deeply rooted as is the derision provoked by Malvolio, because
its object remains unseen. Dromio's target is a figure of fantasy upon
which comic hyperbole can be hung.

Laughter that partakes both of aggression and emotional neutrality
is proper to farce. It is no accident that the character whose speech
calls forth that laughter is of a sort played to perfection by Will
Kemp, one of the great farcical actors of all time.[32] Kemp was the
rough clown and dancer of jigs for the Lord Chamberlain's men.
Dromio, along with his brother of the same name, begins a line of
farcical servants and artisans—Grumio, Launce, Launcelot Gobbo,
Bottom, Dogberry—who were probably all played by Kemp. These
characters' most memorable scenes tend to be virtuoso set pieces that
invite farcical action. The detached laughter they earn is deliberately
used to guide the playgoers' emotional responses to other parts of
the plays.

As a succession of bawdy jokes set down with that combination
of aggression and flippancy, hostility and lightheartedness proper to
farce,[33] Dromio's speeches about his kitchen wench elicit much laughter.
Funny as the scene would be out of context, in an actor's anthology
of Shakespearean pieces, it is both funnier and more telling in context
because it simultaneously intensifies and undercuts the romantic passage
that immediately precedes it. Dromio's situation is closely analogous
to his master's: he is mistakenly and relentlessly pursued by a woman
with a greasy face and wide hips; Antipholus is mistakenly and relentlessly pursued by a woman with a weeping eye and a scolding tongue.
This scene begins with Dromio running onto the stage, fleeing from
the woman who claims him. It follows a scene in which Antipholus
figuratively flees the woman who claims him by attempting to make
love to her sister. As Luciana walks off to fetch Antipholus's pursuer,
Dromio gallops on, flying his.

A production can call attention to this analogy by having the entering
Dromio and Nell collide with the departing Luciana. Dromio's subsequent set piece will be more effective if Nell does not remain on
stage while he describes her. Her presence would diminish with reality

his imaginatively hyperbolical anatomization, which the actor would want to deliver with suitably extravagant gestures. But the director may choose to begin the scene with Nell chasing Dromio; such a chase would create many opportunities for farcical business. The servant's scene is a commentary in a farcical mode on his master's scene. The dramatist creates in his farcical scene a striking contrast with its serious counterpart, since Dromio's pungent prose is set against Antipholus's and Luciana's quatrains of closely woven, abstract argument such as would not be out of place in Shakespeare's sonnets.

By drawing attention to the physical counterpart of a moral dilemma, Shakespeare achieves simultaneous effects of undercutting and substantiation. Characters who treat the moral or spiritual aspects of love to the exclusion of the physical are undercut because the audience is forced to see their limitations. Meanwhile, the erotic situation itself is made more substantial because more of its nature is revealed. Love stories figure prominently in all of Shakespeare's comedies, but however his earnest lovers sigh and groan, speaking of essences, eyebeams, arrows, blind boys, yearning hearts, and wondering souls, the audience is not long allowed to forget that love involves the liver's ardor as well as the white, cold, virgin snow upon the heart. If Luciana and Antipholus talk in a sort of spiritual sonnetese, Dromio's description of the fat kitchen wench reminds the audience of what else is at stake if the wrong man is attached to the wrong woman.

Shakespeare's early poem *Venus and Adonis,* although no stage comedy, employs analogous farcical techniques and achieves similar effects of undercutting and substantiation. Most of the first part of the narrative poem is taken up with an elaborate dialogue similar in style and substance to but more extensive than the dialogue between Luciana and Antipholus. Venus tries to persuade Adonis to become her lover, and the young man puts her off. On numerous occasions Shakespeare draws attention to physical details that reflect on this dialogue. The most extensive of these is the description of Adonis's courser's desire for the breeding jennet. Like the ongoing interchange between Venus and Adonis, it is a wooing scene. Yet this passage, like the scene in which Dromio describes the kitchen wench, does not coincide in every particular with its parallel. In Shakespeare's comic writing there is always sufficient difference between the romantic scene and its farcical counterpart to call particular attention to the similarities upon which the playwright wants to focus without blunting the essential comparison by excessive repetition of detail. Thus, the situations of Adonis and his horse are precise opposites. While the young horse is the ardent wooer, the young man is the object of ardent wooing. Although the mare in heat physiologically resembles Venus, she occupies a position analogous to Adonis's. Shakespeare is putting his emphasis on the act of wooing itself. The trampling courser wants what the eloquent goddess wants, but since he lacks her eloquence, his desires are described in such terms as make for Bergsonian laughter. Attention is drawn to his braided hanging mane, his flaming eye, his stamping hoof, and his melting buttock. He is described as breaking his reins and girths, and as biting the poor flies in his fume: "His nostrils drink the air, and forth again, / As from a furnace, vapours doth he send" (273–74).[34]

Many other comic uses of physical detail can be found in the poem. One such is a bit of narrative fact, that Venus begins to sweat in the midst of her oration. The touch undercuts the abstract commonplaces that the goddess has been developing at some length. At the same time, it makes of her a more substantial figure, actuated—goddess though she be—by human desire and limited by human imperfection. A broader comic effect is achieved by a similar use of physical detail. Stunned by a cold look from Adonis, Venus swoons and he revives her: "He wrings her nose, he strikes her on the cheeks, / He bends her fingers, he holds her pulses hard" (475–76). The passage's humor derives from a naturalistic revival for a swoon whose like can be encountered only in romance. Looks may be metaphorically described as killing or stunning, and Shakespeare here employs the Bergsonian device of taking the metaphor in its literal sense.

In such passages as these, Shakespeare comically undercuts Venus's and Adonis's elaborate discourse by drawing attention to limitations in the characters' awareness of what they are talking about. By dwelling on physical desire and some of the physical consequences of passion, the passages extend the reader's awareness by treating such things that the would-be lover and her would-be shunner do not discuss. Love is the poem's chief subject, and Shakespeare makes the subject more substantial for his readers by telling them more of the truth about it. Moreover, by calling attention to physical details and consequences, he better prepares his readers for the ultimate physical consequence, the death of Adonis.

Like many of the lovers in Shakespeare's comedies—Antipholus and Luciana, Proteus and Julia, Lysander and Hermia, Claudio and Hero, Sylvius and Phebe—Venus and Adonis take a grave and incomplete view of love. Part of their comedy springs from their tragic self-perceptions. Shakespeare uses laughter to call attention to the disparity between the spectators' understanding of them and their understanding of themselves.

Comedy customarily deals with a more substantial range of experience than does tragedy.[35] Aldous Huxley develops this notion in the essay, "Tragedy and the Whole Truth." He calls attention to the passage in the *Odyssey* that describes Odysseus's and his shipmates' reactions when one of their comrades is lost to the Cyclops. Although they are grieving, they prepare and eat their supper before they give way completely. Since their grief is mixed with exhaustion, they soon fall asleep. This attention to eating and sleeping, argues Huxley, is incompatible with tragedy, which would concentrate on the passion of grief. Homer tells the whole truth. Hungry men, however grief-stricken, will eat, and exhausted men will sleep.[36]

In his Ovidian narrative, Shakespeare tells the whole truth about love. He does so with the Bergsonian device of leading readers to expect a moral or spiritual treatment and then surprising and delighting them with the comic incongruity of a physical one. He gives his physical treatment in such a manner that it both undercuts and substantiates the intensely felt but only partially perceived experience communicated in Venus's and Adonis's dialogue.

The same sort of device is used time and again in the comedies. All his serious lovers have their undercutters and substantiators: Launce and Speed, Puck and Bottom, Beatrice and Benedick, Touchstone and Rosalind. In *The Two Gentlemen of Verona*, a comedy probably written about the same time as *Venus and Adonis*,[37] Launce and his dog are the chief agents of undercutting and substantiation. The very appearance of Crab on the stage—whether the role is taken by a live dog, a synthetic dog, or a human actor, or whether the creature's existence is mimed by his master—will get big laughs. So will Launce's tales and his manner of telling them. Like Dromio's description of Nell, these tales require the exaggerated, energetic gestures of an actor who is both raconteur and mime. Laughter will be provoked by the details of the stories—the mother's bad breath, or Crab's making water against Silvia's farthingale.

One of Launce's set pieces follows the painful events of Proteus's wooing Silvia in Julia's presence and Silvia's contriving her escape. Launce and Crab provide comic relief in the precise sense of that term. Their presence constitutes a reassurance: no audience will worry too much about the outcome of a play that has such creatures in it. But the scene also provides by farcical analogy a complex and keen criticism of Proteus's behavior. Launce has already established himself as a moral critic, being the first character in the play to state plainly that his master is "a kind of knave" (3.1.261).[38] Now his selfless devotion to Crab is implicitly compared to his master's duplicity. Moreover, he tells the audience that he has given Crab as a gift to Silvia from Proteus. Thus Crab becomes Proteus's representative. The dog is analogous to Proteus in the same way that the courser is analogous to Venus. Crab steals Silvia's capon's leg, makes water against her farthingale, and defiles the duke's table. When this act is smelt out, the dog is threatened with hanging and is saved only when Launce takes the fault on himself and is whipped. The dog, then, is a thief and a defiler, and he makes others suffer for his faults. Precisely the same things may be said of Proteus. He steals Silvia from Valentine, defiles Valentine's friendship and Julia's love, and makes nearly everyone in the play suffer for his faults. Although Proteus is appalled to learn that Launce has given Crab to Silvia, the playwright could not have found for this character a fitter emissary.

As with other scenes of farcical analogy, the audience will doubtless not think all this through as it listens to Launce's story, but the visual and verbal establishment of Crab as Proteus's representative will make more substantial the idea of Proteus that the play communicates. This idea can be strengthened in production with desirable comic effect if once or twice the actor playing Proteus assumes doglike postures in his attempts to woo Silvia. The idea grows even more firmly fixed when Proteus enters, accompanied by his new emissary, the disguised Julia. For a brief moment of emblematic spectacle, which harks back in its whimsical way to the *psychomacheia* of the morality plays, Proteus is on stage with Julia, the representative of all that is good in him, and Crab, the representative of all that is vile.

Shakespeare's subsequent farcical scenes and characters are not different in their nature and function from those in the earlier comedies. While the quartet of Athenian lovers in *A Midsummer Night's Dream* grows increasingly quarrelsome and frenzied under the spell of love-in-idleness, Bottom, on a pinnacle of serenity and self-assurance that they will never reach, calmly accepts as his due the love of the fairy queen, and in lordly fashion commands her attendants to scratch his head. With Dogberry's peculiar use of the English language in *Much Ado About Nothing*, he both undercuts some of the other characters' linguistic pretensions and makes more substantial the notion of faulty communication that the play dramatizes. And Dogberry is the most appropriate figure to avert the near-tragedy that grows out of this faulty communication. In *As You Like It* Touchstone's scenes with Audrey call attention by farcical analogy to the sexual desire implicit in all the play's other wooings. In *Measure for Measure* the rough denizens of the Viennese brothels and prisons give the audience a worm's-eye view of the duke's machinations. Indeed, the play invites comparison between Pompey as pimp and the duke as procurer and perpetrator of the bed-trick.[39] And in *The Tempest* Caliban's talk of quick freshes, pig-nuts, jays' nests, and marmosets gives the audience its most substantial appreciation of Shakespeare's strangest setting. Moreover, the scatological byplay among Caliban, Trinculo, and Stephano enriches the spectators' sense of the play's other murderous plotters. I observed Nicholas Pennell, playing Stephano in the 1982 production at Stratford, Ontario, give a thrilling theatrical demonstration of this enrichment. When he perceived that he had a genuine chance to become king of the island, he transformed himself with a sneer and a terrifying snarl from buffoon to tyrant. In a moment at once hilarious and disturbing, he communicated to the audience a clarified and deepened understanding of the corrupting effects on Antonio, Sebastian, and even Prospero, of the desire for power and of its exercise.[40]

While Shakespeare's audience may not feel, as Bergson, Freud, and others hypothesize that it should, a total absence of sympathy when it laughs, the farcical characters and scenes do not often call forth from the audience a great rush of fellow feeling, an access of Sidneyan delight. A low comic character may elicit a moment of sympathy, such as that excited by Dromio of Ephesus when his comic mask falls away and the audience perceives the beaten slave beneath it (4.4.27–37).[41] But such moments of intense feeling, however memorable, are rarely excited by the comedies' clowns and gulls. Neither is the laughter they elicit often provoked by scorn or deep malice. I observed at the outset of this chapter that scornful laughter is a frequent activity in Shakespeare's comedies, but the plays are usually so disposed that the audience is not invited to share in the malice. Often the impulse to laugh is suppressed by feelings of sympathy and pain such as I will examine in the next chapter. But as often, the laughter is divorced from derision.

In *The Comedy of Errors,* for example, the playwright could have easily elicited a great deal of malicious laughter at Adriana's expense. He had sufficient warrant for such a strategy from his main source, Plautus's *Menaechmi*. In that play, Menaechmus and his parasite have cruel fun at the unseen wife's expense in the opening moments, and the play closes with the jubilant breaking of matrimonial bonds.[42] Shakespeare deviates from his source by making Adriana a figure central to the play's action, one of the unwitting agents of its furious farce. Although Adriana's behavior is censured by her milder sister and she never wins lasting sympathy, neither is she allowed to become an object of sustained derision, as is her Plautean counterpart.

In her ever-increasing frenzies of jealousy and despair, Adriana comes to embody the mad and violent spirit of farce. As is the case with Malvolio, the actress will play the part most effectively if she achieves a seamless identification with her role. Indeed, she should strive for the fervor and emotional truth of tragedy. The farcical detachment will grow out of the contrast between her genuine frenzy and the blunders that cause it. The more seriously she takes herself, the more hilarious will her scenes become. Adriana's earnestness and precipitancy are matched by equal measures of both qualities in her husband and his twin. All three characters act quickly and decisively, reflect not at all, and, plunging ever deeper into error, compound mistake on mistake with astonishing rapidity that should leave actors and playgoers breathless.

Madness, violence, and confusion can be elements as proper to tragedy as to farce, but speed and context render these elements farcical in *The Comedy of Errors*. The audience knows well that all the play's events have been set in motion by a simple, mechanical mistake. From their first laugh at the wrong Dromio's encounter with the wrong Antipholus, the spectators are serene in their assurance that the twins will meet and the confusion evaporate. To be sure, even this early farce has its deeper implications, which good productions do not obscure.[43] But the play offers little occasion for, nor do most productions strive for, the sustained emotional engagement of the later comedies. With actors in constant motion, perhaps supported by sets that ingeniously employ as many moving parts as possible, this play creates an impression like that of a whirligig, spinning faster and faster until Aemilia puts out her hand at the right moment and stops it.

Farcical scenes in later plays usually feature a manipulator, a character as rapid of wit as tongue who exercises his imaginative will upon the other characters. Petruchio manipulating Kate and her family, Puck

leading lovers and artisans in an ever wilder dance, Sir Toby and
Fabian managing Viola and Sir Andrew into their duel, Mistress Page
and Mistress Ford maneuvering Falstaff into the buck-basket, and
Autolycus terrifying the shepherd and his son with tales of torture
are all characters of such a description. All these parts, even the drunken
Toby, are most effectively played by actors of enormous energy whose
verbal and physical virtuosity will astound the audience.

Petruchio is a farcical Richard III. Like the crook-backed killer,
he overwhelms all the characters in the play with his audacity, wit,
eloquence, and imaginative force. With his size, commanding presence,
and booming voice, Len Cariou as Petruchio in a 1982 Stratford,
Ontario, production verbally and physically dominated the play. The
character can be in constant motion—caressing Kate, backing her father
into corners, striking his servants. Alternately, he can be a stationary
ringmaster with the other characters moving to his apparent control.
However he is played, he must command the stage and the action.

Like Adriana, Kate is actuated by grief and rage, and the actress
will best serve the play if she strives for a similar emotional truth
in playing her role. As with Adriana, Shakespeare depicts in Kate's
early scenes just enough of her emotional torment to mitigate such
scorn as she might otherwise provoke. She may be described as possess-
ing a froward humor that must be purged, but she does not attract
such malicious laughter as figures like Jonson's Bobadil or Molière's
Harpagon draw upon themselves when they are shamed. The derisive
laughter that might have been hers gives place to the detached laughter
of farce, laughter that Petruchio causes and controls.

The force of his eloquence makes his imaginings more vivid than
Kate's reality:

> I tell you, 'tis incredible to believe
> How much she loves me—:, the kindest Kate!
> She hung about my neck, and kiss on kiss
> She vied so fast, protesting oath on oath,
> That in a twink she won me to her love.

(2.1.298–302)

The spectators have seen no such behavior. Kate may be quite overwhelmed, speechless with rage, or she may have fallen in love with
him at first sight, as Barbara Jefford made her do in a 1954 R.S.C.
production.[44] But for whatever reason, she is bereft of the power

to deny Petruchio's magnificent lie and assert the truth of her own senses.

The preeminence of imaginative force in Shakespeare's farcical manipulators becomes even clearer when Petruchio is compared to his analog in *The Taming of a Shrew*. This play appeared at about the same time as Shakespeare's, and it may either have been his source or a feeble redaction of his work.[45] Petruchio's counterpart Ferrando lacks Petruchio's power of fantasy. He paints no glorious picture of Kate's secret love for him; instead, Kate, in an unprovoked aside, tells the audience that although Ferrando puts her off, he is yet better than her prying father and jeering friends.[46] Later in the play, Ferrando simply commands Kate to leave her father's home after the wedding, asserting: "This is my day, tomorrow shalt thou rule."[47] For no apparent reason, Kate chooses to leave with him.

By contrast, Petruchio uses his power of invention to force Kate to leave her house before her own wedding feast has begun. Shakespeare's Kate fiercely asserts her intention to defy her new husband: "You may be jogging whiles your boots are green" (3.2.207). Petruchio conjures an imaginary attack. Under the guise of rescuing her—the actor may mime a fight with an invisible army—he sweeps her from the stage, leaving wedding guests and audience breathless.

In his subsequent battles with his wife, imagination continues to be his chief weapon. To be sure, he causes her continuous physical suffering, depriving her of sleep and food, taunting her with the sight of new garments that she may not have. But the audience is made to concentrate not so much on the abuse as on the series of lies and pretenses that justify the abuse. The truest indication that Kate is indeed tamed is her allowing the hard evidence of her senses to give place to her husband's imagination:

> Then, God be bless'd, it is the blessed sun;
> But sun it is not, when you say it is not;
> And the moon changes even as your mind.
>
> (4.5.18–20)

This is the first moment of genuine concord between them. When she seconds and amplifies Petruchio's fantastical virginification of the withered old Vincentio, she and her husband speak with one imaginative voice. They will speak with that voice for the rest of the play.

Largely controlled by Petruchio, events involving Kate move so quickly that the audience has little time for either scorn or sympathy. Only in the relatively leisurely final scene does the pace relax and allow the audience to reflect. And upon reflection, the playgoers find that although Kate may have been manipulated, she has not become a Bergsonian marionette. She is capable of arousing feelings; indeed, considerable critical debate rages over what those feelings are. Of all Shakespeare's comedies, *The Taming of the Shrew* is one of three that are closest to pure farce; yet in its treatment of its title character it strains mightily against farce's emotional limitations.

As Shakespeare matures, his comedy grows so complex that generic classification or theoretical distinctions among kinds of laughter grow less and less able to describe its achievement. In his greatest comedies he thoroughly mixes the kinds of laughter he calls forth in his audience. He passes easily and swiftly among laughter inspired by derision, accompanied by emotional neutrality, or rising on waves of sympathetic identification. Such mingling can be exemplified by many sequences and characters in his mature comedies, but it can be nowhere better illustrated than in the treatment of Benedick in *Much Ado About Nothing*.

Benedick is a character of many aspects. In the play's early scenes, he is governed by a humor of misogyny that renders his behavior predictable and makes him a proper object of Bergsonian laughter. At the same time, he is a laughing critic, satirizing Claudio, Don Pedro, and Beatrice, and inviting the audience to laugh with him at their expense. The spectators cannot easily sustain an unmitigated campaign of derisive laughter against one who is so well able to entertain with his eloquence and wit. He is at once *alazon*—dupe, imposter, character possessed by a humor that must be purged—and *eiron*—self-deprecator, self-ironist, recognizing his own foibles and vulnerabilities. In this he resembles Falstaff, and the laughter he excites can be profitably compared to the laughter provoked by the fat knight.[48]

Such mixed laughter is elicited by Benedick's comic monologue preceding the scene in which he eavesdrops upon his friends and hears the false information that Beatrice is in love with him. In this speech the character addresses the audience directly, and it would not be inappropriate for the actor to take on the manner and presence of a stand-up comic, spicing his satiric commentary with extravagant, entertaining gestures. Unlike such early commentators as Launce or Grumio, or such late ones as Lavache or Autolycus, Benedick reveals something of himself and thereby incurs laughter at his own expense.

The revelation begins when he turns from his excoriation of Claudio's folly to an expatiation upon his own imperviousness: "One woman is fair, yet I am well; another is wise, yet I am well; another virtuous, yet I am well" (2.3.23–24). With each repetition, the actor can reveal the character's diminishing confidence; although he affects the form of detachment, he is deeply engaged. Laughter that Benedick means to earn by virtue of his wit mixes with laughter elicited by his unintentional self-revelation.

Benedick's second solo speech toward the end of this scene is different in kind from the first. It communicates the process of internal conflict, change, and growth. Rather than simply announcing the result of change, it conveys a kinetic experience and is thus quintessentially dramatic.[49] Put in the simplest terms, Benedick does not know at the speech's beginning how it will end. The spectators know how the speech will end, but they cannot predict any better than he can the elaborate twistings through which he will arrive at his conclusion. Much of the audience's laughter arises from the earnestness with which the character performs his emotional pirouettes. As is logically the case with a speech of this complexity, many fruitful approaches offer themselves to the actor. He may choose to address the spectators as if they were a group of confidantes, his equals in intelligence and wit. Since the spectators know so much more than he does, ironic laughter will spring from his placing himself on an equal footing with them. Alternately, the actor may choose not to speak directly to the audience, entering instead into a private meditation that the playgoers happen to overhear. In our production the actor became still and grave, showing that the character was sobered by knowledge of Beatrice's apparent love and his responsibility to prove worthy of it. He conveyed an initial bewilderment and went on to show with absolute conviction the character's astonishment and pleasure at the nature and force of the resolution he arrived at by the speech's end.

Benedick's ability to make such a speech suggests that he is more than a creature governed by a Bergsonian mechanism. Yet even when he shows himself capable of incipient growth, he complicates the audience's response by appearing to exchange one mechanism for another. His subsequent behavior as lover is as predictable and laughably mechanical as his former conduct as professional woman hater. But having watched him begin a process of growth, the audience can never again react to him simply as an automaton. His soliloquy shows a living creature beginning to disengage himself from the mechanical thing that has been encrusted on him. It reverses Bergson's comic formula by showing a thing in the act of becoming a man. This act calls forth the happy laughter of recognition and sympathetic identification.

What happens when the highest degree of imagination, the keenest wit, and the greatest verve are given to a character who is his play's chief butt? The butt I refer to is for many the embodiment of that untamable and indefinable thing known as the comic spirit. He is Falstaff, and the play in which he is victimized is *The Merry Wives of Windsor.*

Now Falstaff is universally acknowledged to be one of Shakespeare's great creations, but it is still widely held that the Falstaff of this farce is a debased version of the Falstaff of the history plays. Indeed, until recently it has been fashionable to despise the play as a piece of hackwork and bring in for evidence tales of quick composition and royal commission.[50] Yet as Allardyce Nicoll demonstrates, Shakespeare in *The Merry Wives of Windsor* shows an important kinship with the makers of the Comedia del'Arte.[51] The devisers of these scenarios customarily put well-known characters into fresh situations. Shakespeare, Nicoll argues, is doing once, as an experiment, what for the makers of the Comedia is a quotidian practice. The chief difference between Falstaff in Windsor and Falstaff in Eastcheap is one of situation rather than conception or execution.

The apparent change in his character springs inevitably from the play's situation. In *Henry IV, Part I,* Falstaff is usually the dupe, while the prince, Poins, or the gods of battle are the tricksters. In this play he is not the intended victim but the intended practicer, setting up his plots to possess the merry wives' persons and their purses. In the Boar's Head he must evade each crisis as it arises, reacting to what others initiate. At Windsor he initiates the action, devising a long-range goal and forgetting about scrapes that his pursuit of that goal may bring about. He forgets to evade, to dodge, or to improvise because his imagination of himself as a great lover thoroughly blinds him to what is apparent to everyone else on the stage and to everyone in the audience. This imaginative conception becomes the mechanical thing encrusted on him and renders him a fit subject for mocking Bergsonian laughter. In *Much Ado About Nothing,* the audience sees a living man disengage himself from a mechanical thing. In *The Merry Wives of Windsor,* the audience sees a mechanical thing take possession of a living man. The Falstaff of this play, made inflexible by vanity and lust, can find no trick, no starting-hole to evade the buck-basket, the cudgel, and the horns.

Humored thus, he draws as much malicious laughter as does any character in Shakespeare. But he draws it more from the other characters on the stage than from the audience. As with Benedick, the spectators will give him the occasional scornful guffaw, but he is not an object of continuing malice. Even though his plot against the merry wives is ugly enough to incur considerable dislike, Shakespeare diminishes potential scorn by drawing on the well-known persona he has previously created for the fat knight. Like Benedick, Falstaff makes the audience laugh often enough by virtue of his wit to convert potentially malicious laughter into the detached or even affectionate laughter of admiration for a good entertainer. Although seized by a form of Bergsonian automatism, Falstaff still has in his nature and actions an abundance of what Suzanne Langer calls "the comic rhythm, the rhythm of felt life."[52] It is impossible to laugh with continuing malice at such a figure. Falstaff outflanks the audience by laughing at his own defeats:

> Well, if I be serv'd such another trick, I'll have my brains ta'en out and butter'd, and give them to a dog for a new-year's gift. . . . and you may know by my size that I have a kind of alacrity in sinking . . . I had been drown'd . . . a death that I abhor; for the water swells a man; and what a thing should I have been when I had been swell'd! (3.5.10–15)

The greed, lust, and vanity that make him so easy to dupe are balanced by an imagination that renders him secure from most of the audience's malice. Falstaff has the imagination of Homer and can make of his encounter with Ford epic narrative:

> I quak'd for fear lest the lunatic knave would have search'd it; but Fate, ordaining he should be cuckold, held his hand. Well, on went he for a search, and away went I for foul clothes. (3.4.94–97)

Although scorn is an element in their complex laughter, the spectators cannot laugh in continuing scorn at anyone who talks like that.

Falstaff comes in for a fair amount of violence in this play; he is beaten, nearly drowned, and pinched black and blue. In addition to such physical violence, tendered in a manner proper to farce, the play offers the emotional violence of Ford's obsessive passion. Many observers, both of the play and of Verdi's comic opera based on it, have feared this passion too weighty for comedy.[53] With Ford, Shakespeare seems to be looking with one eye toward such comical figures as Jonson's Kitely and Middleton's Harebrain, but he is looking with the other eye toward his own serious and disturbing creations, Othello and Leontes. Like laughter provoked by most of the comic figures of Shakespeare's maturity, such laughter as Ford provokes mixes at times with deep feeling that would seem to be incompatible with laughter. Time and again in his plays, Shakespeare demonstrates how thin is the line between laughter and pain. Ford stands on that line.

2
PAIN

THE EFFECTS OF FARCE DEPEND HEAVILY ON CONTEXT, and the context in which Ford's rage and pain are presented tends to suppress sympathy and invite laughter. The play emphasizes the preposterousness of the idea that Falstaff can be an illicit lover. Although Shakespeare forcefully demonstrates in subsequent plays that jealousy needs no reasonable foundation, he still invites his audience to bear in mind that Cassio and Polixenes, the respective objects of Othello's and Leontes's jealousy, are proper men and feasible lovers. Falstaff is neither, and the audience is encouraged to laugh at the presentation of jealousy founded upon so ludicrous an object.

Neither Ford's language nor his perception of his pain is of a nature to invite sympathy. Othello and Leontes, both committers of appalling crimes, are yet given some of the most affecting verse in English to express their agony. Ford, who does no real harm and suffers considerable humiliation, talks in workaday prose. Although he tries to convey with his prose a sense of loss, what he sees himself as losing is expressed in terms so unexpectedly banal that the audience laughs. Compared to the unbearable pain of Othello and Leontes, Ford's is a passion in miniature, a Lilliputian rage. His wife, reduced to the stature of one of his threatened possessions, is placed in a series with his butter, his cheese, his horse, and his bottle. The character is in constant, violent motion—ransacking the buck-basket and firing his birding-piece up the chimney.

To be sure, occasional moments of stillness will enrich the playing of Ford. In his 1968 performance, Ian Richardson demonstrated with a few quiet, tender moments in the play's last scene that it would have been possible for him to make the audience perceive Ford's jealousy in a more serious and disturbing light.[1] But for the rest of the performance, he played in the farcical mode that the text suggests. Like most actors who assay this role, he created a character whose rage drove him to hilarious physical excess. He tore about the stage with the extravagant ferocity of a tornado, leaving as much havoc behind him.

Ford is a rarity among Shakespeare's characters because he suffers without moving the audience to participate in his suffering. The dramatist's usual way when he presents suffering characters is to invite the audience to share their pain. He does so by creating a sense of sympathy between characters and spectators—that is, by making the spectators feel some measure of what the characters are feeling. I use the word *sympathy* as it is used in Shakespeare's own writings.[2] His most revealing use of the word occurs in *Venus and Adonis*, the Ovidian poem from which so much can be learned about the playwright's comic practice. Readers of the poem will recall that when the beautiful young man is killed, Venus mourns him while the surrounding foliage seems to partake in his experience of death.

> No flow'r was nigh, no grass, herb, leaf, or weed,
> But stole his blood and seem'd with him to bleed.
> This solemn sympathy poor Venus noteth. . . .
>
> (1055–57)

The sympathy described in the poem is not a conventional gesture of pity. It is instead a participation in the experience of one creature by other creatures.

When the word occurs in Shakespeare's plays, it denotes a like sharing, an experience held in common by the creatures who are said to sympathize with each other. At the end of *The Comedy of Errors,* for example, Aemelia invites to a feast and to an explanation "all that are assembled in this place, / That by this sympathized one day's error / Have suffer'd wrong" (5.1.395–97). Everyone on the stage has either made mistakes or suffered through mistakes. Thus everyone has shared in the day of error, and Aemelia's phrase most properly denotes that sharing. Her lines take in the spectators as well, presuming their sympathy. The word carries the same denotation when Falstaff uses it repeatedly in his love-letter to Mistress Page:

> You are not young, no more am I; go to, then, there's sympathy. You are merry, so am I; ha! ha! then there's more sympathy. You love sack, and so do I; would you desire better sympathy? (2.1.8–9)

It is a critical commonplace that one of Shakespeare's supreme

achievements in tragedy is to make his audience both apprehend the
terrible things his protagonists are doing, and at the same time share
these protagonists' terrible anguish.[3] As R. S. Crane observes, the
audience feels that the death of Macbeth is necessary. He must be
stopped for the sake of the people he is causing to suffer as well
as for his own sake. The audience cannot bear to feel what Macbeth
feels, to become the monster he is becoming, any more than it can
bear to witness his crimes.[4] The spectators are brought to this perception because the playwright makes them know what it feels like to
be Macbeth. Although Shakespeare's comedies do not inflict upon
their characters or their spectators the intensity of suffering achieved
in *Othello* or *Macbeth*—they could not do so and remain comedies—
they often work upon the audience in similar ways. They present
characters who suffer outer and inner pain, and they make the spectators
know what it feels like to be those characters.

Shakespeare's simplest way of eliciting fellow feeling in his audience
is by creating wholly virtuous characters who quickly win the spectators' affection, and then making these characters suffer through the
plots of villains and traitors. It is relatively easy for a skilled dramatist
to move his audience to pity and pain by depicting torment inflicted
upon good people by bad ones. This is the standard stuff of melodrama.
That the dramatist draws on simple, black-and-white conflicts at every
stage of his career as a writer of comedies suggests that he does not
entertain the prejudice against melodrama held by many of his critics.
Indeed, he returns to melodrama whenever he attempts a new direction
in comedy, in *The Two Gentlemen of Verona, All's Well That Ends
Well, Pericles,* and *Cymbeline.* These comedies rise out of the simplest
dramatic conflicts. Shakespeare pits characters of unalloyed virtue
against characters who prove almost entirely bad–Julia, Valentine, and
Silvia against Proteus; Helena against Bertram and Parolles; Pericles
and Marina against Antiochus, Cleon, and Dionyza; and Imogen
against Iachimo, Cloten, and the wicked queen. Concerned with various new problems of dramatic artistry, he does not complicate his
labors in these plays by creating mixed characters.

The earliest of these plays, *The Two Gentlemen of Verona,* is a
comedy of the workshop. Shakespeare here tries many things for the
first time in his career as a comic playwright, and one can learn
much about his stagecraft by noting what he continues to use and
what he abandons. He represents for the first time in comedy a genuine
betrayal and its consequences in human suffering.[5] The abandoned

Julia is his most successful early portrayal of a suffering figure in comedy.

Julia wins the audience's interest by expressing her passion's force in verse that is perhaps crude in comparison to what Shakespeare writes later in his career, but is still sufficiently affecting for Thomas Hardy to choose a line and a half of it as the epigraph for *Tess of the D'Urbervilles*. At the same time, she is able to mock her passion even as she recognizes its strength, indulging in witty wordplay with her maid and commenting in wry soliloquy:

> Since maids, in modesty, say 'No' to that
> Which they would have the profferer construe 'Ay'.
> Fie, fie, how wayward is this foolish love,
> That like a testy babe will scratch the nurse,
> And presently, all humbled, kiss the rod!
>
> (1.2.55–59)

Such portrayal of simultaneous passion and self-mockery becomes one of Shakespeare's surest means of winning sympathy for his comic heroines. The spectators grow to care deeply about Julia, and her scenes of humiliation and lament are the most painful in Shakespeare's apprentice comedies.

The playwright derives the character of Julia mainly from Felismena, a figure in Jorge de Montemayor's *Diana Enamorada,* a Portuguese romance. The incorporation into comedy of such pain and wonder as he finds in narratives of Montemayor, Bandello, Boccaccio, or Painter allows him to move beyond his early farces toward the rich and complex form that he is developing throughout his career. His evolving methods for communicating his characters' pain to his audience is revealed by the striking way in which he modifies Montemayor's material. Like Julia, Felismena is betrayed by her lover and goes wandering in man's disguise. But Felismena is a roaring girl of romance, an Amazonian shepherdess who slays savages and knights. Shakespeare takes over the strong love, the betrayal, the journey, and the sexual disguise but leaves out the martial prowess. Julia is the least heroic of his heroines. She has less control over her destiny than any of Shakespeare's other comic heroines.[6]

The playwright lavishes wondrous resources on his subsequent heroines, but he goes against a tradition in romance by giving to none of them strength and skill in physical combat. Indeed, he frequently shows how little able they are to defend themselves and how vulnerable they can be to physical danger. This forces the audience to take their sufferings more seriously than it might be able to do could the heroines simply unhorse and behead their assailants. Thus, in writing *Cymbeline*, the dramatist again departs from his sources to deprive his heroine of martial prowess. Imogen's counterpart in Boccaccio has "adventures in the eastern Mediterranean, rising to high office under the sultan of Alexandria." In other of the story's analogs, the heroine becomes a great soldier.[7] Though Imogen is capable of terrifying rage of a sort that Julia never achieves, Shakespeare makes her in her pathetic adventures with her unknown brothers and with the Roman army as unsoldierlike as can be imagined. She is given resources that enable her eventually to take more control over her affairs than Julia can, but like Julia, she impresses herself most keenly on the audience as a sufferer.

Whenever Shakespeare is wrestling with new sorts of comic material, he makes his audience enter into the feelings of virtuous, suffering women who embody the pathetic rather than the heroic. Even so, the parts of these suffering comic heroines are written with great variety, and actresses who play them need not make them sound like constant whiners. The speeches and actions of Imogen, Helena, and even Julia give performers many opportunities to display the characters' wit and resilience. Although the heroines are denied physical prowess, audiences' responses to them are enriched by the surprising abilities they do display.

Helena, in *All's Well That Ends Well*, endures amorous rejection and performs medical miracles. In her dual role as sufferer and wonder-worker, she may be viewed as Shakespeare's prototypical comic heroine. He endows her with the courage, generosity, and wondrous optimism that he gives to his most winning heroines. He also gives her the humor that springs from self-irony. No sad forlorn lover, however disinterested, will long retain the audience's sympathy. Such dreariness is forestalled by Helena's bantering scene with Parolles early in the play: "Bless our poor virginity from underminers and blowers-up! Is there no military policy how virgins might blow up men?" (1.1.114–16). These lines wittily anticipate the scheme by which she will contrive to undermine her man by losing her virginity. Although she has not the quicksilver wit of Beatrice or Rosalind, the scene with Parolles adds to the audience's impression of her resourcefulness, and it helps keep her many sad scenes from growing oppressive.

The brief scene in which Parolles tells her that her husband is going to leave her and commands her to lie to the king frankly appeals to the audience's pity. But pity does not amount to sympathy. The audience can feel sorry for Helena without knowing what it feels like to be Helena. Shakespeare contrives in this scene not only to move pity, but to make the audience share Helena's apprehension. A Fletcherian seesaw of a soliloquy in which joys and fears play tag with each other through limpid verse would be just the sort of thing to cool genuine sympathy and heat voyeurism. Shakespeare avoids this trap and instead produces a scene best calculated to create fellow feeling—the tiny dialogue between Helena and the clown.

The clown is an ally and representative of the old countess, and by this point in the play she and Helena are so intricately tied to each other that they seem to share each other's feelings. Thus, the clown's riddling insistence that the countess is "not well" works on Helena's fears. She may momentarily enter into the countess's vague distemper: "If she be very well, what does she ail that she's not very well?" (2.4.6). This moment of unease will help the actress persuade the audience to enter into the character's apprehension. The clown's own unhappiness—a characteristic explicitly noted by Lafeu toward the play's end and implicit in all his scenes—will contribute further to the disturbing sense that the scene subtly conveys.

Shakespeare gives his heroine no expression of joy in her new marriage. Instead, he reveals her doubts and makes the audience share them. Her suffering is spread out over several scenes as the playwright brings her by degrees to a full knowledge of her abandonment. These scenes owe their poignancy as much to what is left out of them as to what they contain. Certainly the playgoers will expect Bertram to say no word such as a new husband might speak to a new wife. But the playgoers might expect from Helena speeches of reproach or sorrow in response to her husband's cold contempt. They hear only her reiterated fear that she has overreached herself by contriving marriage to an aristocrat:

> And ever shall
> With true observance seek to eke out that
> Wherein toward me my homely stars have fail'd
> To equal my great fortune.

(2.5.72–75)

This speech is enormously difficult in performance, since the actress may exhibit neither irony, self-pity, nor reproach. But that the feeling informing the words is of the first importance in an effective playing of Helena was demonstrated by Roberta Maxwell when she performed the role in Michael Kahn's 1970 production at Stratford, Connecticut:

> Any potential stridency in her character was mitigated by an aura of vulnerability, by what the director perceived as "a wonderful sense of 'am I overstepping?'"[8]

Characters who linger over their own troubles frequently cool an audience's emotional response. It will be remembered that Ford, with his repeated use of the first person pronoun, provokes a pennyworth of pity to an intolerable deal of laughter. Helena's lack of self-pity and self-regard, coupled with her essential resilience, renders her among the most sympathetic of Shakespeare's characters.[9]

Even before she knows that her husband never means to see her again, she is deeply hurt by his manner of saying good-bye to her. Her pain is most strongly conveyed to the audience in a short speech of broken phrases:

> Something: and scarce so much; nothing, indeed.
> I would not tell you what I would, my lord.
> Faith, yes:
> Strangers and foes do sunder and not kiss.

> (2.5.82–85)

I call particular attention to the two syllables "faith, yes," which express her resolve to ask for the kiss her husband will not give. They stand by themselves in a line of verse, and from their placement as well as their import the actress may infer that they are to be heavily stressed as befits the speech's climactic words, and are to be surrounded by pauses that will express the uncertain quality of Helena's resolution. The speech as a whole, with its many stops and changes of direction, provides the most appropriate dramatic expression of her humiliation.

As the play proceeds, the spectators will be urged to participate in Helena's feelings in spite of a fundamental and irreconcilable difference between her feelings and theirs. They may come to loathe Bertram, while she strongly loves him. If when she gets him the playgoers despise him so much that they do not want her to have him, they will leave the theater baffled, uneasy, irritated. The playwright counters such feelings by his manner of revealing his heroine in the early scenes. There are striking similarities between this method and the way in which Hamlet is first introduced to his audience. Knowing in *All's Well That Ends Well* that he will be asking his audience to sympathize with a young girl's love for a man it may come to despise, he perhaps cannot do better than to borrow for this play devices by which he initially presents the most sympathetic of all his characters.

Like the Danish prince in the early council scene, the poor physician's daughter in the opening scene of leave-taking stands quietly but tensely by, speaks a few highly charged words, and then, when the stage is finally cleared, explodes into soliloquy and unloads her heart to the audience. Her soliloquy, like Hamlet's, begins with "O!"—an expressive sigh that conveys pain and release. The scenes in both plays seem to be conducted in the presence of death. The dead King of Denmark is very much on the minds of the living royalty, while the dead Count of Rousillon, the dead physician, and the apparently dying King of France are silent witnesses to what their descendants and dependents say and do. Both Hamlet and Helena are dressed in mourning and seem to be grieving for departed fathers. Even when the prince and the maid reveal that they are hiding other stronger griefs beneath the show of mourning, the audience is more likely to sympathize with these feelings, having been moved to pity by the spectacle of young people in black. Both Hamlet and Helena take the audience so completely and forcefully into their confidence in their early soliloquies that spectators are inclined to sympathize with subsequent decisions and actions that in other characters they might question.

Of course, there are also important differences between Hamlet's initial appearance and Helena's. The comic heroine is preceded by no ghost come from the grave to bode the world's rottenness. Indeed, in comparison with the world of *Hamlet*, the world of *All's Well That Ends Well* is a paradise of virtue. This difference is immediately manifested in the characters' costumes. Hamlet's suit of mourning contrasts with the doubtless splendidly festive court clothes surrounding him and shows him immediately at discord with his world; all the characters who enter at the beginning of the comedy are dressed in black. Moreover, the countess and Lafeu immediately establish themselves as benevolent voices that quickly command and continually hold moral authority. Since the play makes clear that they are Helena's allies, the audience comes swiftly to understand that Helena, unlike Hamlet, is not alone in her world. This apparent concord allows the playwright a deliberately oblique presentation of Bertram, and upon that initial presentation, coupled with the presentation of the play's heroine, will depend Shakespeare's success at sympathetically portraying Helena's love.

Much is suggested about Bertram's inner nature, but nothing is revealed with certainty. More important, everything that is suggested turns out to be half true at best. So oblique is Bertram's initial scene that it can be argued that Shakespeare is deliberately misleading the audience's expectations.[10] While I do not go so far as A. P. Riemer, who argues that the audience is initially led to expect that Bertram and Helena are lovers, that the old countess is opposed to a match between them, and that the play's chief action will arise from the young people's separation, I hold that the initial presentation of the young people does lead the audience to expect that they are or will soon become lovers.

When Helena opens her heart to the playgoers after the stage has been cleared, they will still have echoing in their ears Bertram's last words to her, which certainly bode no ill and may give cause for hope: "The best wishes that can be forg'd in your thoughts be servants to you! Be comfortable to my mother, your mistress, and make much of her" (1.1.68–70). This brief farewell is one of the play's many difficult sequences for the actors. Bertram may choose to show the audience that he holds a genuine fraternal affection for his mother's ward, and Helena ought to conceal for the moment the full extent of her passion. The scene is charged with tension, much of which may be dissipated if Helena telegraphs to the spectators what she will reveal in her ensuing soliloquy.

The playwright continues to deceive the audience about Bertram during the first two acts by making the young man say relatively little and by making those characters whom the audience has learned to take as moral guides put the best interpretation on the little he does say. There need be no indication that he has not inherited his father's moral parts about which the audience hears so much, or that he does not deserve the full affection of the countess, the king, and Helena. In the 1970 production at Stratford, Connecticut, director Michael Kahn dealt with the problem by having Peter Thompson play the character as a very attractive unsophisticate. Kahn explained to the company: "In thinking about Bertram we have to keep in mind Rousillon—a beautiful chateau, in the country, inhabited by elegant and marvelous people— but *country*. This accounts for a great deal in Bertram's character and behavior. What happens to the boy from the country when the girl from home arrives as he begins his new life in the city?"[11]

The first truly unpleasant thing Bertram does is publicly to reject Helena toward the end of the second act. Even this rejection has some color of justification about it:

> My wife, my liege! I shall beseech your Highness,
> In such a business give me leave to use
> The help of mine own eyes.
>
> (2.3.104–6)

The actor's challenge is to show that the character is truly staggered by being forced into this marriage. In another context, in another comedy, the audience might well sympathize with such words. If the actor cannot discover a way to enrich and complicate his emotional reactions in this difficult scene, the play's subsequent events may prove unacceptable to the spectators. Reviewing Trevor Nunn's 1981 R.S.C. production for the *London Times,* Irving Wardle notes that Bertram recoiled from Helena as from a loathsome fruit, making nonsense of their final reunion.[12]

By making the audience enter so completely into his heroine's feelings and by delaying the full revelation of her husband's faults, Shakespeare makes it possible for the playgoers to want Helena doubly to win Bertram even though they dislike him. Although the audience has a clear and unsentimental view of Bertram, Shakespeare does not allow it to indulge in easy and unmixed loathing. At Bertram's worst it is possible to perceive some good in him, as do the sober French lords who engineer the unmasking of Parolles. Helena's reconquering Bertram at the play's end may engender uneasiness; the final scene does not culminate in unalloyed bliss.[13] But the audience would not have patience even to journey with Helena as far as this final scene had not the playwright complicated its distaste for Bertram with some small hope for the young man's redemption.

That the playwright works so elaborately to manipulate his audience's reactions suggests how deeply problematic is this play. Bertram and Helena are among Shakespeare's most challenging roles, and the rewards may not match the challenges. It is more fun to play Beatrice and Benedick. Yet the Royal Shakespeare Company's 1981–83 international success with *All's Well That Ends Well* demonstrates that the play, like the flawed young count at its center, is by no means beyond redemption.

Shakespeare's audiences experience discomfort that amounts at times to pain because they are rarely permitted to suppress their sympathy for characters even as repugnant as Bertram. The dramatist forces his audience to dislike characters who cause suffering and to fear that harm or grief may come to sympathetic victims like Helena or Julia. At the same time he forces the spectators to admit, however painful the admission, that such characters have points of view that demand recognition. The author of the lines, "When my love swears that she is made of truth, / I do believe her, though I know she lies," knows perhaps better than anyone the complex and seemingly contradictory ways in which human beings can react to each other.

Even as early as the workshop comedy *The Two Gentlemen of Verona*, Shakespeare invites interest and some measure of sympathy for the traitor Proteus. In future comedies he does not use all of the devices that contribute to his depiction of Proteus, but he repeatedly employs and enormously improves upon his principal means of complicating the audience's response to this first of his comic villains. Keeping the audience constantly and keenly aware of the wrong the character is doing and the pain he is causing, the dramatist at the same time tries to give a sense of internal conflict and inner anguish. This is not done to mitigate the impression of the character's vileness but rather to create the impression that he is experiencing pain even as he causes it. Proteus's early scenes with Valentine and Julia encourage the actor to play the character as a genuinely affectionate young gentleman. Later, the actor may show that the character is horrified by what he contemplates and performs. If Proteus charms the spectators, they may be disposed to give his story the attention and imaginative participation it requires.

Few would point to Proteus as a signal success for the playwright, but it cannot be denied that showing inner suffering in a character who causes suffering ultimately brings about some of Shakespeare's greatest triumphs in the portrayal of character: Shylock, Angelo, Leontes, Othello, and Macbeth. One reason for the relative failure

with Proteus is that his speeches of inner anguish contain verse apprecia-
bly weaker than the verse spoken by his victims. This contributes
to an impression that such pain as he suffers cannot be compared
to the pain he causes. Another problem may arise from Shakespeare's
manner of presenting the character's change. Proteus in the first few
scenes is a passionate lover; his nature and situation are commonplace
in the various comic traditions upon which Shakespeare draws. What
happens to Proteus when he meets Silvia is not so much a change
of nature as a change of direction. Love is still his primary passion.
To it friendship and loyalty give way. His change is depicted as all
but mechanical and instantaneous. After a speech of self-chiding, he
switches his affection from Julia to Silvia.

Shakespeare seems to realize that this is not the best method of
portraying inner change in a character with whom the audience is
invited even partially to sympathize. Although he presents many more
lovers and a fair number of wrongdoers who inspire condemnation
and sympathy, he never again presents a suffering wrongdoer who
changes his affection so swiftly and suddenly.[14] In *Twelfth Night*, a
play whose central situation resembles that in *The Two Gentlemen
of Verona*, and for which the earlier comedy has been claimed as
a major source,[15] Shakespeare initially presents Orsino as desperately
in love with Olivia. In all the renditions of the story on which he
draws, Orsino's counterpart is made first to love Viola's counterpart
and then to cast her off. Although Viola, like Julia, suffers carrying
messages from the man she loves to the woman he loves, Shakespeare
spares her the humiliation of being that man's cast mistress. Orsino,
for all his faults, is not portrayed as a suddenly changing lover, and
the audience will probably accept more readily his eventual happiness
than Proteus's final bliss.[16]

When Shakespeare next assays in comedy a causer of pain with
whom the spectators are invited in some measure to sympathize or
whose nature they are at least encouraged to explore, the result is
Shylock, perhaps the most controversial figure the playwright ever
puts on the stage. Actors from Kean to Olivier have tended to make
Shylock a sort of unacknowledged tragic hero. Some productions have
borrowed from Verdi's Rigoletto and interpolated a silent scene in
which the old man returns to his despoiled house to find that Jessica
has been kidnapped by her Christian lover.[17] In a production made
over for television, Olivier showed Shylock's death, and the performance ended with a recitation of the *Kaddish*, the traditional Hebrew

prayer for the dead. Perhaps in response to overromanticizations in the theater, critics and scholars from Stoll to Hecht insist that Shylock must be viewed in the context of the terrifying history of European anti-Semitism, and they call their readers' attention to the case of Dr. Lopez, the tradition of religious disputation, and the overtly Christian symbolism in the characterization of Portia. Stoll sees Shylock in the tradition of the bottle-nosed, money-loving, monstrous Elizabethan stage Jew, and Hecht suggests the blood libel, the notion that Jews kill Christians to use their blood in making the Passover *matzoth*, as a possible explanation for Shylock's determination to have Antonio's flesh.[18] The very existence of these opposing traditions of interpretation suggests the extent to which Shylock arouses strong, contradictory reactions.

Stoll and his followers are correct in insisting that to distort the play into Shylock's tragedy by giving the audience too strong an impression of his pain is to be false to Shakespeare's text. At the same time, the comic villain, the conventional stage Jew, is an equally unsatisfactory representation of the character Shakespeare gives us. The spectators are not permitted to view Shylock simply, as do Salanio, Salarino, Gratiano, and Antonio. He is neither the tragic hero of Kean nor the comic villain of Stoll. His whole is greater than the sum even of these parts.

As does Proteus before him, Shylock reveals to the audience much of his hidden nature and inner anguish, but he makes these revelations in stronger scenes and speeches. Significantly unlike Proteus, Shylock does not in midplay mechanically change directions. His daughter's elopement makes his ancient grudge against Antonio break to new mutiny, but his essential nature never changes. His earliest serious profession in the play is a rooted hatred of Antonio and all Christians. His first long aside (1.3.37–43) reveals the force that drives the character and informs the play.

Shylock's hatred is intricately bound up with the Christians' hatred for him. The play demonstrates that the usurer's nature is bent into a monstrous shape by mistrust and alienation. It may be assumed, certainly a number of the play's Christian characters do assume, that his malevolence is natural to him because he is a Jew. But the play taken as a whole does not dramatize that assumption. The scenes in which Shylock's character is most fully revealed rather dramatize the painful spectacle of mutual hatreds feeding each other fat. In his 1976 performance at Stratford, Ontario, Hume Cronin gave us an angry and beset man, duped and robbed by his daughter, mocked by enemies that he despised as thoroughly as they despised him, driven by hatred so intense and by so maniacal a desire for revenge that at times he became grotesque, almost farcical. . . . This dynamo of cunning deviousness, malice and vindictiveness was recognizably a man in torment, and perhaps for that reason he gained our sympathy in far greater measure than a watered-down version could have done, however less might have been the risk of outraging modern sensibility. . . . Mr. Cronin's performance made us recognize that *The Merchant of Venice* is a play about prejudice, more perhaps about its effects on those who hold it than about the consequences for their victims. The Christians lost their humanity when they were dealing with Shylock. He lost his when he insisted on blood.[19]

Shakespeare's Richard III and Aaron the Moor are also haters and outsiders. Comparing Shylock with these characters yields a clearer understanding of the pain Shylock and his play elicit from the audience. Aaron is a racial outsider, and his hatred for the society to which he is alien is nurtured by their like hatred for him. Where he differs from Shylock is in the pleasure he takes in his monstrosities. Richard III is also an outsider:

> I have no brother, I am like no brother;
> And this word 'love', which greybeards call divine,
> Be resident in men like one another,
> And not in me! I am myself alone.
>
> (*3 Henry VI*, 5.6.80–83)

This could be part of Shylock's creed. But Richard also differs from Shylock by taking intellectual and emotional pleasure in his evil ingenuity and in his ability to cause pain. Both Richard III and Aaron are descendants of another stage Jew, Marlowe's Barabas, who dominates a play that has been described as "savage and serious farce."[20] These characters are creatures of splendid melodrama. The spectators are never allowed to forget the suffering they cause, but the audience's sense of that suffering is mitigated by a sense of their pleasure in causing it.[21] The audience roots for the villains, carried along by sheer glee in evil.

Glee is precisely what Shylock lacks. He is not a joyous trickster. The audience sees him experiencing rage and suffering pain, but taking no pleasure in anything. This aspect of the character was stressed by Patrick Stewart in John Barton's 1979 production at the R.S.C.'s Other Place. Stewart's Shylock forever narrowed his eyes as if frugal even of his sight and frequently returned the remains of his thread-thin cigarette to its case for later use.[22] The old man's shames and defeats in no way mitigate the audience's perception of the harm he does, not even so much as the glee and pride of Richard III, Aaron, and Barabas mitigate perceptions of their crimes. Spectators' perceptions of the pain Shylock suffers rather intensify their perceptions of the pain he causes.

The scholars of Elizabethan stage conventions, history, and theology compel an examination of uncomfortable facts that no one undertaking to produce the play or act Shylock can ignore. There can be no question that the bulk of Shakespeare's audience was anti-Semitic and that their doctrinal distrust and dislike of Jews—who in an essentially Jewless England were exotic, alien, and unknown—had been stimulated by the recent Lopez business. Whether Shakespeare himself was anti-Semitic is a question that, like so much else in the playwright's mental and spiritual life, will provide matter for endless speculation and will never be satisfactorily resolved on the extant evidence. *The Merchant of Venice* suggests that Shakespeare's views were complex, conflicting, seemingly contradictory—in other words, of the essence of the dramatic. He may, as Derek Cohen disturbingly argues, have been willing to use the cruel stereotypes of anti-Semitism for mercenary and artistic purposes.[23] Nevertheless, had he entertained such simple views about Shylock as do many of his characters and critics, he would have produced a very different play.

The play he did produce goes beyond the assumptions held by the Elizabethan audience. A function of first-rate drama is to challenge the assumptions of its audience, to force that audience to extend the range of its thinking and feeling. Drama that reinforces commonly held thoughts and feelings and encourages complacency can be precisely described as sentimental. Shakespeare's way of challenging assumptions in this play is exemplified in the central trial scene, in which Shylock appears at his most monstrous and in which he is thoroughly beaten. In the hands of a conventionally complacent, anti-Semitic dramatist, the conclusion of this scene might have provided ample occasion for Jew baiting. There is nothing of the sort in Shakespeare's scene. After Shylock goes off, beaten and unwell, there is hardly a word more about him. There is Jew baiting aplenty during the scene, but the sole baiter is Gratiano. His raillery is consistent with his character, but he is scarcely to be taken as a moral spokesman for Venetian Christian society. Moreover, before Shylock is defeated, he conducts himself in response to Gratiano with dignity and moral assurance, and he has the dramatic best of their encounter. Gratiano's continued baiting after the old man's defeat has multiple effects on the audience. It gives the playwright a means of satisfying the craving for condemnation of what Shylock is and does that will have been engendered by the scene's principal events. At the same time, Gratiano's railing at a beaten and humiliated man takes on a brutish quality. The speech about godfathers and gallows that covers Shylock's long, anguished final exit adds considerably to the pain and disturbance that this character creates by both reminding the spectators of his monstrosity and simultaneously making them perceive his suffering, greater at this moment than any suffering he has caused.

Disturbing effects also arise from Portia's method of defeating the usurer. Margaret Webster has noted that one reason for her delay may be that she does not know how she will pursue the case, and she is frantically searching through Shylock's bond and through books of law to find a loophole by which means she can save Antonio.[24] But Alan C. Dessen, reviewing Michael Addison's 1978 production at Ashland, Oregon, which employed such a staging as Webster suggests, points out that Portia's frenzied search through legal tomes contradicts the logic of her preceding speeches.[25] The manner and substance of her lines suggest that her strategy for dealing with Shylock has been well worked out before she enters the Venetian court. She proceeds slowly to judgment, going through the ritual awarding of the pound of flesh as a way of giving the old man every chance to change his mind, to show that he does not really intend to slice a pound of flesh from Antonio's living body. What she is doing makes perfect dramatic sense if one bears in mind the duke's first words to Shylock:

> . . . the world thinks, and I think so too,
> That thou but leadest this fashion of thy malice
> To the last hour of act; and then, 'tis thought,
> Thou'lt show thy mercy and remorse, more strange
> Then is thy strange apparent cruelty . . . (4.1.17–21)

In order morally to justify the completeness of Shylock's defeat and humiliation, Portia must establish that the old man's cruelty is not apparent but actual, that he will lead his true malice beyond the last hour of act and use his knife on Antonio.

The audience must see flesh and metal meet if it is to find the defeat dramatically satisfying. Tyrone Guthrie understood this dramatic necessity and in his 1954 production at Stratford, Ontario, Antonio was stripped and bound to a hurdle and "never came closer to losing his pound of flesh than he did in this performance."[26] The duke's lines to Shylock are partly rhetorical plea, but they spring also from a common reaction to the idea of cutting a pound of flesh from a living man. The human mind veers away from contemplating this action and seeks shelter in the notion that this is only the sort of thing one finds in fairy tales. But as well as offering the wonder and ritual repetitions of fairy tales, the play offers the fairy tale's terror. The story of Shylock's monstrous intention and crushing defeat will not be complete unless this terror is made manifest to the playgoers' eyes. The scene must be staged as Guthrie staged it so that Shylock is in the act of slicing Antonio's flesh when Portia springs her trap.

Shylock's anguish in defeat is conveyed to the audience through the peculiar medium of mercy. The idea of mercy has run through the play from its beginning, and one would expect after Portia's famous speech that the Venetian court that she has come to represent will treat the usurer with greater mercy than he has been willing to offer the merchant. His life is spared, and he loses only half his wealth. He is forced to convert to Christianity, and scholars teach us that this too is an act of mercy since it saves him from certain damnation.

The role permits many valid interpretations, and actors have differed widely in their playing of the character's final moments on stage. George C. Scott, for the 1962 New York Shakespeare Festival, leapt savage and snarling at the Venetians when he learned that he would have to convert to Christianity.[27] In a 1967 performance at Stratford, Connecticut, Morris Carnovsky exited down a flight of stairs, staring ahead sightlessly. At the second step he stopped and sat, struggling for strength enough to go on. A moment later he was up—eyes blazing, head high—a man defeated but not conquered.[28] Patrick Stewart, in the 1979 Barton production, demonstrated his apprehension of mercy by groveling in obsequious acceptance of the forced baptism. Bereft of revenge, Stewart's miserly Shylock would do anything to retain his money.[29] In their varying ways, all these performances communicated the character's anguish and humiliation.

Shylock's feeling pain where mercy is offered has complex and contradictory effects on the audience. Spectators may indeed perceive him as the inhuman wretch he is so often described as being, since he is not only incapable of rendering mercy himself but may be incapable of recognizing mercy when it is shown him. But his defeat is so dramatized that the audience cannot choose but keenly perceive his pain. No explicit mention of salvation is made in connection with his forced conversion. Earlier in the play, questions of damnation and salvation have been discussed, usually in Launcelot Gobbo's theologically pointed patter, but the discussion is not continued here. Discussions of Shylock's damnation and salvation are left to the scholars and conducted off the stage.

The audience's attention is precisely focused not on the Venetian court's clemency, but on the beaten man's agony. There can be no sequence more theatrically emblematic of this precise focusing than Shylock's statement that he is not well and his final exit accompanied by Gratiano's jeer. Even here, Shakespeare is not asking his audience to pity his creature any more than Shylock ever asks pity for himself. But the audience is asked to bring a complex and painfully expanded understanding to the character. At the heart of this understanding are the simultaneous apprehensions of Shylock as monster and as victim.

The 1976 Stratford, Ontario, production with Hume Cronin demonstrated that the play may appear to best advantage if Shylock is seen throughout as a drab creature in the midst of a bustling society that has about it the nature of a Mardi Gras.

> In a world of frock coats and waistcoats, he wore his gabardine. It marked him as the alien: the stranger whose refusal to conform confirmed the worst suspicions of those who would not have accepted him, even if he had conformed. On Mr. Cronin the gabardine became Shylock's symbol of contempt for the society that had shut him out, a declaration of his superiority.[30]

The play can be so staged that the Venetians are always seen in acts of extravagant consumption, such as Salanio and Salarino gambling or eating or Bassanio distributing largess. By contrast, the members of Shylock's household can appear confined and pinched in their garments and gestures. When Gobbo changes masters, he can change costumes from Shylockian bleakness to Bassaniesque splendor, and when Jessica becomes Lorenzo's wife, her appearance can change from dowdy to gaudy.

Shylock's driving hatred is nowhere more forcefully revealed than in the well-known speech containing the line: "Hath not a Jew eyes?" Yet actors from Keane to Olivier have tended to make it into a plea for pity. At Stratford, Connecticut, in 1957, Morris Carnovsky moved into a center stage spotlight and delivered the speech as a sort of aria.[31] Such a playing would make for a deeply moving sequence, but it might blunt the effects of the character's hatred to the detriment of his subsequent scenes. Perhaps in reaction against such interpretations, Jonathan Miller in his BBC production directed Warren Mitchel to speak with a thick Yiddish accent and had Salanio and Salarino laugh loudly at his words and manner. A thick accent detaches the audience's emotions from a character and provokes scornful laughter. Shakespeare uses French, Welsh, and Irish accents for such purposes in *Henry V* and *The Merry Wives of Windsor*. Shylock may choose to speak with an accent that contributes to the needed sense of his alienness. But if the accent distances the audience from Shylock, much of the play's disturbing richness will be lost. Rather than obscuring Shylock's words with their competing laughter, the actors playing Salanio and Salarino may display quiet boredom, or may show that their characters are stunned to silence by his cold fury.

Far from being a statement of common humanity, Shylock's words profess his doctrine of revenge. The speech is indeed the precise opposite of Prospero's doctrine of forgiveness expressed toward the end of *The Tempest*. Like Prospero, Shylock insists that his senses, affections, and passions are identical to those of his wrongers. But the old usurer reaches the contrary conclusion. If the Christian's humility is revenge, then the Jew's sufferance must also be revenge. The expression of this doctrine is calculated to elicit pity neither from the other characters nor from the audience. Its chilling tone is set by its opening line—Shylock's response when he is jeeringly asked what Antonio's flesh will be good for: "To bait fish withal. If it will feed nothing else, it will feed my revenge" (3.1.44–45). Taunted by urchins, poked at with sticks, mocked by Salarino and Salanio, and with blood on his injured brow, Antony Sher's Shylock achieved his eloquent climax with the word "revenge." "From being a representative of a wronged race, he had become a vindictive individual."[32]

There are other moments in the play when derisive laughter, the only reaction he elicits other than anguish and disturbance, does become an appropriate response to the character. Shakespeare uses the laughter to give his audience relief from the intense pain that Shylock evokes one way and another. Such laughter is prompted early in the play when he anticipates Jessica's elopement: "There is some ill a-brewing towards my rest, / For I did dream of money-bags to-night" (2.5.17–18). Hearing these lines, the audience is invited to join some of the play's characters and laugh at the old man's greed. The bulk of such laughter as Shylock draws will come shortly after his interchange with Salarino and Salanio. In the subsequent scene with Tubal, in which Shakespeare draws most heavily on the convention of the avaricious Elizabethan stage Jew, Shylock expresses his grief and rage at his daughter's treachery in marrying a Christian: "I would my daughter were dead at my foot and the jewels in her ear; would she were hears'd at my foot, and the ducats in her coffin!" (3.1.74–75).[33] The fact that he laments equally for his lost daughter and his lost money will raise mocking, scornful laughter: ". . . and I know not what's spent in the search. . . . The thief gone with so much, and so much to find the thief" (3.1.77–78). He sounds for a moment like Jonson's Sordido or Molière's Harpagon. His erotic relation with his possessions is the stuff of searing satire, and the scene in which this relation is explored diminishes him temporarily into a miserly figure of fun. Further derisive laughter is called forth by Shakespeare's manner of dramatizing the internal conflict between the old man's grief at Jessica's treachery and his joy at Antonio's losses. Tubal alternates pieces of news about Jessica's prodigality with pieces of news about Antonio's wrecked ships, and Shylock switches mechanically from capers to groans and back again. In the best Bergsonian fashion, laughter rises from the sheer automatism of these emotional responses. The scene is quite difficult to play since the actor must communicate the emotions with absolute conviction and make the contrasts between them as sharp as possible. Commenting on Michael Redgrave's performance of this scene, Kenneth Tynan noted: "It needs a continental actor to switch from fun to ferocity in a split second. Englishmen take at least half a minute to change gear."[34] The actor's emotional virtuosity will make the spectators laugh as they realize that the character is totally unconscious of the contradictions in his extremes of passion.

This scene and other isolated moments of scornful laughter at Shylock's expense do not temper the audience's sense of the anguish the character causes and suffers; rather, they give brief respite from that anguish and reduce the scope of the conflict so that it will admit of comic resolution. By inviting the audience to indulge its spleen, Shakespeare cuts the character down to a size that can be contained in comedy. Making the old man for the time being into a miserly butt is the playwright's first intimation that the evil he creates can be satisfactorily purged without the shedding of blood.

For all the pain and disturbance that accompany him, Shylock is a comic figure and must be dealt with in an appropriately comic manner. He must neither cause nor suffer death. He must not even cause permanent injury. The punishment he receives can be appropriately harsh, but it too must involve no bodily harm. All these strictures governing comedy from its earliest days Shakespeare scrupulously observes.

But whenever Shakespeare makes his comedies veer toward tragic catastrophe, he does not want for critics who take him generically to task. That *tragicomedy* may be the only appropriate generic term for most of Shakespeare's plays, although first stated with overwhelming authority more than two centuries ago, seems to need reiteration in every generation. Thus in our time L. G. Salingar argues that Shakespeare is by conscious choice working on different types of comedies.[35] Salingar points to an important distinction among the kinds of sources on which Shakespeare draws. Plays based on English romances differ in kind from plays based on Italian narratives.[36] The plays based on Italian tales convey to their audiences greater apprehension and give their critics more problems than plays based on English ones. Comedy that contains too abundant an infusion of pain has given problems to critics, from the Italian commentators who raged against *Il Pastor Fido*[37] to commentators of our own generation who meditate on the mold-cracking properties of *All's Well That Ends Well* and *Measure for Measure*.[38] But the mingling of mirth and pain does not seem to have bothered Elizabethan playwrights working for the popular theaters. These writers, perhaps taking as their precedents the mixing of solemnity with farce in many of the medieval miracle plays and moralities, put the boisterous braggings of Huff, Ruff, and Snuff into *Cambyses,* the farcical rough-and-tumble of Dick, Robin, and the horse-courser into *Doctor Faustus,* and the deaths of the Lamberts and Searlsbys into *Friar Bacon and Friar Bungay.*

It is chiefly from Robert Greene, the man who famously blasts him as an "upstart crow," that Shakespeare learns about comic hybrids.

In the play about Prince Edward and his friend Lacey both wooing the fair maid of Fressingfield, Shakespeare perhaps finds a precedent for his play about Valentine and his friend Proteus both wooing the duke's daughter of Milan. And this play of love and treachery is the first of those painful, problematic comedies that Shakespeare produces throughout his career down to *Cymbeline* and *The Winter's Tale*. Shakespeare does not until his four last comedies break the law of death that Greene breaks in *Friar Bacon and Friar Bungay*. Indeed, until these late plays, Shakespeare contrives his comic actions so that none of his characters is even physically harmed. Yet he goes far beyond Greene or any other comic writer in the exploration in comedy of agonies of the mind and spirit.

In *The Merchant of Venice* the dramatist brings his audience to a complex understanding of a particular character. In his next comedy, *Much Ado About Nothing*, a play which is also based principally on an Italian narrative, he brings his audience to a complex understanding of a difficult situation. Out of this situation arises much pain for the characters, and the spectators are invited both to understand and to share it. Yet even at its keenest, the pain is kept in comic bounds. Bandello's tale, on which Shakespeare chiefly draws, contains potentially tragic material, for it is not unlike Cinthio's tale, on which the playwright bases *Othello*. But in the play based on Bandello, he is keeping the worst demons at bay. As A. P. Rossiter remarks, Shakespeare is showing his audience problems that might make for tragedy but saying, "not now, not yet."[39] The entrances of Dogberry hard on the heels of the most potentially tragic scenes, the fact that the central incident of slander and betrayal is never staged but rather given over to Borachio's drunken narrative, and the dominance over all the play's moods held by Beatrice and Benedick insure that the play's events will never stray beyond the sociable comic realm.

Indeed, the problem for most directors and actors is not that potential tragedy threatens to overtake and overwhelm the comedy, but that Shakespeare makes a dull business of the credulity and slander. Two of his most fascinating and endearing characters seem grafted on to one of the most incredible and tedious of his romantic plots. An examination of the play's stage history reveals the great names of theater attaching themselves to Beatrice and Benedick and not to Claudio, Hero, Don Pedro, and Leonato.[40] None of these last named characters is individually of extraordinary interest. But all four characters, together with Beatrice and Benedick, collectively generate and experience pain that is profitably comparable to the pain Shylock gene-rates and experiences in *The Merchant of Venice.*

The presentation of the play's serious elements remains a problem for directors and performers. Nevertheless, these elements become so important a part of the play's wit that spectators who are not persuaded to be sympathetically attentive to the pain will not fully comprehend and appreciate the laughter. Claudio's hot rage at his wedding springs from a conviction that the audience knows to have resulted from the young lover's credulity and the bastard's treachery. But the actor's task is to convey this rage as forcefully as actors playing Othello or Leontes convey their rages. Hero's pain and humilia-tion when she is disgraced at the altar and hurled by her quondam lover back to her father must be conveyed with a like sincerity and power.

The arrangement of scenes and characters does not allow the wit to be separated from the melodrama. The playwright here employs different storytelling methods from those he uses in previous comedies. His comedies typically involve large groups of characters and tell several stories at once. The action frequently moves back and forth from one group of characters to another, and often from one location to another. *Much Ado About Nothing* does not alternate between Beatrice's and Benedick's affairs and those of Claudio and Hero. In-stead, the story of the witty lovers is at every turn combined with, affected by, and affecting that of the other characters. Indeed, it is not accurate to say, as did the program note for the New York run of Terry Hands's R.S.C. 1983–84 production,[41] that the play tells two stories. Shakespeare is telling a single, complicated story that embraces a relatively large group of people. A profitable comparison can be made in this regard to *The Taming of the Shrew,* another comedy of love with an eccentric couple at its center. In that play, Petruchio's and Kate's most important relations are with each other, and their story is carried on more or less independently of the story of Bianca and her suitors. The scenes of Kate's taming can be excised from the play and can stand on their own, as Garrick made them do.[42] Unlike Petruchio and Kate, Beatrice and Benedick do not spend most of their stage time with each other. Their five scenes together are all brief. The longest of them, the aftermath to the aborted nuptials, can be played in five minutes. Taken together, their scenes with each other comprise no more than twenty minutes of stage time in a play whose performance should not exceed two and a half hours. The greater part of their time on stage is spent talking to and interacting with the play's other characters. Benedick spends a significant amount of time with the prince and Claudio;[43] Beatrice spends a comparable amount of time with Leonato, Hero, and Hero's women.[44] Consequently, the play requires its performers to show the audience as much about the witty lovers' social context and their relations to the other characters as to each other.

These lovers deserve and get most of the attention in the performance, but their story will be less than complete and its reception will be less than satisfactory if the actors and director do not try to persuade the audience to take a sympathetic interest in the painful events entangling all the characters. Terry Hands's production placed Beatrice and Benedick in their contrasting social settings by creating an enclosed aristocratic world "where the soldiers' masculine friendships were sharply set against the very different emotions of the women."[45] Scenic designer Ralph Koltai fashioned a maze of reflecting surfaces that summoned up the narcissistic society of Messina. Yet in spite of these production values and highly acclaimed performances by Derek Jacobi and Sinead Cusack, Frank Rich complains that "the ruptured wedding and its aftermath still seem inconveniences that must be endured."[46] Yet this wedding is a part of Beatrice and Benedick's central scene of mutual discovery and self-discovery, which cannot be understood without it. Beatrice shares her cousin's pain and humiliation and breaks finally into terrible fury on Hero's behalf. Benedick is astonished: "For my part, I am so attired in wonder, / I know not what to say" (4.1.144–45).

The events that occasion these serious emotions depend largely on Claudio. As Walter Kerr observes in his review of the Terry Hands production, the role of Claudio cries for help, but it does not receive sufficient help from Hands or from actor Christopher Bowen.

Shakespeare didn't bother to tell us what very odd quirk in this singular young soldier caused him to blow so hot and so cold so quickly. Perhaps he knew how the actor in his company who had been assigned to the role would play it without further amplification from him. (It's also possible that the part bored him, but we'll try not to think that. In any event, something must be interpolated—by gesture or physical business—to explain this young fellow's unsympathetic behavior and make him sympathetic again. We do want sympathy restored to him because he's one half of the concluding love story.) The trick can be pulled off and has been pulled off in one production or another. There are various ways of doing it, the most convincing of which in my theatre-going experience stems from the early description of this warrior as "a lamb." When an actor makes Claudio young enough and callow enough to be both impetuous and insecure, the combination works. A Claudio who depends heavily on the approval of others and is constantly checking to see if his betters regard him as sufficiently sophisticated and sufficiently mature may very well behave as Shakespeare's rattled youngster does behave. He may even be caught in a kind of torment, personally ravaged by his treatment of Hero at the same time that he is doing his mistaken best to show himself as manly and knowledgeable. There are of course other ways of adding weight and dimension to the underwritten role, but some effort must be made if the evening's second half or second plot is to be kept afloat.[47]

When I undertook a production of *Much Ado About Nothing*, my cast and I were well aware that we would have to find ways of giving weight and dimension to the serious lovers. Benedick's many references to Claudio's youth and Beatrice's ease in advising Hero how to conduct herself with potential wooers suggest a significant difference in age between the couples. Following this suggestion, we chose to play them as about ten years older than Claudio and Hero. This choice permitted us to portray Claudio with such qualities of youth, insecurity, and impetuosity that perhaps best serve the part. The play's text also suggests that Beatrice and Benedick are socially and financially dependent on their friends. Beatrice is her uncle's ward, while Hero is his only heir. Don Pedro and Claudio are respectively a prince and a count, while Benedick has no title but Signior. His two friends twit his lack of a house and means, and they occasionally treat him as if he must fulfill a jester's function of making them merry. The witty couple's social inferiority and financial dependency colored many of our production's scenes. Leonato's banter about his niece's inability to catch a husband was edged with concern that she might become a perpetually dependent spinster. The prince and Claudio's affection for Benedick was tinged by patronization, and Beatrice's taunting him as "the Prince's jester" took on a peculiar sting.

Even though the witty lovers are older and poorer than their friends, they are at first deeply involved in the artifice and deception that define their world. The painful events at the play's center cause them to turn away from this world and toward each other, and that turning away constitutes this funny play's serious action. All our choices in production were guided by our desire to focus the spectators' attention on Beatrice and Benedick's gradual abandonment of their society's artifice and convention. Accordingly, our set was deliberately artificial—a garden painted on tapestries that hung about the stage. Painted among the plants and flowers were Benedick's "quondam carpet-mongers," the lovers of myth and romance—Hero and Leander, Troilus and Cressida, and, preeminently, Europa and the bull. The costumes were designed to heighten the contrast between the play's two couples. Beatrice and Benedick were dressed in earth tones and textures, rough greens and browns, while Claudio and Hero appeared in fairy-tale white and gold.

The play is a delightful comedy of love and at the same time a searing indictment of the codes and conventions that govern courtly lovers. The sexes are separated by seemingly impassable barriers, which only Beatrice and Benedick, for all their professed misanthropy and misogyny, can surmount. By virtue of his authority in the play's world and his function in its plot, Don Pedro enforces and embodies these codes and conventions. His practices on all the lovers depend on sexual separation and on the consequent importance of hearsay.

Robert Speaight, reviewing Ronald Eyre's 1971 R.S.C. production, observes that Don Pedro does not carry the weight of character to support his function in the plot, and he notes the custom of casting in this role a "good actor but not quite good enough to be given Benedick."[48] But Don Pedro is not a second-string Benedick. The Prince of Arragon is his play's chief temporal authority and manipulator, performing a function in this play similar to those performed by Vincentio in *Measure for Measure* and Prospero in *The Tempest*. Like them, he unifies his play by acting important scenes with all its major characters. Just as Vincentio must reckon with Barnardine and Prospero acknowledges Caliban, Don Pedro recognizes Dogberry and accepts the true justice that the constable has restored. It is noteworthy that neither Beatrice nor Benedick ever appears on stage with the play's other great humorist. Also like Vincentio and Prospero, this prince designs and executes many of the elaborate plots and stratagems that drive the action forward. If Speaight is right, the actor's job becomes all the harder, since he must impart a sense of urgency to his plots and lend the character sufficient force of personality to impose his will on his coconspirators and unify his play. Paul Scofield, in the classic *Much Ado About Nothing* of Gielgud and Leighton, and Anthony Nichols, in Douglas Seale's acclaimed 1958 revival, each played the character with vigor and authority, making important contributions to the successes of their respective productions.[49]

A number of this character's speeches and actions suggest that he is keenly sensitive to the quirks and needs of the play's reluctant lovers. He observes Benedick's wittily expressed outrage at being called "the Prince's jester" turn gradually into the disturbingly uncontrolled rage of "so, indeed, all disquiet, horror, and perturbation, follows her" (2.1.216–32). A little later in the same scene he is the recipient of Beatrice's indecorous hint that she is attracted to him. There is an awkward moment as she draws from him a half-serious proposal that she must gracefully turn down.

> *Beat.* Good Lord, for alliance! Thus goes every one to the world but I, and I am sunburnt; I may sit in a corner and cry 'Heigh-ho for a husband!'
> *D. Pedro.* Lady Beatrice, I will get you one.
> *Beat.* I would rather have one of your father's getting. Hath your Grace ne'er a brother like you? Your father got excellent husbands, if a maid could come by them.
> *D. Pedro.* Will you have me, lady?
> *Beat.* No, my lord, unless I might have another for working-days; your Grace is too costly to wear every day. But, I beseech your Grace, pardon me; I was born to speak all mirth and no matter. (2.1.286–97)

In its fusion of wit and pathos, this scene anticipates Chekhov. Beatrice's mask momentarily slips, revealing uncertainty and sadness. In our production, we attempted to show the unease beneath the wit. Beatrice's nimble tongue stumbled over suddenly difficult words, and her face crumpled. Don Pedro's habitual smile changed to an expression of concern, and his voice grew grave. The actor playing Don Pedro shared with the audience his character's perception that both Benedick and Beatrice were exhibiting a growing disturbance. The prince's subsequent scheme for bringing the reluctant lovers together lost none of its humor, but I hoped the audience would accept it also as an act of compassion arising out of his shrewd observation of Beatrice's and Benedick's behavior.[50]

For all their benevolence, Don Pedro's practices could only be effective in a world governed by elaborate sexual conventions. The masked dance in the second act is a theatrical metaphor for the codes of courtly love that the comedy indicts. The spectators observe masked couples moving in elegant, formal patterns and conversing in elegant, formal prose. For all the spectacle's grace and beauty, it engenders an atmosphere rife with misconceptions, half-truths, and plain lies. The dancers do not know with certainty the identity or intentions of their partners. It is small wonder that Don John's lie takes so strong a hold on Claudio. In the formal perfection of its appearance and the confusion, unease, and inchoate danger inherent in its actual nature, the dance symbolizes the courtly conventions and codes of behavior that govern the serious lovers and from which the witty lovers are trying to disengage themselves. The Gielgud production used the dance as symbolic action. Describing the staging, Alan S. Downer writes:

> The director has used the physical resources of his production to develop the central idea of the action. The dancers of the second act, bearing their false faces on wands, perform a ballet of misprision and resolution which draws the dark deceit of Don John, the malapropisms of Dogberry, the fortunate gulling in the arbor and even "Kill Claudio" into a pattern, a thematic and artistic unit.[51]

As the dancers leave the stage to the plotting Don John and the petulant Claudio, Beatrice and Benedick speak three lines anticipating the turn the play will take:

Beat. We must follow the leaders.
Bene. In every good thing.
Beat. Nay, if they lead to any ill, I will leave them at the next turning.
 (2.1.132–35)

The courtly dance leads to terrible ill at the failed wedding, and Beatrice does leave the leaders of that dance when she rages against Hero's accusers. The climactic fulfillment of her witty prophecy occurs when the prince and Claudio leave the stage after they have denounced Hero. Benedick chooses not to accompany them and stays behind with Beatrice. In our production we tried to show that this was a conscious and difficult choice. The actor playing Benedick began to exit with his friends. Turning for a last look at Beatrice, he saw that she was glaring at him with shock and disappointment. With a troubled expression, he slowly rejoined the forlorn group clustered around the fallen Hero. Our aim was to suggest to the audience his growing realization that in staying behind with Beatrice he was leaving forever the courtly dance, the comradely but conventional world of his friends.

The play makes clear both through its wit and its scenes of emotional turbulence that this world is marred by an all-embracing sexual mistrust. Beatrice and Benedick, gaily and trenchantly mocking at the courtly lovers, are sufficiently mistrustful of each other to be susceptible to hearsay. The second and third acts quietly and ominously dramatize the notion of sexual separation. When Benedick is made to believe that Beatrice is in love with him, the tricksters are all men and they talk in jocular, hearty prose. When Beatrice, in a parallel scene, is tricked into a false opinion of Benedick's affection for her, the tricksters are all women talking in delicate, mellifluous verse. It is almost as if men and women speak different languages. Qualities of staging and acting can reflect the differences between the masculine and feminine worlds. In Walton Jones's production for the Yale Repertory Theatre in 1983, both scenes were staged farcically with first Benedick and then Beatrice crashing through a gazebo at identical spots. While the staging called attention to the parallel plights of the reluctant lovers, the second scene seemed a feeble and unnecessary repetition of the first.[52] By contrast, Terry Hands effectively differentiated between the scenes. He gave Benedick's scene a hilariously busy farcical staging, with Benedick constantly on the move in his unavailing attempts to keep the conspirators from spying him. Beatrice in her scene was immobile, taking the criticisms of herself very much to heart.[53]

Men and women are kept apart in these scenes, and they are again separated in a later pair of parallel scenes in which the reluctant lovers are respectively mocked. During the play's epitasis, the sexes are restricted to their own scenes. These scenes might have provided Claudio and Hero a chance simply and naturally to converse, but the playwright denies them that chance. Even Leonato shifts quietly to the masculine world. He no longer talks to his daughter and his niece as he has done during the early scenes; rather, he is drawn by his friendship for Don Pedro to participation in the men's scenes. Thus Shakespeare keeps Hero from her father and her lover until all three meet at the wedding.

The scene of the failed wedding must be understood in this context. The characters are rendered easily credulous by the sexual mistrust and confusion that has pervaded the play from its beginning. The incredibility of the device that fools them underscores their own credulity. The play in production must help the audience to care about this painful event and the conventions that shape it, or the climactic scene with Beatrice and Benedick that it occasions will be greatly diminished, if not wholly lost. This scene elicits in the audience simultaneous effects of laughter, pain, and wonder, which I shall discuss further in a subsequent chapter.[54] I stress here that it must also be understood in the context of the four lovers' complex mutual involvement.

Since a modern audience's complete acceptance of this play's events depends so heavily on its understanding and acceptance of conventions different from its own, directors have continued to seek means to render these conventions credible and to give them a compelling and consistent portrayal. Many directors of *Much Ado About Nothing* have achieved these ends by moving the play to other times and places deemed more familiar or more suggestive, but characterized by similar social stratification and the attendant codes governing relations between the sexes. Many of these temporal and spatial transplants have resulted in successful productions. John Houseman and Jack Landau produced a Wild West version in 1957 at Stratford, Connecticut;[55] A. J. Antoon set the New York Shakespeare Festival's 1972 production in Theodore Roosevelt's America; John Barton in 1977 moved the play to an Indian garrison and provided it with a Sikh Dogberry;[56] and Douglas Seale's 1958 production was set in mid-Victorian England. In a comment that can be profitably applied to all intelligently conceived and meticulously executed temporal transplants, M. St. Clare Byrne credits Seale's production with shaking her out of her theatrically induced habits and making her attend to the Hero story as never before.[57]

Different as they were from each other, all these productions displayed directorial imagination and invention in the service of bringing the play completely to life on stage. But this play's problems are often deemed so vexing, its serious roles judged so ungrateful, that many directors will concentrate exclusively on Beatrice, Benedick, and Dogberry, or will impose a theatrical stylization that plays against the text instead of serving it. This sort of stylization was displayed in Franco Zeffirelli's National Theatre production in 1965. That production prompted the usually sympathetic Robert Speaight to observe that the director

reduced the play to insignificance. . . . The wit is ironical and the melodrama is perfectly serious. To smother them both with slapstick is not only to destroy the substance of your play, but to invite your play to answer back. In the present case, it did so pretty sharply, and the result was the most spectacular suicide I have ever seen in the theatre. . . .

What is lacking to so many of our young directors is not imagination but integrity, and with integrity, intelligence. Mr. Zeffirelli's *Much Ado* rippled with invention and radiated a good deal of visual beauty, but it remained the most unintelligent production of Shakespeare I have ever seen.[58]

In *Much Ado About Nothing* Shakespeare invents Beatrice and Benedick and uses them to transform and complicate a ready-made tale of love, slander, and jealousy. In *Measure for Measure* he invents or greatly expands the duke, Lucio, and Mariana and uses them to complicate and transform a ready-made tale of a corrupt judge, a beset virgin, and a brother condemned to die.[59] Both these plays give more than their share of problems to actors, directors, and critics, and the persistent cognomen "problem comedy" seems affixed to at least one of them.[60] If one has a whimsical turn of mind, one may note that both plays feature constables who invent their own languages based on English, and who point to similar slippages of meaning.[61] The carry-over from Dogberry to Elbow may suggest that Shakespeare himself recognizes a peculiar relationship between these two plays.

While I should not like to push this point too far, the constables call attention to the plays' aesthetic similarities. Different as they are in theme and treatment, both plays represent, in essentially comic form, material that comes close to tragedy. In both plays pain grows out of a complex situation involving a large number of characters whose varying relations the audience is asked to follow and comprehend. Spectators are not asked to give unqualified sympathy to a single virtuous and suffering character, a Julia, Helena, or Imogen; nor are they encouraged to understand a single complex character like Shylock who causes and suffers pain. Like Shylock, Angelo is a suffering villain, and the audience is made both to understand his internal anguish and to condemn him as a causer of anguish. But the deputy does not dominate his play in the same way that the usurer dominates his. Like Helena and Imogen, Isabella is horribly beset, but her austere piety keeps her from winning unalloyed sympathy. Behind all the characters, profoundly affecting their fortunes and the way the audience perceives them, stands the duke, mysterious, controversial—for characters and spectators alike perhaps this problem comedy's chief problem.

But for many critics, the play's chief problem is unevenness. The alleged unevenness differs interestingly from the unevenness ascribed to *Much Ado About Nothing*. The comedy of love and slander is attacked for attaching two fascinating characters to an incredible and tedious plot. The comedy of justice and mercy is attacked for giving the audience two and a half acts of tragic intensity and then, as the duke becomes ever more dominant, changing for two and a half acts into a comedy of grimy intrigue and lukewarm emotion. The last half of the play is often viewed as an emotional and aesthetic letdown, and there are commentaries rife with speculation about Shakespeare changing his mind in midcourse, or grafting new material on to an old and indifferent play, or experimenting with a comic denouement that extends for two and a half acts.[62]

The circumstances of character and situation that define the near-tragedy of Claudio, Angelo, and Isabella are delineated with such clarity and force that there can be no problem for the director, the actors, or the spectators in understanding how they work or why they achieve their emotional effects. The problem in performance is more one of execution than interpretation. What director and actors must ponder is the relationship to these three characters and their painful situation of Mariana, Lucio, the lowlifes of brothel and prison, and preeminently the disguised duke. Just as the director and actors must recognize in *Much Ado About Nothing* that the fortunes of Beatrice and Benedick are integrated so thoroughly into those of Claudio, Hero, Don Pedro, and Leonato that all make for one complex story, so they must come to understand here how the play's many characters, particularly the manipulating duke, affect from the beginning the rapidly intensifying dilemma of Claudio, Isabella, and Angelo. With such an understanding, they may be able to keep the play in production from falling into two discrete halves with the second half falling so far short of the first.

Since the playwright apparently does not choose to make clear the duke's motives and intentions, a wide range of interpretations is available to actors and directors. In order to unify their productions and to achieve psychological coherence, some directors adopt specific tones and angles of vision and invent silent prologues that aim to provide such illumination for the duke's course of action as cannot be found in the character's lines. Thus Jerry Turner's 1978 production at Ashland, Oregon, was set in Freud's Vienna and was seen through a lens of inner torment. Dan Kramer as the duke

descended a staircase, seated himself and pounded his book of state while Viennese waltzes played in the background. While the music turned discordant, Kramer rapped his legs with a riding-crop in obvious anguish. The audience perceived behind him the shadowy figure of a naked woman hanging by her wrists being whipped. Ultimately, the duke broke off this vision and in a shaken voice called out for Escalus.[63]

David Giles's 1969 production at Stratford, Ontario, opened with muffled characters slipping silently on to the darkened arena stage,

> some grappling with one another, others coupling like animals in a corner. A sober citizen was jostled and then stabbed. Suddenly, all were gone except one. He slowly took off his swathing-hood and his beggar's weeds, and lo he was the duke. His curious commission to Escalus and Angelo following immediately was understandable. In these first two minutes, the chilling sense of violence, lawlessness and sexual immoderation had gripped us. We wanted them curbed . . . yet it would, we felt, have to be someone other than this spectator-duke who had watched the scene before him so passively.[64]

But something of the richness and mystery suggested by the play's text may be lost if the actor and the director invent traits and motives that may not be suggested by the character's lines and actions. Reviewing Turner's Ashland production, Alan C. Dessen warns that a psychologically coherent *Measure for Measure* may substitute one kind of excitement, modern and psychological, for another, "harder to define and pinpoint, but inherent in the original script."[65] David Giles's 1969 production at Stratford, Ontario, received mixed reviews,[66] and it may be that William Hutt's spectator-duke was unable to take a sufficiently firm grip on the action and pacing of the play's second half. When Hutt played the part again six years later for Robin Philips, he

> played the duke as authority—implacable, apparently capricious, frequently impersonal, inscrutable and secret. . . . Following the clear evidence of what the duke does rather than non-existent evidence of why he does it, he turned attention to the nature of authority itself, which tends to obscure the character of the individual who wields it.[67]

This approach may perhaps have satisfied Dessen's hope that performance preserve the essential complexity and mystery inherent in the script. Equally important, it allowed Hutt's duke to control the pace and flow during the second half.

For all this character's inherent mystery, a close examination of his lines and actions may offer directors and performers some useful aids in understanding him and bringing him to full stage life. These lines and actions suggest that the duke is a frequent witness to pain. If he is a sufferer as well, most of his suffering must be invented, as Turner and Kramer invented it. Relatively early in the play, the disguised duke visits Juliet, the young girl who is pregnant by Claudio. He catechizes her, tests the quality of her repentance and finds it true. She goes as far as a suffering young girl can in setting forth a deep repentance: "I do repent me as it is an evil, / And take the shame with joy" (2.3.35–36). So far, the duke is seen in the best possible light, as a confessor bringing a sinner to grace. But he does not leave it there. He advises Juliet to rest in her repentance and immediately takes that rest from her: "There rest. / Your partner, as I hear, must die tomorrow, / And I am going with instruction to him" (2.3.38–40). Having brought freshly to mind her pain, the duke leaves her to utter some of the play's most anguished lines:

> Must die to-morrow! O injurious law,
> That respites me a life whose very comfort
> Is still a dying horror!
>
> (2.3.40–42)

The lines are doubly painful since Juliet is referring both to her own life, which has been spared to a premarital widowhood, and the life of her child, who will be born to the horror of a dead father.

This scene reveals much about the duke's function in the play and his effects on the action. It is of the first importance in creating an impression of this enigmatic figure, because it is the first scene in which the audience sees him putting into practice his plan of disguised visitations to his subjects. What the audience sees is a man who wishes to appear, and who may in fact be, thoughtful and benevolent. At the same time, the character may be so deeply involved in his own schemes or so carried away by a sense of his mission that he does not take into account the effects of human passion. His reminder to Juliet that Claudio is about to die is, to say the least, ill-timed and tactless. His bringing her from the calm acceptance he has helped her to achieve to an extreme of anguish can be an unforgettable moment in production. J. C. Trewin was so deeply moved by this scene in a 1978 R.S.C. production that he found himself fumbling through his program to learn who was playing Juliet.[68]

Something of the same sort happens when the duke, much later

in the play, breaks to Isabella the false news that her brother has
been beheaded. Her verbal response is brief but passionate.

> O, I will to him and pluck out his eyes!
> . . . .
> Unhappy Claudio! Wretched Isabel!
> Injurious world! Most damned Angelo!
> (4.3.116, 118–19)

Throughout the duke's long speech adjuring her to take command
of herself and follow his directions, the lines make clear that she is
weeping profusely. The duke's deception of Isabella may have the
most benevolent purpose: "To make her heavenly comforts of despair
/ When it is least expected" (4.3.106–7). Her conviction of her brother's
death does make more poignant and meaningful her subsequent plea
that Angelo be spared. By the play's end, the audience will perceive
that the duke has mined her austere piety and found a rich vein
of mercy. Yet his benevolence of purpose may be corrupted by his
presumption of omniscience and omnipotence. In the 1975 Stratford,
Ontario, production, the duke's display of theatrical power in this
scene "was linked to sexual power as his wandering hands emphasized
the complex ironies of his lines to Isabella."[69] However the actor's
gestures reinforce the character's lines, Isabella's tears, insisted on by
the text, provide a visual counterpoint to the duke's words and cause
the audience at least to question the wisdom and goodness of his
course.

    In his scenes with Juliet and Isabella, the duke causes pain where
he seems bent on relieving it. The pain is of such a nature and in
such a context that the audience is moved to share it. In both instances,
the duke either fails to or chooses not to recognize that the women
he is attempting both to manipulate and to serve will necessarily respond with overwhelming grief to what he says to them. At the
very least, these scenes point up a limitation in his understanding
of people and a concomitant limitation in his ability to manipulate
the theatrical power for which he has traded his political authority.
These limitations are revealed as well in many of the play's scenes
of laughter. The duke fails duly to consider in his calculations the
effects of human fractiousness as well as those of human anguish.
He shows himself repeatedly unable to silence the scurrilous Lucio,
and he fails to persuade Barnardine to die conveniently: "I swear I

will not die today for any man's persuasion" (4.3.56). There is no better emblem of unruly life refusing to bow to passionless manipulation.

In our production, we tried to draw the spectators' attention to both the duke's strengths and his limitations. We chose to portray him as a commanding figure committed to what he believed was a wise course. His objectives were to help and to heal, to save his city from sliding more deeply into decadence, and to prevent his subjects from abusing each other. The strength of his conviction resulted in urgent quickness of delivery, which kept the pace brisk during the last two acts. His limitations were dramatized by the other characters' reactions to him. Much of the dramatic tension grew out of his seeming inability truly to find the remedies he was forever seeking.

Much of the critical controversy about Vincentio grows out of a perceived disparity between his stated intentions and his actions and achievements.[70] He lacks two important attributes of providence: he is neither omnipotent nor omniscient. When Shakespeare next creates in Prospero a providential figure who dominates his play's action, he gives that figure powers that make him more than human. Yet even Prospero must learn something of human compassion and the extent of his own angry passion before his play is through. Vincentio, unlike Prospero, does not really appear to learn or change. He is the instrument of profound changes in Isabella and perhaps even in Angelo, but the play does not unequivocally show a like change wrought in him. He manages to perform a great deal of good. As a result of his machinations, a rigid and unworkable justice is seasoned and softened by mercy. But the play does not spare in revealing his limits in power and understanding. Perhaps the most just assessment of the character can be borrowed from another tale about a would-be providential figure who wants to do good, who does good in spite of himself, but whose powers and understanding are similarly limited. When the Wizard of Oz is unmasked, he says to Dorothy: "Oh no, my dear, I, I'm a very good man. I'm just a very bad wizard."

The encounter between Vincentio and Juliet provides an example of one of Shakespeare's most striking ways of moving his audience to share his characters' pain. With Juliet, the playwright does not employ complex dramaturgical devices. He simply gives the character an anguished outcry that, by virtue of its suddenness and force, takes the audience along with it. Such suddenness and force can most effectively disturb or even alarm an audience. The dramatist who presents in his early tragedies and histories events like the stabbing of young

Rutland by Clifford or the stabbing of young Mutius by his father knows this well. Although such acts of physical violence are out of place in comedy, Shakespeare enriches and deepens all his mature comedies, even the sunniest of them, with keen sudden moments of emotional or spiritual pain.

No discussion of Shakespeare's ways of eliciting pain in his audience is complete without a glance at such moments. As a conclusion to this chapter, I want to look in isolation at two such moments that render rich and strange his most nearly perfect comedy. They both occur in the last act of *Twelfth Night*.

In the first of them, Orsino threatens to murder Olivia, then spares her and threatens to kill Viola instead. This sequence makes dramatic sense only if the actor playing Orsino makes clear to the audience his homicidal intentions and the women he threatens react as to real and immediate danger. In a 1974 production at Ashland, Oregon, and at a 1985 production at Stratford, Ontario, the duke did not make his purposes sufficiently clear. On both occasions I observed that the spectators grew puzzled and their attention lapsed. The audience hitherto has been encouraged to view the duke—wallowing in self-pity, farcically starting and stopping his musicians,[71] boasting of his strongly beating heart and tough sides—as something of a figure of fun. Now it is made clear that the character's passion can lead to danger, and the audience sees without warning the most deadly manifestation of love's madness.

Sir Toby's drunken entrance, hard on the heels of Orsino's threats, brings another sudden moment of pain. For much of the play he and Sir Andrew have been comedy's oldest and most enduring couple, the knave and the fool.[72] They have provided much laughter and entertainment. But there have been moments—the near duels with Antonio and Sebastian—when a quarrelsome, dangerous side to Sir Toby could be glimpsed. Now his contempt for Sir Andrew, which has always been apparent to the spectators but has been concealed from the foolish knight beneath a mask of camaraderie, is revealed in stark and ugly nakedness. "Will you help—an ass-head and a coxcomb and a knave, a thin fac'd knave, a gull?" (5.1.197–98). In the BBC production Robert Hardy as Sir Toby tempered the drunken rage with no merriment or good humor. Ronnie Stevens as Sir Andrew crumpled with shame and humiliation.

The duke's threats and Sir Toby's insults demonstrate how suddenly and unexpectedly the mirth in Shakespeare's comedies can be displaced.

Such juxtapositions of laughter and pain make for greatness in comedy. They can be found in Aristophanes, Jonson, Molière, and Chekhov, as well as in Shakespeare. Shakespeare is highly skilled but not unique in his ability to manage them. Where he shows his true uniqueness as a writer of comic drama is in his juxtaposition of laughter and pain with such scenes as that which follows immediately after Sir Toby insults Sir Andrew. For now Sebastian, the man who has wounded the drunken knights, makes his appearance and his apology. The audience has been expecting almost from the beginning the simultaneous appearance on the stage of Sebastian and Viola and the consequent resolution of the play's many errors. What it has perhaps not been expecting is the mutual reaction of the sister and brother when each discovers that the other is alive. This reaction quite overwhelms the laughter and pain that have preceded it. Fabian, one of the play's tricksters, recognizes its strength when, changing from his usual jocular prose to meditative verse, he tells Olivia:

> And let no quarrel nor no brawl to come
> Taint the condition of this present hour,
> Which I have wonder'd at.
>
> (5.1.343–45)

This speech registers a change from sudden pain to sudden wonder.

3
WONDER

THE MEETING BETWEEN SEBASTIAN AND VIOLA IS ONE
of Shakespeare's great scenes of wonder. Other characters who witness
the scene and whose lives are miraculously changed by its revelations
properly guide the audience's reactions. The brother and sister have
each thought the other dead, and now each reacts as to a resurrection.
Sebastian is certain that his sister has drowned. He looks at what
appears to be his own semblance:

> Do I stand there? I never had a brother;
> Nor can there be that deity in my nature
> Of here and everywhere.
>
> (5.1.218–20)

At first he can attribute the apparition only to an occurrence of the
supernatural, and he wonders whether he is possessed of the godlike
power of ubiquity.

Viola's case is different from her brother's. From the play's beginning
she has feared that Sebastian was drowned, but the captain held out
the hope of her brother's survival. Now she suffers the most painful
imaginable suspension between hope and fear:

> Such a Sebastian was my brother too;
> So went he suited to his watery tomb;
> If spirits can assume both form and suit,
> You come to fright us.
>
> (5.1.225–28)

Sebastian does not deny that he is a ghost. Rather he affirms it:

> A spirit I am indeed,
> But am in that dimension grossly clad
> Which from the womb I did participate.
>
> (5.1.228–30)

His words carry a sense encountered from time to time in Shakespeare's plays that simply to be living is miracle enough. But Sebastian recognizes an even greater miracle—that his sister is living too:

> Were you a woman, as the rest goes even,
> I should my tears let fall upon your cheek,
> And say 'Thrice welcome, drowned Viola!'
>
> (5.1.231–33)

All that remains is for Viola to confess that she is wearing masculine attire, and the two can rejoice in their mutual resurrection.

Significantly, she is not yet ready to make that final confession. Instead, with "My father had a mole upon his brow" (5.1.234) she initiates one of the most remarkable exchanges in Shakespeare's comedies. Her line subsumes the romance tradition with its emphasis on bodily marks and other physical means of identifying long-lost relatives. Shakespeare draws on this tradition throughout his career, from *The Comedy of Errors* through *Cymbeline* and *The Winter's Tale*. But where Guiderius's natural stamp or Perdita's fardel, for all their symbolic value, are necessary to the romantic plots in which they figure, the brother's and sister's reminiscence here of their father's mole and of the hour of his death is hardly necessary to a plot that has already established their true identities and all but brought about their recognition of each other. These speeches can be taken as both obligatory nod toward and parody of the romance tradition. Parody is not inappropriate in a play that has employed every other comic device, but the lines do not evoke the laughter proper to parody. At my own production of *Twelfth Night* and at all the others I have attended, the audience was hushed and still. What the lines chiefly derive from the romance tradition is the solemnity which that tradition at its best can convey. The slow and stately cadences, the repetitions, and the ornateness of the language carry a strong sense of incantation—an aspect of ceremony not far removed from prayer. The brother and sister create a ceremonial remembrance of their father that gives to their mutual resurrection a formal perfection and an appropriate gravity. At this moment when death seems temporarily to have been defeated, it is proper that they recall their own mortality by reminding themselves and each other of their father's death.

This play explores the transience of every human state, and it frequently demonstrates the nearness of joy to pain. Thus, only after the children recall their father's death does Viola announce that she is in disguise. She and her brother experience and communicate joy that is paradoxically too great for physical expression and too fragile to endure without what Shakespeare calls in another place "a badge of bitterness."[1]

Although the dramatist is bringing the play to a happy conclusion, he deliberately denies to characters and spectators a final consummation and completion. The brother and sister never embrace, and the spectators never behold Cesario transformed into Viola. She pushes her final transformation into offstage futurity, but she gives the scene of recognition its most appropriate close by triumphantly asserting her true identity, which has throughout been suppressed and beset:

> If nothing lets to make us happy both
> But this my masculine usurp'd attire,
> Do not embrace me till each circumstance
> Of place, time, fortune do cohere and jump
> That I am Viola.

> (5.1.241-45)

Although the spectators do not see the physical transformation from man to woman, as they do in *As You Like It*, they are made to feel in these lines, which resound with a trumpet's clarity and brilliance, the release and clarification that accompany Viola's resumption of herself. The lines will achieve greatest force in the theater if the syllables "I am" and the first syllable of "Viola" are given strong and equal stresses.

The scene's participants respond strongly to what they take to be a miracle. By this point in the play the characters have worked their way so deeply into the sympathies of the audience that it shares their feelings. Albertus Magnus describes with notable accuracy such reactions as this scene can elicit in its spectators:

Now wonder is defined as a constriction and suspension of the heart, caused by amazement at the sensible appearance of something so portentous, great and unusual that the heart suffers a systole. Hence, wonder is something like fear in its effects on the heart.[2]

To communicate the scene's emotions with sufficient force, the actor and actress playing Sebastian and Viola must throughout the play convince the audience of the depth and sincerity of their characters' feelings for each other. Viola's part opens with an extraordinarily difficult emotional transition. She must pass from the genuine grief of "My brother he is in Elysium" to the desperate hope of "Perchance he is not drown'd. What think you, sailors?" Her joy at the play's end will make its full impression only on spectators who are made to believe in her conflicting grief and hope at its beginning. Eric Bentley tells us how difficult it is to communicate joy to an audience. "High-spirits and hilarity we can on occasion manage . . . but joy—as an actor would say—'There is nothing harder to do.'"[3] Joy cannot be conjured by directorial invention. One works to find actors possessed of the rare gift of expressing it, one helps them achieve a detailed understanding of their characters in relation to the play, and one exercises sufficient restraint not to interfere with them. Berners W. Jackson stresses this point in his review of Cathleen Widows's performance in the 1975 Stratford, Ontario, production:

> Because she is an actress capable of expressing great joy by what appears to be a process of inner radiation, Miss Widows made the recognition scene totally memorable.[4]

To the actor playing Sebastian falls the comparably difficult task of communicating joy that must grow out of and contrast with the character's sustained and deep grief. The portraying of Sebastian's abiding sadness without falling into dreary monotony requires an actor of considerable ability. Yet in a play featuring such attractive roles as Malvolio, Feste, Sir Toby, and Sir Andrew, Sebastian is often a throwaway, given to anyone from central casting who happens to look like the actress playing Viola. Even this is a mistake since Viola alters her appearance and manner to imitate her brother.[5] The character's essential seriousness, on which the final scene depends, must be communicated in his scenes with Antonio. If the playgoers are encouraged to leer at these scenes, the ending will be ruined. Like Viola, Sebastian is resilient and generous. The similarity in nature between brother and sister is as important to the play as their similarity in appearance.

Even if Sebastian and Viola give astonishing performances, the playgoers cannot be astonished by the scene's events. Wonder is the proper reaction to a miracle or a surprise, but the audience knows that what it beholds is no miracle. It is not even a surprise, since the spectators have been led by the play's form to expect it almost from the beginning. How can the audience experience wonder equivalent to that experienced by the characters? Although the audience will not be astonished by the event, it will be astonished by the verse. This verse moves by degrees from the utterance of every day—"I am sorry, madam, I have hurt your kinsman" (5.1.201)—to an utterance whose use of metaphor, assonance, and proparalepsis makes it lofty and remote— "He finished indeed his mortal act / That day that made my sister thirteen years" (5.1.239–40). Spondees and inverted iambs render the verse rhythmically compelling. With their figurative language and canny circumlocution, the characters rise to the highest pitch of eloquence. Their lines are, in the Longinian sense, sublime.

The ancient, post-Classical and Elizabethan treatises on rhetoric that Shakespeare knew and used teach that the grand style properly moves in its hearers the strongest passions.[6] For the rhetoricians and for the writers who draw on them, wonder is an appropriate response to a miracle or a sudden, surprising event. It is also a proper reaction to poetry; indeed, it can be described as an end of poetry.[7] One of the strongest tenets in the long tradition of rhetorical and poetic theory, from Aristotle through Longinus down to Sidney, is that poetry at its most elevated can move wonder, or to use Sidney's phrase, can "stir the effects of a well raised admiration."[8] Effects of astonishment can result from unusual diction and rhythm as well as from unusual events. Wonder can be a response to style as well as to subject.

That Shakespeare's verse can move wonder has been attested to by nearly everyone who has seen or read his plays. Two early encomia may serve as representative examples. Ben Jonson, in verses written for the First Folio in 1623, offers an assessment almost as well known as its subject: ". . . Soul of an age; / Th'applause, delight, the wonder of our stage."[9] The twenty-two-year-old Milton, writing verses for a new impression of the Folio in 1630, amplifies Jonson's theme: "Thou in our wonder and astonishment / Hast built thyself a livelong monument."[10] What chiefly moves wonder in these poets is the verse.

Yet in drawing upon rhetoricians, literary theorists, and philosophers who develop the idea that wonder is a reaction to both miracles and poetry, one comes flush against the insistence that wonder is an emotion proper to tragedy but not to comedy. Indeed, whenever tragedy and comedy are defined by ancient, medieval, or Elizabethan theorists, these two major forms are seen as precise opposites. The hold on the heart that Albertus Magnus describes, the feeling akin to fear, is a definitively tragic response—the *fobos* of Aristotle, the admiration of Sidney, or the wonder named by Horatio in *Hamlet*. Despite the weight of theory and tradition, Shakespeare so fashions the last act of *Twelfth Night* that wonder is one of the play's emotional effects. It is as integral to this comedy as it is to the tragedy of *Hamlet*. In that tragedy, the commentator Horatio cites wonder as a proper response to the spectacle of sudden death. In this comedy, the commentator Fabian cites wonder as a proper response to the spectacle of sudden resurrection. The dramatist is working with wonder as an accompaniment to both the woe of tragedy and the joy of comedy. His evocation of wonder in comedy as well as in tragedy may be the most significant respect in which he combines the comic with the tragic.

In such combination, Shakespeare is directly at variance with the tradition of precise opposition between the forms. That he often works toward the mutual interpenetration of these types of drama, making each a part of the other, has long been established as a point of either praise or blame. He has been called to account by critics from his own century to ours for indecorously mingling agony and mirth.[11] It takes the greatest of English critics, Samuel Johnson, to recognize the extent to which Shakespeare fuses tragedy and comedy and to perceive this fusion as a virtue. Johnson argues that all Shakespeare's plays are tragicomedies because the dramatist is preeminently the poet of nature, and nature is tragicomic. Johnson's pronouncement is that Shakespeare writes neither tragedies nor comedies,

> . . . . but compositions of a distinct kind exhibiting the real state of sublunary nature, which partakes of good and evil, joy and sorrow, in which at the same time, the reveler is hasting to his wine and the mourner burying his friend; in which the malignity of one is sometimes defeated by the frolic of another, and many mischiefs and many benefits are done and hindered without design.[12]

From the beginning of his career, Shakespeare seems bent on mingling the tragic element of wonder with his comedies.

But the introduction of wonder into comedy is not original with Shakespeare. Elements of the marvelous can be found as far back as Aristophanes, preeminently in *The Birds*, and indeed can be traced even further back to the origins of comedy in ritual.[13] In the relatively recent past of his own country, Shakespeare can find works for the stage that combine the comic with the wondrous, namely the medieval miracle plays and moralities. His immediate forerunners in comedy,

Lyly, Peele, Greene, and many lesser writers, often mix elements of
the supernatural into their comedies. Although none of them evokes
the sort of wonder that Shakespeare evokes in *Twelfth Night*, it can
be argued that Peele, in *The Old Wives' Tale*, and Greene, in *Friar
Bacon and Friar Bungay*, are making serious attempts.

Shakespeare's manner of drawing on Plautus for *The Comedy of
Errors* suggests how strongly the fusion of wonder and comedy appeals
to him, even at the beginning of his career. The play is mainly an
adaptation of Plautus's *Menaechmi*, a typical Latin farce. But one
of the play's central scenes is probably suggested by Plautus's *Am-
phitruo*—atypical Plautus in that it comes nearer to tragedy than any
of his other plays and relies to a greater extent on the supernatural.
For Aegeon's narrative at the beginning and the reunion of the old
man with his long-lost wife at the end, Shakespeare draws on the
tale of Apolonius of Tyre in Gower's *Confessio Amantis*, a work on
which he also draws for *Pericles*.[14] This mixture of romance and farce,
of the literature of wonder and the literature of laughter, is a recurring
combination in the sources for Shakespeare's comedies.[15]

The playwright goes beyond the mechanical combining of events
from romance with events from farce. He enriches Plautus's ambience
of cuckoldry and cozenage by adding darker and stranger threats of
enchantment and demonic possession:

> They say this town is full of cozenage;
> As, nimble jugglers that deceive the eye,
> Dark-working sorcerers that change the mind,
> Soul-killing witches that deform the body,
> Disguised cheaters, prating mountebanks,
> And many such-like liberties of sin . . .
>
> (1.2.97–102)

The jugglers, cheaters, and mountebanks are recognizable denizens
of new comedy from Menander to Middleton. They are urban perils
and take their natural places in comedies of the city. But the dark-
working sorcerers and soul-killing witches are creatures from the world
of legend, fairy tale, and dream. That Shakespeare places such perils
beside the typical urban dangers is an early indication of his comic
manner of combining the mundane with the magical.

This combination persists throughout the play. Nothing explicitly
supernatural occurs, but characters fearfully refer to witches, spirits,

and devils. Such creatures are so thoroughly integrated into the play's imagery that Ephesus takes on the nature of a haunted town.[16] To be sure, fear of witches and devils enriches the means by which Shakespeare keeps his farce moving. Fear of the demonic can create just such a situation as makes for farcical confusion, violence, and laughter. But fear of cozenage alone would serve the purpose of farce equally well. By mixing in his characters a fear of the natural and explicable with a fear of magic, Shakespeare makes an early essay in that exploration of the supernatural that contributes so much to his dramatic and poetic uniqueness.

The playwright's interest in things rich and strange in this early play also manifests itself in Aegeon's last-minute reunion with his wife, long thought dead, and in the final coming together of the two sets of twins. The error-making presence of identical twins and their ultimate reunion create a striking resemblance between this comedy and *Twelfth Night,* a resemblance that has leapt at commentators ever since John Manningham noted it in his diary in response to the performance of *Twelfth Night* at the Middle Temple.[17] There are also obvious and important differences between the plays, and among these is that, despite the demonic imagery and the joyous reunion, no wonder is elicited from the audience in the early play. Indeed, relatively little wonder seems present in the rejoicing characters. Despite the desire expressed in the first act by Antipholus of Syracuse to find his brother, the twins, upon meeting, speak no words of wonder as do Viola and Sebastian in the later play. Neither does Aegeon speak amazedly when his wife is found and his life is saved. To be sure, at this early stage in his career, Shakespeare is not capable of truly sublime verse, and his not attempting such verse may be a tacit recognition of his own limitations. To paraphrase a remark that C. S. Lewis makes of his own early fairy tales, the play partakes of wonders but it possesses no wonder.[18]

A similar observation can be made about Shakespeare's other early comedies. At the center of *The Taming of the Shrew* is an occurrence that can be described as miraculous—the transformation of Katherina. "She has chang'd, as she had never been" marvels her father; "Here is a wonder, if you talk of a wonder," observes Lucentio (5.2.106, 115). Yet these fleeting references constitute all of wonder that the characters express. Spectators are invited to acknowledge that a miracle of sorts has occurred, but they are not invited to respond to it. In *The Two Gentlemen of Verona* one can detect at least the potential for poetry that rises to wonder. But Shakespeare does not rise to the sublime in this play. He attempts in the final scene to represent dramatically the miracle of Valentine's resuming his friendship with the repentant Proteus and offering Silvia to his friend. However, he still lacks sufficient power either as dramatist or poet to make credible Proteus's repentance or Valentine's offer.[19] One may perceive in this unsuccessful ending the playwright's interest in presenting astonishing events. In the play's last speech, Valentine promises the duke: "Please you, I'll tell you as we pass along, / That you will wonder what hath fortuned" (5.4.168–69).

These attempts to weave wonder into comedy reach their first complete success in *A Midsummer Night's Dream*. The play is remarkable for many qualities, not the least of which is verse that gives full expression to the marvels the dramatist represents. The king and queen of fairyland astonish the spectators with their language as well as their power. Titania's attendants and even Puck are creatures of a different order from the contending sovereigns of fairyland, and the difference should be made clear in production. In Shakespeare's time Oberon was played by an adult actor, Titania by the star boy, and the other fairies by children of lesser abilities. In a 1978 R.S.C. production the attendant fairies were puppets, and in Peter Brook's famous production, as well as in several others not so well known, all the fairies, including Oberon, became trapeze artists.[20]

The manner in which the fairies' verse contrasts with the verse of their king and queen suggests differences of degree and kind. The fairies and Puck characteristically speak in tetrameter or pentameter couplets. They exult in and exalt the diminutive. Their verse is full of dewdrops, cowslips, long-legged spinners, and hedgehogs. The mischiefs in which Puck delights are typically farcical pranks—tempting lusty horses, humiliating old ladies, or spoiling the beer. Oberon and Titania speak mostly in blank verse that grows ever more majestic. In describing and enacting their continuing quarrel, the king and queen make clear that their discord is reflected in all sublunary nature. Shakespeare is here varying a rhetorical device that he uses throughout his career. But Titania and Oberon are not mortals like Romeo or Richard II, who imagine all nature to be participating in their grief and rage. Rather these are the very spirits of nature, the originals of natural turbulence. What they describe is not an imagined but an actual result of their anger.

To express this turbulence, the playwright gives Oberon and Titania

verse that employs striking rhythmic and figurative resources. The
ear encounters inverted iambs and spondees, which force strongly
stressed syllables into direct alignment with each other. There is also
frequent enjambment and a flexible use of the caesura, which occurs
often in the middle of a foot and occasionally in the middle of an
inverted foot. The rhythm of a line like "Fall in the fresh lap of
the crimson rose" has a twofold effect: the juxtaposition of strongly
stressed syllables forces the speaker to retard; accented syllables and
the caesura, all occurring in surprising places, create an impression
of emotional agitation. Moreover, the prosopopoeia and antonomasia
in these speeches invest the unseasonal prodigies with human passion
and torment:

> The human mortals want their winter here;
> No night is now with hymn or carol blest;
> Therefore the moon, the governess of floods,
> Pale in her anger, washes all the air,
> That rheumatic diseases do abound.
> And thorough this distemperature we see
> The seasons alter: hoary-headed frosts
> Fall in the fresh lap of the crimson rose;
> And on old Hiems' thin and icy crown
> An odorous chaplet of sweet summer buds
> Is, as in mockery, set. The spring, the summer,
> The childing autumn, angry winter, change
> Their wonted liveries; and the mazed world,
> By their increase, now knows not which is which.
> And this same progeny of evils comes
> From our debate, from our dissension;
> We are their parents and original.
>
> (2.1.101–17)

A key to Titania's speech can be found in a word near its end
that Shakespeare typically charges with many meanings. The fairy
queen speaks of "the mazed world," calling to mind her earlier reference
to "the quaint mazes in the wanton green" (2.1.99). The world in
its confusion has become literally and figuratively a maze, a labyrinth
in which no right path can be found. But the word takes on also
its second sense of "amazed," that is, astonished, struck with wonder
by the alterations. The speech in performance will stand or fall on
the actress's ability to convince the audience of her character's astonish-

ment and shame that she and Oberon are damaging the natural world. To be sure, they are engaged in a farcical love-brawl, but love that is capable of such effects is a great and terrible passion that evokes a Sidneyan admiration. The rage and power of Oberon and Titania stir potentially tragic responses. Peter Brook's recognition and manipulation of these responses may constitute his famous production's greatest achievements.

No Shakespearean comedy offers wider scope to the imagination of directors, designers, and actors, and in no Shakespearean comedy is it more necessary to observe Bruno Walter's admonition to select from among the limitless imaginative possibilities those essential to the play as a whole. Although many of the play's scenes require spectacular visual display and startling or hilarious stage business, the second-act quarrel between Oberon and Titania must guide the audience to focus on language and passion. The director's principal responsibility in this scene is to find actors who possess the talent to speak verse with beauty and power. Having found and worked with such actors, the director must insure that the scenery, lighting, and costumes aid the spectators' response without competing for their attention.

Peter Brook notes that certain of Shakespeare's scenes—most often the prose scenes—can be "enriched by our own invention. The scenes need added external details to assure them of their fullest life."[21] But Brook warns that passages in verse require a different sort of treatment.

> Shakespeare needs verse because he is trying to say more, to compact together more meaning. We are watchful. Behind each visible mark on paper lurks an invisible one that is hard to seize. Technically, we now need less abandon, more focus, less breadth, more intensity.[22]

Surely no director has given the supernatural elements in *A Midsummer Night's Dream* a fuller and more astonishing life than Peter Brook. Yet, true to his own dictum, Brook stilled his acrobatic fairies during Oberon's great speeches, and Alan Howard delivered those speeches unforgettably. I cannot now read or hear "I know a bank where the wild thyme blows" without recalling Howard's slow, deliberate cadences.

But Brook did not adhere to his own doctrine in staging Titania's speech. Sarah Kestelman was an intensely sensual Titania. Her crimson feather bed was the only object of color in the stark white brightly lit set. But she gave the impression that she was nothing more than a sexually indulged creature who was somehow responsible for creating the problem that the charming and authoritative Oberon had to solve. In an interview for the *New York Times*, Brook discussed the

> most extraordinary, demonic notion of Oberon having his queen fornicate with a physically repellent object, the ass. And why does Oberon do it? Not out of sadism, anger or revenge, but out of genuine love. It is as though in a modern sense a husband secured the largest truckdriver for his wife to sleep with to smash her illusions about sex and to alleviate the difficulties in their marriage.[23]

This assessment of the couple's marital relations was reflected in Brook's staging of their quarrel. While Titania spoke, Oberon stroked her leg. His action commanded the audience's attention, drawing it away from her words. To the spectators, she seemed to be merely talking about the weather while Oberon generated the scene's true erotic power. The sense of natural turbulence growing out of the fairies' domestic discord was lost. More important, Sarah Kestelman's Titania was diminished into a creature of sensuality without power. The effect was astonishing, but it was astonishment different in kind and quality from the wonder that arises out of Titania's verse. Brook's production was ruled by its Oberon and its Puck,[24] but Titania's scenes were less enriched by a sense of her magnitude than they could have been.

Something of the wonder that Titania's words create remain with her throughout the play. Although she is bewitched into a ridiculous amour, she never fully loses her original stature. Funny as they are, there is a peculiar power in her scenes with Bottom. Much of this power is drawn from her speeches in the second act, and some of it accrues from the astonishing manner in which Oberon introduces the magic herb that will bring about her dotage. Like his consort, he employs striking rhythmic and figurative devices:

> Thou rememb'rest
> Since once I sat upon a promontory,
> And heard a mermaid on a dolphin's back
> Uttering such dulcet and harmonious breath
> That the rude sea grew civil at her song,
> And certain stars shot madly from their spheres
> To hear the sea-maid's music.
>
> (2.1.148–54)

Oberon invests the herb with the power of the music he is describing. The playwright diverts attention from the fact that the fairy king is actually playing a rather petty and cruel practical joke on his wife. The diversion by no means mitigates the laughter that the trick will bring about, but it suggests that the device and its accompanying laughter contain elements of wonder. Although what happens to Titania is similar in kind to what happens to the quartet of human lovers, it is raised to a greater order of magnitude.

Even the human lovers, foolish, passionate, and ridiculous in their pain, are not untouched by wonder. When Theseus's huntsman wakes them after they have been released from their enchantments, they are still enraptured by the fading memory of the dream they have shared. "Methinks I see these things with parted eye, / When everything seems double" (4.1.186–87). "And I have found Demetrius like a jewel, / Mine own, and not mine own" (4.1.188–89). Lysander's line to Theseus suggests to directors and actors how all four lovers should speak and act in this scene: "My lord, I shall reply amazedly, / Half sleep, half waking" (4.1.143–44). After the jangling couplets and farcical stage business of their protracted quarrel, the lovers' quiet scene of awakening possesses a startling beauty.

Even Bottom is moved to wonder after his fashion at his night's adventures. Twisting Biblical phrases about the wondrous works of God, he lists the particular incapacities of the various human senses and faculties to conceive or report his vision.[25] The speech is funny, but if the actor plays it quietly and convinces the audience of the character's genuine amazement, wonder will mix with the laughter. Bottom realizes that his dream is good enough to be made into a ballad to grace the end of the tragedy that he and his companions plan to perform at the duke's wedding. What better thing can come at the end of a tragedy than something that moves wonder?

All five of the humans whose lives have been touched by love-in-idleness sense that they have traveled to terrain that lies on the far side of reason. Theseus maps and then dismisses this terrain in his famous speech toward the play's end. But that speech takes on reverberations for the audience that go beyond his conscious intentions because the spectators have seen and dwelt for a time with the fairies, and he has not. Even in Brook's production, in which Theseus dreamed himself into Oberon, Alan Howard's Theseus gave the impression that his conscious mind was tendering a stringent warning to his half-conscious fantasies. The rich counterpoint between Theseus's skepticism and the spectators' memory of the magic can be strengthened in production if, while the actor is talking urbanely about lovers and madmen, his bearing and movement recall those of Oberon and the lighting subtly reminds the audience of the haunted grove.

Albertus Magnus asserts that wonder can be called forth in one who is in suspense as to a cause, the knowledge of which will make him know instead of wonder.[26] It follows from this assertion that reason can dispel wonder. If reason finds out the cause of a seeming miracle, then reactions proper to a miracle are no longer either necessary or possible. As Guildenstern argues in Tom Stoppard's play—which owes more than its plot to Shakespeare—the miraculous unicorn shrinks to a horse with an arrow in its forehead. Now Theseus is using his reason with just such an intent when he ascribes the lovers' wonder to their amorous fancies. But Hippolyta speaks for the audience's larger experience when she raises a caveat that Theseus never answers:

> But all the story of the night told over,
> And all their minds transfigur'd so together,
> More witnesseth than fancy's images,
> And grows to something of great constancy
> But howsoever strange and admirable.
>
> (5.1.23–27)

Her last word, used as Sidney uses it, makes clear that she partakes of the lovers' wonder. The playwright contrives his action and his verse so that the spectators share her response.[27]

After his first comic masterpiece, Shakespeare continues in his comedies to demonstrate his interest in things supernatural and causeless and in the admiring responses those things call forth in characters and audiences. With the possible exception of the farce *The Merry Wives of Windsor*—and even that play is not without its fairies—each of the subsequent comedies contains at least one seeming miracle and at least one dramatically represented moment of wonder. Yet characters in these comedies again and again try to set up reason as a means to dispel wonder. Hymen says at the end of *As You Like It*, when Rosalind appears as a seeming miracle, "Feed yourselves with questioning, / That reason wonder may diminish . . ." (5.4.132–33). In *Much Ado About Nothing*, the friar similarly offers to dispel the wonder at Hero's seeming resurrection:

> All this amazement can I qualify,
> When, after that the holy rites are ended,
> I'll tell you largely of fair Hero's death.
> Meantime let wonder seem familiar . . .
>
> (5.4.67–70)

In *All's Well That Ends Well*, Bertram in effect charges his wife to convert his wonder into knowledge: "If she, my liege, can make me know this clearly, / I'll love her dearly, ever, ever dearly" (5.3.309–10). And the king too wants to look into the causes of the miracles: "Let us from point to point this story know, / To make the even truth in pleasure flow" (5.3.318–19). In *Measure for Measure*, the duke's last words promise an abundance of explanations: "So, bring us to our palace, where we'll show / What's yet behind that's meet you all should know" (5.1.536–37). Even in the late comedies, plays so deeply concerned with mysteries and magic, such explanations are demanded and promised. At the end of *The Winter's Tale*, Leontes accompanies his newly resurrected wife, his daughter found by miracle, and everyone else to a session of questions and answers:

> Lead us from hence where we may leisurely
> Each one demand and answer to his part
> Perform'd in this wide gap of time since first
> We were dissever'd.
>
> (5.3.152–55)

And in *The Tempest*, the only comedy besides *A Midsummer Night's Dream* to make explicit and extended use of the supernatural, Prospero promises to qualify everyone's amazement:

> At pick'd leisure,
> Which shall be shortly, single I'll resolve you,
> Which to you shall seem probable, of every
> These happen'd accidents.
>
> (5.1.247–50)

As the characters in these comedies process offstage to their feasts and discussions, one cannot escape the suspicion that they are indulging in an activity against which Lafeu, the old lordly commentator in *All's Well That Ends Well*, issues an eloquent warning:

They say miracles are past; and we have our philosophical persons to make modern and familiar things supernatural and causeless. Hence is it that we make trifles of terrors, ensconcing ourselves into seeming knowledge when we should submit ourselves to an unknown fear. (3.3.1–6)

Having found in *A Midsummer Night's Dream* the means to represent wonder dramatically and to express it poetically, does Shakespeare, with these repeated promises of explanations, allow reason to diminish wonder and replace unknown fear with seeming knowledge?

As with most questions rising from Shakespeare's plays, the answer is yes and no. The audience is made to react in each play to the dissolution of wonder by knowledge. Yet the playgoers marvel that such strong love and gratitude can exist, and they marvel even more at the language in which these are expressed. Shakespeare typically does not baffle his audience with mysteries but illuminates it simultaneously with clear reason and undiminished wonder. In most of his comedies, as we have seen, wonder is evoked partly by the strength and quality of the characters' feelings and chiefly by the sublimity of their verse. Yet this assertion contains only part of a truth, the rest of which defies explanation. There is always a mystery at the heart of a great artist's power. Since the ability to evoke wonder in an audience so strongly depends upon the quality of the verse, the evocation itself must have something mysterious about it.

There is a mystery, moreover, at the heart of what the verse expresses. Again, in spite of all the characters' promised explanations and in spite of all the facts the spectators possess, there is something astonishing in the love and joy that the plays' chief figures experience and communicate. The audience knows all along that Beatrice and Benedick, half in love with each other from the start, will be successfully maneuvered into matrimony. Everyone can laugh heartily at the progress of the tricks. Yet when Beatrice and Benedick move beyond their original selves to find a love that goes almost hand in hand with reason, the audience moves beyond laughter to wonder. When Benedick proclaims, "A miracle! here's our own hands against our hearts" (5.4.91), the playgoers' laughter will be enriched by awe. Similarly, toward the end of *As You Like It*, Rosalind speaks a simple line of blank verse once to her father and once to her lover: "To you I give myself, for I am yours" (5.4.110–11). The spectators are surprised by this line of verse coming from one who has for so long been a mistress of trenchant prose. The urgent love that she has mocked for so long now takes full possession of her and forces her at least momentarily to feel and express its unalloyed force. Although the audience has been expecting it, the moment is astonishing.

In Shakespeare's comedies, wonder is not the price of irony. The audience is almost never astonished by what astonishes the characters, but is frequently astonished by the quality of their astonishment. Shakespeare does not seem unaware of the mystery and paradox at the heart of his evocation of wonder. In his last great play, Prospero promises to explain everything. But spectators must take this promise in juxtaposition with the fact that no one else in the play, not even Miranda, knows of Ariel's relation to Prospero. Indeed, the old magician puts his daughter into a charmed sleep to keep her from seeing the sprite. Now that Prospero has broken his staff and drowned his book, does he intend to reveal all his magic secrets? Is there an explanation for such things as Ariel? The play leads one to ask these questions. Many answers are implied in its text, but no explicit answer is given. Shakespeare is prompting the audience to wonder how much of his mystery Prospero will preserve when he retires to Milan, where every third thought shall be his grave.

At the midpoint of his career, the playwright offers a theatrical emblem that figures forth his recurrent collocation of the explanation and the mystery. At the end of *As You Like It*, Hymen seems to promise an explanation of the apparent conjuring of Rosalind by an offstage but omnipresent magician. The explanation is simple: Rosalind is Ganymede. But what is Hymen, and how has he come into the forest of Arden? Is he a supernatural and causeless being, the god of marriage graciously appearing to bless this miraculous quadruple wedding?[28] Or can his presence, like Rosalind's be simply explained? Most productions invent an explanation, having him played by the old shepherd Corin, whom Rosalind has persuaded to represent Hymen in a wedding masque. Thus Terry Hands's 1981 R.S.C. production reached its "climax with the arrival of nuptial corn-dollies under the supervision of Corin's Hymen."[29] M. St. Clare Byrne, reviewing Byam Shaw's 1957 R.S.C. production with Peggy Ashcroft observed:

If Rosalind, Celia and Touchstone did not knock off those verses and fix the whole thing up with their neighbours overnight, they are not the people I take them for.[30]

For Byrne, the ending is comparable in its rustic mummery to the Pyramus and Thisby play or the show of the nine worthies. But Hymen enriches and complicates the rustic mummery. When Joe Papp, always suspicious of the supernatural in Shakespeare, cut Hymen from the 1973 New York Shakespeare Festival production, Jack J. Jorgens noted that the "ceremonial air of the conclusion was diluted."[31] The unexplained appearance of the god of marriage makes its small contribution of wonder to the play's last scene. Whatever Hymen is, whether god or shepherd or something of both, he is not explained, even though he puts himself forward as a chief explainer. Reason's putative representative is, in fact, a representative of wonder.

Most of this comedy's dialogue is in witty prose, a medium hardly calculated to inspire wonder. But the playwright creates in the Forest of Arden a setting that establishes an astonishing counterpoint to the characters' usual manner of discourse. It is a place of many surprises. The forest surprisingly furnishes the clown Touchstone with a lover. Oliver's conversion is a surprise. His fourth-act entrance and sudden amorous attachment to Celia make for astonishing matter for which the play has in no way prepared the audience. Of Hymen's appearance I have already spoken, and Jaques de Boys's entrance and announcement make for a crowning surprise. This forest of unnamed magicians, convenient lionesses, sudden appearances, and even more sudden changes of heart is a world of wonders where anything conceivable becomes possible. Since the quality of the dialogue makes this pastoral comedy one of Shakespeare's most satirically urbane plays,[32] the necessary counterpoint created by the pastoral imagery and the many surprising events associated with the forest can be strengthened in production by imaginative scenic and lighting design. Terry Hands's 1981 R.S.C. production luxuriated in a setting that "changes with the seasons from a fleece-lined box to a glade bursting with crocuses."[33]

The creation of such counterpoint by means of imagery and setting is a typically Shakespearean device. Many of the comedies are partially set in what Northrop Frye calls "the green world."[34] Characters journey to magical places and are there transformed, renewed, or reborn. Of such places, the Forest of Arden is the archetypal example. For Shakespeare's company, the creation of such worlds was brought about more by the evocative art of the poet than by the plastic art of the scene designer. But the contemporary of Inigo Jones who wrote his last plays for Blackfriars cannot have underestimated the importance of spectacle in aiding imagination and increasing wonder.

Wonder is a part of the life and meaning of each of the major comedies. Yet wondrous events must not occur too often. One of the defining characteristics of any miracle—as Shakespeare's characters never tire of pointing out—is its rarity. Shakespeare's strong evocations of wonder are rare, and his wondrous scenes are relatively brief. But unsurprisingly, the frequency and strength of such scenes increases in the late comedies, plays that treat astonishing and supernatural events and in which the quality of the verse approaches the miraculous. Even *Pericles,* notoriously uneven and likely a partial reworking of someone else's play, rises in its final scenes of restoration to one of Shakespeare's strongest evocations of wonder.[35]

Unlike other scenes of wonder, the meeting between Pericles and his daughter is of considerable length, extending over one hundred and seventy lines and probably taking about ten minutes to perform. The dramatist's task is to sustain the scene at a high pitch; he must not diminish the wonder by attenuation. Accordingly, much of this scene is taken up with questioning, doubt, and fear that the grand apprehended truth may dissolve into illusion before the reasonable faculty can comprehend it. The scene also communicates an almost musical recapitulation of the play's events. Adopting a method analogous to that of a composer employing sonata form, the playwright makes fleeting references to former themes. These recapitulations create a sense of symmetry that gives weight and permanence to the meeting between father and daughter. The shipboard setting augments the sense of recapitulation. Pericles has suffered the greatest of his losses at sea, and it is spiritually and artistically appropriate that his greatest restoration also come at sea.

Pericles has been absent from the stage for several scenes. His humanity has in the interim given way to his sufferings, and his appearance now will shock the audience. Director, designers, and actor will create the appropriate effects by striving to create an impression of the character's insanity and bestiality. In costume, manner, and sound, Pericles must seem more than half animal. In his *London Times* review of Ron Daniel's 1979 production, John Barber called attention to Peter McEnery's ghastly appearance as the grieving father.[36] The character has long been silent, and his voice might be harsh and rusty from disuse. When the prince realizes that his daughter has been restored to him, he regains his humanity. The wonder of this restoration will be most forcefully conveyed to the audience if the audience is made to understand how much of that humanity Pericles has been in danger of losing.

Marina plays the angel to Pericles' beast. She is both a wonder in herself and a worker of wonders. In this play, which has so much to do with the power of artifice, it is fitting that a character central to its dramaturgy and themes should be an artificer of god-like abilities.[37] By her art Marina rescues her father from certain ignominy, just as Shakespeare, by his art, rescues his story from certain disaster.

The playwright brings the scene of restoration through many emotional vicissitudes before the characters are allowed to experience and the audience is allowed to share the final sense of wonder. Marina tries and fails to move Pericles with her singing, and when she attempts to speak to the old man, he strikes her and pushes her away.[38] The action is brutal, a moment far worse in its horrific violence than anything that has been done or threatened in the brothel. At the same time, the actor and actress create between them an almost palpable sense of electricity. Even at Pericles' bestial nadir, the actors can suggest to the audience that their characters are mysteriously drawn to each other. Ian Richardson and Susan Fleetwood achieved an "agonized ecstasy" in the 1969 R.S.C. production.[39] The sense of this mutual bond grows even stronger for characters and spectators when Marina begins to reveal what she knows of her own history. On an instinctive level that precedes reason and has nothing to do with doubt, the two have already recognized each other, but like Sebastian and Viola, they draw back from their instinctive recognition into remembrance of their sufferings. By making her father relive his grief, Marina forces him to purge himself of sorrow: "I am great with woe, and shall deliver weeping" (5.1.105). This metaphoric birth, a recapitulation of Thaisa's terrible childbed at sea, is a necessary step to the miracle of rebirth toward which the scene is moving. When the old man at last realizes that he has found his daughter, he utters one of Shakespeare's great speeches of joy and wonder. If it is delivered pianissimo, the actor will create the impression that the character's body, wracked by this sudden storm of joy, almost lacks the strength to give that joy utterance. But he draws energy from the joy of his discovery, and in the speech's final lines he can crescendo, rising in volume to match the thunder he invokes. As Pericles gives his happiness a voice, he continues to recapitulate his pain. His speech insists upon an idea central to each of Shakespeare's mature comedies, that joy does not supplant pain but rather merges with it:

O Helicanus, strike me, honour'd sir;
Give me a gash, put me to present pain,
Lest this great sea of joys rushing upon me
O'erbear the shores of my mortality,
And drown me with their sweetness. O, come hither,
Thou that beget'st him that did thee beget;
Thou that wast born at sea, buried at Tharsus,
And found at sea again! O, Helicanus,
Down on thy knees, thank the holy gods as loud
As thunder threatens us. This is Marina.

(5.1.189–99)

Like Lear, Pericles is in some measure restored when he becomes certain that the lady before him is his daughter. But as with Lear, the restoration is not complete. Lysimachus recognizes that Pericles is not yet fully recovered: "It is not good to cross him; give him way" (5.1.228). The old prince of Tyre is most like the old king of Britain because his very joys threaten to become dangers. Shakespeare demonstrates in *King Lear* how a heart caught "'twixt two extremes of passion, joy and grief," can "burst smilingly."[40] The play insists that the old prince is swept very near to death by the sudden joy. The difference between Lear and Pericles is the difference between catastrophe and anastrophe. In the comedy, the gods themselves seem to send Pericles music that charms him asleep and permits him to recover fully. The text implies that the music is a gift from Diana. In the 1969 R.S.C. production, the music was audible only to Pericles and Marina, and the actors made clear to the spectators its supernatural character.[41] The goddess sends Pericles the sleep that completes the restoring of his life, just as she sends him the dream that completes the restoring of his family.

The vision, the subsequent journey to Ephesus, and the restoring of Pericles and Thaisa to each other contain new matter to astonish and delight the characters. But for all the joy the characters claim at the play's end, the penultimate scene between Pericles and Marina remains for the audience the genuine crisis and resolution. That Shakespeare may have realized how anticlimactic a second restoration would be to an audience that has been so deeply affected by the first is suggested by the different solution he fashioned for the same dramatic problem in *The Winter's Tale*.

Understanding the scene between Pericles and Marina is a necessary step to understanding all Shakespeare's scenes of wonder, especially those in the plays that follow. In scenes of restoration in *The Winter's Tale* and *The Tempest*, the playwright again moves his major characters through violent, often bestial passions before they find their lost loved ones and their resurgent humanity. These plays further resemble *Pericles* in that qualities of conscious artistry, both in their composition and in the events they depict, figure largely in their scenes of wonder. Like the musical recapitulations in *Pericles*, Hermione's emblematic statue and Prospero's shaping artistry give their plays a sense of stability and permanence.

Since the figure of the artist becomes an increasingly important source of wonder in Shakespeare's last plays, it is instructive to glance at *Pericles'* other scene of resurrection toward the end of the third act. It will be remembered that the playwright vividly portrays Thaisa's seeming death. In the next scene the queen is brought back to life in a manner that moves greater wonder in the audience than does her restoration to her husband at the play's end. Cerimon, the agent of her resurrection, is a forerunner of Prospero in that he, too, is an artist-magician. Although the role is small, it is most effectively played by such an actor as would play the deposed Duke of Milan. The 1973 production at Stratford, Ontario, featured Powers Thomas as a mysterious and moving Cerimon. Martha Henry as Thaisa had awakened to sexual attraction at the moment that she met Pericles. "Her second awakening, this time to loss and loneliness, was all the more poignant."[42] Although Thaisa awakens to loss, her resurrection is a miracle:

> Death may usurp on nature many hours,
> And yet the fire of life kindle again
> The o'erpress'd spirits.
>
> (3.2.87–89)

As it becomes apparent that Cerimon's ministrations will revive Thaisa, the gentleman's words capture the feeling that the production should elicit in the audience:

> The heavens,
> Through you, increase our wonder, and set up
> Your fame forever.
>
> (3.2.100–102)

For all Cerimon's profession that he has studied physic, he seems almost a god. Watching this scene of resurrection, the audience will come to feel that to bring the dead to life is very great magic indeed. Such magic pervades the plays that follow *Pericles*.

Magic certainly pervades *Cymbeline*. Only the queen and Cloten, both of whom can well be spared, die in earnest. But the play is full of seeming deaths and actual restorations. While many comedies end with multiple weddings, *Cymbeline* ends with a multiple resurrection. The increased number of such seeming miracles does not bring about a concomitant increase in the effects of wonder conveyed to the audience. Rather, these effects are vitiated by the manner in which Shakespeare contrives his play. *Cymbeline* is a complex drama that self-consciously calls attention to its complexities. As Granville-Barker argues, the play partakes of a sophisticated artlessness that displays art instead of concealing it. Shakespeare seems to say to his audience: "This is an exhibition of tricks, and what I want you to enjoy, among other things, is the skill with which I hope to perform them."[43] Artistic self-consciousness contributes importantly to the wondrous effects in *Pericles, The Winter's Tale,* and *The Tempest,* but in *Cymbeline* the artifice calls such deliberate and insistent attention to itself that the audience is often encouraged to examine the events rather than to participate in them.

This is particularly true in the scenes of wonder. As an astonishing and supernatural event, Posthumus's vision could potentially elicit such a feeling, but the verse is either so mannered or so undistinguished that the effects of admiration that the spectacle might otherwise encourage in the theater are almost wholly counteracted. The scene calls attention to itself as a theatrical contrivance, and in precise Brechtian fashion the audience is *verfremdet,* estranged.

From the opening moments of bald narrative exposition, the play puts the audience into a mood for a remote fairy tale rather than a dramatic event characterized by the vividness and immediacy of the theater. The spectators are repeatedly distanced from feelings of wonder expressed by the characters. The final scene is indeed as likely to move laughter as wonder. One cannot escape the sense that Shakespeare is burlesquing the tradition in which he writes. The repeated restorations, each with its requisite exclamations of surprise, take on a mechanical, Bergsonian quality. As Bergson points out, and as every canny performer knows, repetition is one of the surest means of getting laughs in the theater. The author of the repeated motto, "Some are born great; some achieve greatness; and some have greatness thrust upon them," cannot have been unaware of this. Although the last scene of *Cymbeline* contains a few moments of genuine astonishment, the delight in this play tends rather to be aesthetic than emotional. The spectators, while intent on the tale that Shakespeare is telling, seldom forego their consciousness of the playwright as teller of tales.

The title, a key incident, and much of the imagery of Shakespeare's next comedy suggest that the playwright is still exploring ways to make the audience grow conscious of and take delight in his abilities as storyteller. But where the display of artifice is deliberately apparent in *Cymbeline*'s dramaturgy, such display is subordinated in *The Winter's Tale* to so great an extent that the dramatist has it both ways. He achieves theatrical immediacy with the full imaginative and emotional participation that such immediacy engenders in the audience, and he simultaneously creates the impression that he is telling a story to while away a winter evening. The pain elicited by Leontes mixes with the laughter called forth by Paulina in such a way as to reassure the audience that all will eventually be well.[44] At the beginning of the third act, Shakespeare briefly interrupts his scenes of rapidly intensifying pain leavened by laughter to suggest that the play will take the audience beyond tragedy to joyous wonder. Cleomenes and Dion, the two lords returning from Delphos with Apollo's oracle, can show the audience that they have been mightily affected by the experience. Their feelings are given strongest expression in the speech that describes the oracle's voice:

> . . . But of all, the burst
> And the ear-deaf'ning voice o' th' oracle,
> Kin to Jove's thunder, so surpris'd my sense
> That I was nothing.
>
> (3.1.8–11)

To be sure, a piece of narrative will not affect spectators so deeply as a piece of theatrical representation. But Cleomenes' speech in performance can evoke a reaction akin to the far stronger response that the play's final scene will call forth. In a 1981 production at the Abbey Theatre,

> This little scene carried such authority that Leontes' dismissal of the oracle in the trial scene seemed genuinely blasphemous, and his cry

to Apollo soon after was a scream of remorse. . . . The statue scene took place among people who were clearly believers.[45]

The play's essential dramatic movement is identical to that in *Pericles*. Both plays leave a grieving father to follow the fortunes of a wonderful daughter. The playwright makes Perdita the creature whose very presence restores her father's humanity. One might think that the scenes in which this redemption is portrayed should evoke the strongest wonder in the audience. But the framing of his appeal to the audience constitutes for Shakespeare a particularly difficult dramaturgical problem. He has already composed in *Pericles* a scene of restoration between father and daughter that can hardly be surpassed. Indeed, so stirring is that scene that Pericles' restoration to his wife savors of anticlimax. Leontes, like Pericles, is now to find, as if by miracle, first his daughter and then his wife. Although little is known about the playwright's working methods, study of his plays suggests that he rarely repeats a triumph without modifying it and that he often repeats and improves upon a dramatic situation that he has previously treated with only partial success.[46]

In *The Winter's Tale*, Shakespeare avoids the repetition of a triumph and corrects a previous dramaturgical error by communicating the discovery of Perdita's true parentage through a scene of narration. The audience is given a thorough understanding of both the events and their effects on the play's principal characters, but this understanding is not heated by emotion. In performance, the speakers need not strive to make the audience share their feelings. Rather, the actors and director can contrive means to detach the spectators from the described raptures. In his 1979 production at Stratford, Ontario, Robin Philips staged this scene with a group of junior officers who "burst in, dying to light up as a relief from the big emotional scene upstairs."[47] Preparing for what may be his greatest scene of wonder in comedy, the playwright insures that his audience will not be emotionally exhausted when it beholds the final revelation. Instead, his narrators instruct the spectators how they should react to the miracle that is to come.

The audience is not ushered directly from one revelation to the next. It will be recalled that in *Pericles* the action hurries from the prince's meeting with his daughter, to his god-sent vision, to his meeting with his wife. This swiftness contributes to the sense of anticlimax. In *The Winter's Tale*, the colloquy among Autolycus, the shepherd, and the clown is sandwiched between the account of Perdita's restoration and the unveiling of her mother's statue, providing the relief of laughter. It insures that the audience will come to the final scene with high expectation, acute judgment, and refreshed emotion.

In that scene the playwright departs from his usual practice of making his characters react with astonishment to events that do not surprise the spectators. Instead, he astonishes the audience with what it should also take to be a miracle. The events of the third act are calculated to convince the audience that Hermione is dead. The coming to life of the statue will be as great a cause of wonder for the playgoers as for the other characters on the stage. It behooves the actress, the lighting and costume designers, and the makeup artist to convince everyone in the theater that Hermione is made of just such stone as the other characters describe. The audience's admiration for the actress disguised as a statue should equal the characters' admiration for the statue itself.

The scene is disposed so that wonder is inspired first by a work of art, then by a miracle, and finally by a work of nature. Only after admiration has been expressed for the statue's resemblance to the queen and its closeness to life does Shakespeare allow its seeming magic to draw an even more wondering response. The wonder increases yet again when the statue proves indeed to be the thing it resembles.

When the statue is first revealed, the characters' immediate response is silence, which Paulina rightly interprets: "I like your silence; it the more shows off / Your wonder" (5.3.20–21). The characters are so rapt in the work of art that they cannot use their senses or faculties for any of their natural functions. Leontes' description of his daughter may be taken as a stage direction:

> O royal piece,
> There's magic in thy majesty, which has
> My evils conjur'd to remembrance, and
> From thy admiring daughter took the spirits,
> Standing like stone with thee!
>
> (5.3.38–42)

Much of the scene's language suggests that one element of this reaction is the admiring response to artistry. "The fixture of her eye has motion in't, / As we are mock'd with art" (5.3.67–68). *Mock* bears the sense of both scoff and imitation. Wonder is an appropriate response to the artificer's skill in imitating life.

It is also an appropriate response to a miracle. Just as the audience has fully shared the characters' reactions to the seeming work of art, it will now respond with the characters as to a work of magic. When Paulina says, "Resolve you / For more amazement" (5.3.86–87), she refers to the latter response. Seeming to conjure life in the statue, the actress must assume the commanding power of a magician. Leontes responds to the succeeding miracle when he says, "If this be magic, let it be an art / Lawful as eating" (5.3.110–11).

Hermione is a product of neither artifice nor witchcraft, although Shakespeare calls forth for her the wonder accruing to both. The greatest miracle is that she is Hermione, and that she has always been alive. So carefully does the dramatist combine and balance his effects in her final scene that even the most meticulous and well-considered directorial intervention may vitiate its force. In the 1969 R.S.C. production and in the 1975 production at Stratford, Connecticut, Hermione was doubled with Perdita. While such doubling reinforces the major theme of time's cyclical nature, it may mar the final moments. In the 1969 production, Hermione was placed on a revolving pedestal. The curtain was temporarily closed, and when it opened again, Judi Dench, who had been playing Perdita, was on the pedestal as Hermione, ready to descend. The spectators were so busy admiring the sleight of hand that the scene's emotional impact was blunted.[48] In his 1979 production at Stratford, Ontario, Robin Philips altered the ending in another way. Hermione stepped toward Leontes and touched his hand. She then left him to embrace Perdita. Her reunion with her daughter became the scene's emotional climax, and the lines referring to her embrace of her husband were cut. This made for an effective but wintry conclusion, "serene but utterly cold."[49] The restoration of Hermione's warm life helps create the scene's effect. Depriving that life of part of its warmth, Philips deprived the scene of part of its wonder.

In a quite literal sense, Hermione, as she is fashioned by her dramatic artificer, is all three of the things that she has seemed to be. As work of art, work of magic, and work of nature, she embodies the principal elements that surprise and delight audiences. It is appropriate that the scene of which she is the center should be one of Shakespeare's most profoundly amazing.

Effects of power and wonder, concentrated in the final scene of *The Winter's Tale*, can be found throughout *The Tempest*. Prospero is literally supernatural—above nature. If Ariel is a spirit of nature, Prospero is nature's commander. Caliban contributes to the play's wonder by virtue of his own strangeness and in his capacity to respond in memorable verse to the island's beauty and to Prospero's power. The play's heroine, like Marina, Imogen, and Perdita, calls forth wonder by her very presence and her accomplishments. As Ferdinand reminds the playgoers, her name denotes the response she invites. The actors playing Ferdinand and Miranda have no small responsibility for sustaining the play's rarefied atmosphere. In the 1975 production with Paul Scofield as Prospero, these scenes were played with sacramental rapture.[50]

A chief cause of the play's wonder is its ability literally to astonish the audience. To be sure, there is no single surprise comparable in magnitude to the discovery that Hermione is alive, but there are several wholly unexpected events. *The Tempest* is so well known that readers and even some actors and directors may overlook its surprises. But understanding these is vital to producing the play. Most of the surprises spring from the playwright's manner of developing his chief character. The old magician is exalted by a god's powers and debased by a man's passions and infirmities. As the play's expository second scene demonstrates, and as Prospero himself confirms in the last act, the deposed duke is driven by fury and thirst for revenge.[51] The tempest whose form he commands Ariel to take is a wide-ranging manifestation of his own ruling passions. The role is as demanding as Lear because it requires its actor to create and sustain a similar inner storm. The great Prosperos of our time, Gielgud, Scofield, and Carnovsky, have also been the great Lears. This angry magician controls and manipulates events more surely than do any of Shakespeare's other managing figures—Hal, Don Pedro, Rosalind, Sir Toby, Vincentio, and Iago. Like these other managers, he imparts to the audience his passions and motives. But unlike all of them, except Vincentio, he does not divulge all his intentions. Although he is fully candid about his plans for his daughter and Ferdinand, the old mage is far less candid about what he will do to the Neapolitan lords and his usurping brother. True, he saves them from the storm that he has made Ariel become. Through Ariel's agency, he saves Alonso and Gonzalo from being killed by Antonio and Sebastian:

My master through his art foresees the danger
That you, his friend, are in; and sends me forth—
For else his project dies—to keep them living.

(2.1.288–90)

The oft-repeated word *project* carries the sense of a magical experiment.
Jonson uses the same word to the same purpose in *The Alchemist*.
But of the precise nature of this project the playgoers are never in-
formed. Consequently, they never know what to expect in the scenes
involving the lords. These scenes prove in production as surprising
and disturbing for them as for the characters.

When King Alonso and his company hear "Marvellous sweet music" (3.3.19) and see "several strange Shapes, bringing in a banquet"
(3.3.S.D.), the spectators are as astonished as the lords and even more
apprehensive. After all, the audience knows that an angry Prospero
has planned and is observing all. Whatever his intention, it cannot
be to give these lords a meal. The "living drollery" (3.3.21) that presents
the banquet creates an evanescent air of festivity, yet this mood is
darkened by Alonso's apprehensions, and when the banquet vanishes
and the harpy appears, the inchoate comedy changes to fear and wonder. The lines suggest that the lords' senses and faculties are wholly
taken up with an amazed contemplation of their crimes. To solve
this acting problem, the actors must relive in sensuous detail all the
events of Prospero's enforced exile—the armies storming the palace,
the ransacking of the ducal possessions, the violent putting to sea
of the defeated duke and his screaming baby daughter. The spectators, not knowing what is coming until it comes, will share the lords'
horror and astonishment. In Yukio Ninagawa's production at the 1988
Edinburgh Festival, the magical banquet was first delivered and then
snatched away by Noh figures in animal masks, to the wonderment
of the Westernized lords.[52]

Ariel holds out a hope of pardon with his reference to "heart's
sorrow, / And a clear life ensuing" (3.3.81–82). But the audience still
has no certain knowledge of the magician's plans. The actor playing
Prospero can continue to imply that the character may be inclined
to kill his enemies. I attended a performance at Leeds in 1975 in
which Paul Scofield played the role with prophetic fury, conquering
his passion in the final act only with the greatest difficulty. M. St.
Clare Byrne describes a similar rage in Gielgud's performance, noting

that his Prospero must "win through under our eyes to the rarer action which is the foregoing of vengeance."[53] The wronged Duke of Milan's decision to free the lords is the play's major turning point. The change wrought in Prospero is as astonishing and moving as Hermione's change from apparent stone to actual flesh. There is no *coup de theatre* here. The drama is within Prospero's soul, and it takes the form of a conflict between fury and reason.

Having renounced his fury, Prospero renounces his magic. The audience will not be surprised by this second renunciation. Throughout the play Prospero has been promising Ariel his freedom, and the play makes clear that the sprite is both agent and embodiment of his master's powers. But the might that Prospero describes even as he gives it up, the sense of finality in the renunciation and the verse's majesty, will move wonder without surprise. The play's final act demonstrates that Prospero, like Pericles and Leontes, is regaining his humanity. He gives up his rage, which has made him less than human, and also his magic, which has made him more. In order for the audience fully to comprehend what is being let go, Prospero conjures and then exorcises his mighty art.

> I have bedimm'd
> The noontide sun, call'd forth the mutinous winds,
> And 'twixt the green sea and the azur'd vault
> Set roaring war. To the dread rattling thunder
> Have I given fire, and rifted Jove's stout oak
> With his own bolt; the strong-bas'd promontory
> Have I made shake, and by the spur pluck'd up
> The pine and cedar. Graves at my command
> Have wak'd their sleepers, op'd, and let 'em forth,
> By my so potent art.
>
> (5.1.41–50)

The magician's determination to abjure this power will be deeply moving if spoken quietly, with a diminuendo beginning on the phrase, "But this rough magic." John Wood's 1988 Prospero at Stratford-upon-Avon spoke a quiet renunciation that created an astonishing contrast with the thunder that preceded it.[54]

Of all Shakespeare's comedies, *The Tempest* is most dominated by wonder. But as we have seen, wonder is of major interest to the dramatist throughout his career, from the imagery of witchcraft and the pieces of Gower's romance grafted on to an urbane Plautean comedy to Hermione's statue and Prospero's magic. Although it is strongest in *A Midsummer Night's Dream, Twelfth Night,* and the posttragic comedies of Shakespeare's last wholly active years as a playwright, it is an element in all the comedies. Perhaps more than any other element, wonder contributes to their uniqueness and accounts for their enduring appeal.

Wonder can be a response to both a work of art and that which the work of art treats. As we have seen, Hermione's statue is perhaps its best emblem, partaking of art, magic, and great creating nature. Like the statue, Shakespeare's best plays are great works of art. They too seem at times to partake of miracle. Yet however much they deal with the supernatural, however strongly they are shaped by artistic conventions and abilities, they are most firmly based in nature.

Miracles occur rarely, either in art or in the life that art imitates. When they do occur, those which move most deeply and remain longest in memory partake of the artistic, the supernatural, and the natural. Just such a miracle occurred three and a half centuries after Shakespeare's death. It happened during a journey to Russia taken by composer Benjamin Britten and the tenor Peter Pears in 1965. At the time, Britten had just completed his settings for six poems by Pushkin, so he and Pears naturally wished to visit the Pushkin house and museum. Peter Pears describes the visit they made in company with their friends, the cellist Mstislav Rostropovitch and the soprano Galina Vishnevskaya. His account suggests how accurately Shakespeare captures the form and essence of wonder and its tripartite relation to art, magic, and nature.[55]

> Before we retired, our host took a torch and showed us Pushkin's house and museum, and outside the front door was the clock tower and its cracked clock which was there in Pushkin's time and still struck its old hours. . . . Our host begged to hear the Pushkin songs. We moved into the lamplit sitting-room with an upright piano in the corner and started on the songs after an introduction by Slava. Galya sang her two and I hummed the others. The last song of the set is the marvelous poem of insomnia, the ticking clock, persistent night noises, and the poet's cry for a meaning in them. Ben had started this with repeated staccato notes, high low, high low, on the piano. Hardly had the little old piano begun its dry tick-tock, tick-tock, then clear and silvery outside

the window, a yard from our heads, came ding ding ding not loud but clear: Pushkin's clock joining in his song. It seemed to strike far more than midnight, to go on all through the song, and afterwards we sat spellbound. It was the most natural thing to have happened, and yet unique, astonishing, wonderful.

4

MOODS

IN EACH OF THE PRECEDING CHAPTERS I HAVE DIS-
cussed a particular response elicited by Shakespeare's comedies. I have
isolated dramatic sequences and emphasized aspects peculiar to each
response. My intention now is to explore the dramatist's ways of
mingling and contrasting these responses and making them modify
and enrich each other. Shakespeare habitually creates many moods
in his plays and evokes in his audience reactions appropriate to those
moods. Samuel Johnson recognizes this attribute when he observes:
"As he commands us, we laugh or mourn, or sit silent with quiet
expectation, in tranquility without indifference."[1]

That the playwright is well assured of his power to guide his audience's emotions is suggested by the Prologue to *Henry VIII*.[2]

> I come no more to make you laugh; things now
> That bear a weighty and a serious brow,
> Sad, high, and working, full of state and woe,
> Such noble scenes as draw the eye to flow,
> We now present.
> . . . .
> Be sad, as we would make ye. Think ye see
> The very persons of our noble story
> As they were living; think you see them great,
> And follow'd with the general throng and sweat
> Of thousand friends; then, in a moment, see
> How soon this mightiness meets misery.
> And if you can be merry then, I'll say
> A man may weep upon his wedding-day.
>
> (Pro. 1–5, 25–32)

Throughout this passage the playwright invokes an idea basic to the
Elizabethan drama, that of decorum in response.[3] It would be as inde-

corous, as inappropriate, to laugh at such spectacles as will be shown in this play as it would be to weep at one's own wedding.

Yet a person may weep on her wedding day, as the author of *Much Ado About Nothing* knows well. So the prologue goes further by suggesting that, even though sadness and tears are appropriate reactions to the play's events, such reactions cannot be elicited unless the spectators allow their imaginations to be guided by the playwright. As in the more famous Prologue to *Henry V*, a frank appeal is made to the playgoers' imaginary forces. A bargain is struck with the audience.[4] If the spectators yield their imaginative consent and participation, the playwright will gain the power to guide their minds and emotions to react appropriately to the play. Arousing the imagination, which has both reason and emotion in its service, he can induce in his audience thoughts and feelings that possess greater substance and solidity than if he appealed to what Eliot calls "undisciplined squads of emotion,"[5] or to unaided reason. Appealing instead to both emotion and reason marshaled by the imagination, he induces in his audience states that are fluid but not fleeting.[6] This power to command the spectators' reactions by appealing to their imaginations is Shakespeare's from his earliest comedies. But he recognizes how important it is that the spectators be in the proper frame of mind and the proper emotional state to be moved and delighted. He has Rosaline in *Love's Labour's Lost* admonish Berowne:

> A jest's prosperity lies in the ear
> Of him that hears it, never in the tongue
> Of him that makes it.
>
> (5.2.849–51)

In *The Comedy of Errors*, Antipholus of Syracuse rebukes both Dromios for jesting when he is not in the mood:

> I am not in a sportive humour now;
> . . . .
> Come, Dromio, come, these jests are out of season;
> Reserve them till a merrier hour than this.
>
> (1.2.58, 67–68)
>
> Your sauciness will jest upon my love,
> And make a common of my serious hours.
>
> . . . .

If you will jest with me, know my aspect,
And fashion your demeanour to my looks. . . .

(2.2.28–29, 32–33)

Viola, in *Twelfth Night*, comments in a similar vein on the necessary skills of the professional fool:

He must observe their mood on whom he jests,
The quality of persons and the time,
And, like the haggard, check at every feather
That comes before his eyes. This is a practice
As full of labour as a wise man's art.

(3.1.59–63)

The jester Shakespeare holds two advantages over the jesters who are his creatures. First, that his hearers have chosen to come to the theater indicates that they are willing to allow him to put them into the proper mood for amusement. Second, he is not bound simply to observe their moods. He can create moods that will make his hearers ever more receptive to his jests, as well as to his more serious moments. So skillful does he become in creating such moods that he can turn riotous laughter into pain and terror all in a moment—and then, dispelling the terror, he can make his audience laugh again.

Yet he does not wantonly combine and vary these responses. Throughout his career he recognizes that a dramatic event of sufficient magnitude can permanently change a play's mood. Mercutio's death changes *Romeo and Juliet* from potential comedy to actual tragedy.[7] Changes in comedy are more delicate, less permanent, and consequently less easy to recognize than in tragedy. Actors and directors must be as sensitive to shifting tones in comedy as to those in tragedy or history. A director who rides roughshod over a delicately changing set of moods will defile the play and cheat the audience.

Let me illustrate Shakespeare's way of mingling and varying his moods in comedy by taking a second look at the scene from *The Winter's Tale* in which the two lords describe their reactions to the oracle. Cleomenes, as I have shown, communicates his unalloyed wonder. By contrast, Dion's reaction is tempered by his concern with the impression he will make on his fellow courtiers when he tells what he has seen:

> I shall report,
> For most it caught me, the celestial habits—
> Methinks I so should term them—and the reverence
> Of the grave wearers.
>
> (3.1.3–6)

In this short speech, the playwright conveys Dion's honest reaction to the oracle and his genuine difficulty in finding adequate language for extraordinary experience and emotion. At the same time, he mildly satirizes the courtier's desire to find the *mot juste.* By combining the courtiers' wonder with this slight suggestion of satire, the dramatist keeps the emotion from obtruding too much on the anguish and torment that dominate this part of the play, and he saves the feeling from any taint of sentimentality. One way of achieving the desired effect in production is to contrast a youthful and frankly astonished Cleomenes with an older Dion, well seasoned in the elegance of manner and demeanor necessary to successful courtly service. The touch of astringency in the scene prevents the audience from expecting Apollo's power to bring about an easy and immediate remedy.

I stress that it behooves actors and directors to shape productions in accordance with such shades and combinations of feeling and the processes by which they change minute by minute as Shakespeare's comedies unfold. For a spectator in the theater, a play is a temporal experience. It develops over a period of time, making its ever-changing impressions on the playgoers' minds, emotions, and imaginations.[8] Contemplating an entire play after a performance or a reading, when the play is complete and frozen in the mind, one can profitably employ spatial metaphors drawn from art or architecture as critical tools. Many critics habitually use such terms as *structure* or *design.* But while the play is being observed or read, such terms are unapt and misleading. For those who prepare a play for production, as well as for those who perceive that production, metaphors drawn from temporal arts like music or dance may be more helpful aids to analysis. Since the process I am concerned with in this chapter is closely analogous to the process by which feelings are varied and combined in musical compositions, I propose to use musical terms, which will enable me more precisely to describe that process.

Grove's Dictionary of Music and Musicians defines modulation as the process of passing out of one key into another. If harmonies belonging essentially to one key are irregularly mixed up with harmonies that are equally characteristic of another, an impression of obscurity arises; but when a chord which evidently belongs to a foreign key follows naturally upon a series which was consistently characteristic of another, and is itself followed consistently by harmonies belonging to a key to which it can be referred, modulation has taken place and a new tonic has supplanted the former one as the center of a new circle of harmonies.[9]

A useful analogy can be drawn between the process of passing from one key to another in a musical composition and the process of passing from one mood to another in a dramatic composition. Shakespeare himself suggests the analogy in a speech given to the dying King Henry IV. The king is telling his son that his troublesome reign has taken its tone from his indirect and sullied way of taking the crown:

> And now my death
> Changes the mood; for what in me was purchas'd
> Falls upon thee in a more fairer sort. . . .
> (2 Henry IV, 4.5.199-201)

The king plays with multiple meanings: "mood" denotes an emotional state and "mode" denotes a "musical scale the character of which alters depending on the note with which it begins."[10] Now modulation as we understand it from the music of Haydn, Mozart, or Beethoven did not exist in Shakespeare's day. But composers with whose music he was probably familiar achieved comparable effects by changing modes. Grove notes, for example, that one can hear remarkably fine and strong effects in the music of Orlando Gibbons, which are produced by means of accidentals. "Gibbons appears to slip from one tonality to another more than six times in as many bars, and to slide back into his original key as if he had never been away."[11] These words might apply equally well to Shakespeare.

Being trained in rhetoric, the dramatist recognizes that he must fashion a style appropriate to the mood he is seeking to create. A change in mood will be accompanied by a corresponding change in style. This recognition, too, is implicit in the dying Henry IV's word-play. The king refers not only to emotional states and musical scales but also to his son's style, or mode, of ruling, which must change with the country's changing mood. The same Shakespearean monarch who calls explicit attention to these principles recognizes them implicitly in his younger days. Toward the end of *Richard II,* King Henry must deal with the clamorous pleas of the old Duke and Duchess of York regarding their conspiring son. The father demands his son's death; the mother implores that he be pardoned. The old people create a few moments of farce in a serious play with their loud knockings on the door and their pleas expressed in rhymed couplets. King Henry cannily observes that comic elements will prevail: "Our scene is alt'red from a serious thing, / And now chang'd to 'The Beggar and the King'" (5.3.79–80).

During his career, Shakespeare develops many ways of passing from one mood to another. He often does so by a shift in his verbal medium: a change from verse to prose or from prose to verse. More subtly, he alters his verse's quality and texture. Verse gives its practitioners a more precise control over tone, atmosphere, and ambience than does prose. Every entrance or exit naturally brings about a change in mood since it effects a change in the relationships among the people on the stage at any given time. The scene of drunken revelry in *Twelfth Night* changes radically when Malvolio enters and changes again when he leaves. Shifts and mixtures can also be brought about by changes in subject or emphasis, by sudden silences or unexpected floods of words. Witness the apparently calm Claudio's outburst on the horrors of death in *Measure for Measure,* or Isabella's silence in the same play when Mariana pleads with her to beg the duke for Angelo's life. Even the merriest scenes, such as Rosalind's badinage with her bewildered lover, have their modulations to sudden sadness. And the scenes of greatest pain, such as the confrontations between Isabella and Angelo, or between Shylock and the Christians in the Venetian court, have their occasional moments of relieving laughter.

An unexpected entrance in *Twelfth Night* combines with a shift in the verbal medium to effect one of the most startling modulations in Shakespeare's comedies. Some of this play's wildest farce occurs when Sir Toby and Fabian maneuver the terrified Sir Andrew and the hermaphroditic Cesario into fighting each other. The very idea of a duel between these creatures will beget laughter, and the laughter will grow enormously when the spectators see the reluctant combatants draw their swords. But the duel is interrupted by Antonio's entrance, and the mood shifts from laughter to danger. A last climactic laugh may be drawn from the audience as the terrified duelists seek protection from each other. In a 1958 R.S.C. production, Dorothy Tutin as Viola flew into the arms of Richard Johnson's Sir Andrew, and they went on clinging together when Antonio intervened.[12] Antonio will cut through the laughter if his words are spoken in such a way as to suggest the absolute seriousness of his intention. He mistakes Cesario for Sebastian, but the humor in the situation is overshadowed by a sense of genuine threat as he makes the quarrel his own. The change is reinforced by his speaking in verse that contrasts markedly with the other characters' prose:

> Put up your sword. If this young gentleman
> Have done offence, I take the fault on me:
> If you offend him, I for him defy you.
>
> (3.4.296–98)

With this new voice speaking a new language, laughter departs from the scene. The swords, which have heretofore been objects of mirth, become objects of dread. The modulation will be most effective in performance if Antonio is played by an authoritative actor with a fine command of verse, who convinces the audience that the character is capable of killing anyone who threatens Sebastian. As Antonio and Sir Toby approach each other with murderous intentions, the violence of farce changes to violence in earnest. For a frightening moment the spectators observe a duel that endangers Viola, a character about whom they have come to care deeply.

Even though bloodshed is averted by the timely entrance of the duke's officers, the scene continues to be painful. Rather than exploiting the possibilities for laughter in Antonio's mistaking Viola for Sebastian, the playwright subjects Antonio to the pain of the seeming Cesario's seeming ingratitude and makes the spectators in some measure partake of this pain. *Twelfth Night* is a play of evanescence, and no single mood is allowed to dominate it for long. But for the time being, Antonio, with his strong passions expressed in strong verse, brings about a change from farcical laughter to the pain that springs from disappointment and dread.

A similar modulation from laughter to pain occurs in *A Midsummer Night's Dream*. This time there is no sudden entrance but simply a change in verbal medium, a shift from rhyme to blank verse. The four wrangling lovers, two of whom have been enchanted by Oberon's love-juice, create a "fond pageant" that gives as much mirth to the spectators as to Puck. The lovers' enchanted vehemence is conveyed in quatrains and couplets, and these modes of discourse create an emotional distance between audience and action. The scene is most effectively played for farce, with rapid delivery and a great deal of extravagant stage business. In the midst of the spectators' laughter and the characters' rhyme, Helena shifts suddenly to blank verse. Convinced that Hermia has joined with both men to mock her, she expresses a deeply felt sense of betrayed friendship:

> Is all the counsel that we two have shar'd,
> The sisters' vows, the hours that we have spent,
> When we have chid the hasty-footed time
> For parting us—O, is it all forgot?
>
> (3.2.198–201)

With this speech, Helena changes the scene's mood. The apostrophes, epithets, showers of oaths, and hyperbole that make for a parody of Elizabethan love poetry give place to an extended description of betrayed childhood friendship.

To be sure, the scene soon recaptures its hilarity. The men plan a duel, and the women carry out their famous bout of name calling. But as the weapons come out, the line grows ever thinner between farcical violence and a threat of actual harm. The spectators can no longer adopt Puck's superior position as detached observer of mortal folly. Instead, they will find their laughter enriched by Helena's distress.

In Benjamin Britten's setting of the play—one of the few operatic masterpieces based on Shakespeare—the composer expresses this change of mood in musical terms. The rhymed protestations of the lovers are accompanied by short, sharp figures in the brass and percussion. The orchestra is expressing the threat of farcical violence and at the same time laughing at the enchanted posturings. The sense of comic chaos is increased as the lovers sing simultaneously. But when Helena begins singing of childhood friendship, Britten modulates in the precise sense of that word by passing from one key into another. Moreover, the orchestral accompaniment changes to sustained chords on the strings and a haunting obbligato shared by the bassoon and the oboe. On the London recording conducted by the composer, Heather Harper, singing Helena, grows more mellifluous, less hysterically impassioned. Her passage, with its quiet accompaniment, is as moving as any in the opera. The composer is sensitive to the change back to farce that follows this passage, and he reinstates the simultaneous singing and short, sharp, instrumental bursts. But in the opera, as in the play, the farce is no longer pure. The auditors are made to perceive that they, unlike Puck, share a common humanity with the lovers. The scene remains funny, but the laughter mixes with sympathy.

Another striking example of dramatic modulation can be found later in *A Midsummer Night's Dream*. When the lovers are released from their enchantments, Shakespeare must pass from the night-rule in the haunted grove to the quotidian atmosphere of Athens without destroying his aesthetic unity. He brings about this transition from one key to another, from one world to another, with a shift in verbal medium and a remarkable use of music. After Titania has been awakened, Oberon calls for music and a dance. As the fairies dance, they speak in pentameter and tetrameter couplets. The audience hears both their music and the pronounced rhymes and rhythms in their talk of enchantments and the fleeing night. As the fairies exit, Theseus, Hippolyta, and the courtiers enter to the hunt. Even as the fairies' music is dying out, the playgoers hear the very different music of hunting horns and Theseus's blank verse about the sweet thunderous cry of dogs on the trail of their quarry. It is necessary that Theseus's court not appear pallid in comparison with the fairies, because it represents the world to which the lovers and Bottom must return. There must be no sense of letdown or anticlimax. So Shakespeare depicts an activity both familiar and natural, and at the same time invested with its own music and power. He invites a comparison between the magic music of the fairies and the natural music of horns and hounds. In so doing, he brings about a modulation from haunted night's dream to the natural morning in which the dreamers awake.

In Peter Brook's production, I found this passage from dream to waking less effective than the parallel passage from waking to dream. Brook famously doubled Theseus with Oberon and Hippolyta with Titania so that the temporal rulers could literally dream themselves into the fairies. But the astonishing moment when Brook's acrobatic spirits first took command of his stage exacted its price during the moment when Oberon and Titania had to reawaken into Theseus and Hippolyta. Joseph Verner Reed, at the time president of the American Shakespeare Festival at Stratford, Connecticut, gave an acerbic description of the scene in a letter to the *New York Times:*

> There is so much pulling on and off of outer robes, bathroom variety, that one cannot be sure whether those on stage are enacting courtiers or creatures of the magic wood. [13]

Brook's precise control of the production seemed momentarily to slip, and the transition from night to day was blurred.

Yet the play's text encourages directors to draw a clear distinction between night and day. Different worlds are set against each other, but there is no sense that they are yoked by violence together. The gap between them is bridged by their common elements of power and music. The dramatic modulation finds a striking parallel in Britten's opera. The opera is structurally different from the play in that Theseus does not appear until the final scenes. Thus, he and his hunting party cannot be introduced when the fairies depart and the lovers awake. Instead, Britten lets the music of the fairies—high, mysterious figures on the strings—continue after Puck, Oberon, and Titania have gone.[14] While the strings are playing, he introduces a new theme, not previously heard in the opera. This theme is played on horns and sounds like a hunting call. The strings and horns play simultaneously in different keys and different rhythms, the former evoking the departing fairies, the latter evoking the world to which the lovers awake. The hearers are conscious of the artistry that makes these disparate motifs form a whole richer than either of its parts.

In *A Midsummer Night's Dream* Shakespeare uses music and changes in the verbal medium to bring about his modulations. In other comedies, simple shifts in emphasis can bring about comparably mingling or varying moods. A characteristically rich scene in *As You Like It* is wholly in prose. This scene consists of a brief encounter between Rosalind and Jaques, followed by a dialogue of some length between Rosalind and Orlando. In her conversation with Jaques, Rosalind outsatirizes and outmoralizes the satirical moralist:

> *Jaq.* Why, 'tis good to be sad and say nothing.
> *Ros.* Why then, 'tis good to be a post. (4.1.8–9)

At the same time, the scene affords a glimpse of the genuine sadness behind Jaques' affectation and shows Rosalind's sympathy with that sadness:

> *Ros.* . . . I fear you have sold your own lands to see other men's; then to have seen much and to have nothing is to have rich eyes and poor hands.
> *Jaq.* Yes, I have gain'd my experience.
> *Ros.* And your experience makes you sad. (4.1.19–24)

These simple statements do not convey a satiric tone but rather bring about a moment of true melancholy. The moment ends as Rosalind's next line modulates back to satire: "I had rather have a fool to make me merry than experience to make me sad—and to travel for it too" (4.1.24–26). The pensive moment is like a brief passage in a minor key set in a piece of music scored mainly in the major.

In the subsequent dialogue between Rosalind and Orlando, the playwright again enriches his satiric mood with moments of pain. Rosalind's professed aim is to cure her lover of his amorous madness. Her real accomplishment is to teach him something about the difference between genuine love and the romantic, literary variety. Her quicksilver wit and her wizardry with words dominate the scene. Orlando can scarcely utter his brief responses. She mocks him, teases him, and revels in his confusion. But beneath her wit is her strong love and her genuine fear that he may not love her as much as he says he does: "Nay, an you be so tardy, come no more in my sight. I had as lief be woo'd of a snail" (4.1.46–47). This amusing line has a sting in it since it makes the audience recall how distraught was Rosalind when she thought Orlando had broken his promise.[15] Perhaps by moving away from him for a solitary moment or by closely studying his face, the actress can show the audience that the character is remembering the unkept appointment. Rosalind is exorcising her own pain through laughter, but the pain is not wholly forgotten.

After telling jokes about cuckoldry and impotence, Rosalind shifts suddenly into a graver mode:

Ros. . . . Am not I your Rosalind?
Orl. I take some joy to say you are, because I would be talking of her.
Ros. Well, in her person, I say I will not have you.
Orl. Then, in mine own person, I die.
Ros. No, faith, die by attorney. The poor world is almost six thousand years old, and in all this time there was not any man died in his own person, videlicet, in a love-cause. Troilus had his brains dash'd out with a Grecian club; yet he did what he could to die before, and he is one of the patterns of love. Leander, he would have liv'd many a fair year, though Hero had turn'd nun, if it had not been for a hot midsummer-night; for, good youth, he went but forth to wash him in the Hellespont, and, being taken with the cramp, was drown'd; and the foolish chroniclers of that age found it was—Hero of Sestos. But these are all lies: men have died from time to time,

and worms have eaten them, but not for love.
Orl. I would not have my right Rosalind of this mind; for, I protest,
    her frown might kill me.
Ros. By this hand, it will not kill a fly. (4.1.78–98)

Rosalind urbanely deflates some of the great legends about love's agony.
Then, by a slight shift of emphasis, she proceeds to tell the austere
truth about death. With her pun on "attorney" and her adoption
of legalistic jargon in response to her lover's facile embrace of death,
she directs a good deal of laughter at Orlando's silly poses. But as
she makes her audience aware of how profoundly the romances lie,
laughter leaves the speech. The most mercurial of Shakespeare's heroines
validates her satire by demonstrating that she knows and accepts the
conditions of death and life that exist outside her chosen targets of
romance.

Reviewing the 1978 production at Stratford, Ontario, Ralph Berry
emphasizes the importance to the role of such control of the spectators'
moods, and he draws particular attention to Maggie Smith's performance of this scene. He describes the fine moment in which she whis-
pers to the recumbent Orlando: "Men have died from time to time,
and worms have eaten them, but not for love."

> The entire audience was hushed at such moments, only to be set laughing
> a second later. I found nothing more admirable in Maggie Smith's per-
> formance than her total and exact control of audience response. . . .
> The elbows go one way, the wrists another, and the audience is convulsed.
> She wills silence and obtains it at once.[16]

Orlando is distressed by Rosalind's talk of death, and his lines invite
the actor to show the character's apprehension at her killing frown.
Love's invisible wounds can still cause him genuine suffering. Rosalind's
observation that her look would not kill a fly is a difficult line, serving
as both culmination and modulation. Vanessa Redgrave's reading of
this line on the Caedmon recording demonstrates the character's understanding that love's metaphoric darts, although they do not kill, can
cause spiritual and mental agony. Redgrave suggests Rosalind's sympathy with the pain her lover is even now suffering, and at the same
time she laughingly mocks his fear. The words are deeply serious,
and they are delivered with a teasing smile.

Partaking of merriment as well as gravity, this line permits Rosalind to move gracefully back to her satirical mode. She does not give her baffled lover a chance to respond to her mocking and serious reassurance. With only a slight pause, her tempo changes from andante to prestissimo: "But come, now I will be your Rosalind in a more coming-on disposition; and ask me what you will, I will grant it" (4.1.98–100). There is again much revelry until Rosalind brings about yet another sudden change in the atmosphere:

> *Ros.* Now tell me how long you would have her, after you have possess'd her.
> *Orl.* For ever and a day.
> *Ros.* Say 'a day' without the 'ever'. No, no, Orlando; men are April when they woo, December when they wed: maids are May when they are maids, but the sky changes when they are wives. I will be more jealous of thee than a Barbary cock-pigeon over his hen, more clamorous than a parrot against rain, more new-fangled than an ape, more giddy in my desires than a monkey. (4.1.127–36)

Once again, Rosalind is telling the whole truth that romances do not tell. This time, the first part of her speech is the painful fact inserted unexpectedly into a passage of light wit. As she predicts her own increasingly outrageous matrimonial conduct, laughter reenters her speech and manner, mixing with and enriching the pain of her initial reflection.

Rosalind's wit and her witchcraft with words do not conceal how deeply the character is in love. When Orlando takes his leave, she responds with a self-dramatizing parody of grief and a prettily phrased injunction that he keep his promise. A slight catch in the breath or an apprehensive look to Celia will help the actress remind the audience of the actual pain beneath the comic extravagance. Orlando's exit naturally brings about another modulation. Laughter still dominates, but its quality changes. Rosalind has been the mistress of mirth; now she becomes its object. Celia, who has been silent through most of the scene, finally breaks into rebukes: "You have simply misus'd our sex in your love-prate. We must have your doublet and hose pluck'd over your head, and show the world what the bird hath done to her own nest" (4.1.180–83). The brief exchange between the cousins initiated by this outburst reveals that Rosalind can be as fancy-sick, as waywardly guided and limited by romance, as Orlando. For all her realistic mockery of love and her painful reflection on death and marriage, she is herself half in love with the seductions of romance. Celia takes on the same relation to her that she has had to Orlando. Rosalind indulges herself with a hyperbolical expression of passion, and it remains for Celia to provide the Bergsonian deflation of physical fact:

> Ros. . . . I cannot be out of the sight of Orlando. I'll go find a shadow, and sigh till he come.
> Cel. And I'll sleep. (4.1.194–96)

Throughout this scene Shakespeare uses changes in subject or in emphasis as means of changing the moods. In another famous love scene, that between Beatrice and Benedick after the failed wedding in *Much Ado About Nothing,* he effects even more startling modulations and combinations without changing his verbal medium. As in *As You Like It,* his subject is the relation of romance to life, and his medium is prose. The circumstances that cause the encounter make for a thorough mingling of conflicting feelings and responses in characters and spectators alike. This is the climax of the trick that has been played on Beatrice and Benedick, the scene that Don Pedro has anticipated with such mirth earlier in the play:

> The sport will be when they hold one an opinion of another's dotage, and no such matter; that's the scene that I would see, which will be merely a dumb show. (2.3.197–99)

What makes the scene other than a dumb show and more than a sport is the terrible anti-marriage to which Claudio has subjected Hero and to which the prince has acted as second. The hilarity springing from the mutually held false opinions of dotage mingles with Benedick's uncertainty and Beatrice's rage. Added to these is a sense of wonder, perceived by characters and spectators, that Beatrice and Benedick should love each other at all.

The fact that one of Shakespeare's funniest scenes begins with the spectacle of Beatrice's tears suggests a thorough mingling of laughter and pain. The actress's difficult task is to convince the audience of the character's anger and grief at her cousin's slander and her own humiliating impotence to undo it. Yet she must simultaneously demonstrate in her comebacks to Benedick's cautious attempts to comfort her that Beatrice is able to mock her own extremes of feeling. Benedick's earnest profession of love is so phrased that, if the actor times its delivery properly, pausing slightly before he asks his question, the line will get a laugh: "I do love nothing in the world so well as you, is not that strange?" (4.1.266–67). Both he and the spectators are alive to the situation's irony and humor. At the same time, Benedick contemplates the miracle that he should be in love with Beatrice and the audience shares his wonder. Beatrice's reply shows that she too shares the wonder: "As strange as the thing I know not" (4.1.268). Yet her words elicit laughter and pain as well. Laughter arises because this witty and clear-sighted woman is so confused about her own feelings. Pain grows out of her depth of passion and her abiding sense that declarations of love are inappropriate at this time and in this place.

Benedick becomes so taken up with telling her how much he loves her and with trying to draw a similar protestation from her that he momentarily forgets the scene's immediate context—the very thing that has prompted him to make his declaration. Beatrice, as deeply in love, does not forget what has happened to her cousin on this very spot where she is now giving and receiving amorous assurances. While Benedick moves into the regions of romance, Beatrice loves and rages at the same time. When he finally succeeds in drawing from her an unequivocal profession of love, he immediately makes the traditional courtly vow of unlimited service. He has forgotten that she needs a real and dreadful service. She has not. She commands him to do the thing she most wants done: "Kill Claudio" (4.1.287). She is expressing a desire that has nothing funny about it. Yet the line elicits laughter from many audiences in many productions.[17] Laughter is likely to arise from the sense of incongruity in the juxtaposition of this dreadful command with Benedick's courtly offer. Such incongruity occurs whenever reality intersects metaphor and literary tradition. The laugh will come if the audience has been allowed to forget, as Benedick has forgotten, the depth and continuance of Beatrice's rage.

The audience must not be allowed to forget this. Reviewing Douglas Seale's 1958 R.S.C. production, M. St. Clare Byrne observes that as Beatrice, Googie Withers

> managed her "Kill Claudio" admirably, in the low-toned intensity of urgent, passionate personal appeal—a close-up with all the force in "kill."

There was no laugh on her line. A controllable one came on Benedick's reply, keyed by his astonishment. My impression was they can kill it if they want to, but do they need to? It made me realize that there was something to be said for both audience reactions.[18]

As Seale's production demonstrated, the laugh most effectively comes not on Beatrice's command but on Benedick's natural and reflexive response: "Ha! not for the wide world" (4.1.288). Yet so fine is the line between laughter and pain in this scene that it is difficult for actors to tread it precisely night after night. Over the run of our production, if the actors' emotional energy flagged or their timing was the slightest bit off, the audience would laugh on "Kill Claudio." On the nights when the scene was alive with the tension and electricity that make for fine theater, there was a hush on "Kill Claudio" and a laugh on Benedick's response. We interpreted the playgoers' reaction to Beatrice's line as a measure of the performance's success.

This exchange brings about another modulation as Beatrice's rage becomes the scene's predominant emotion. All the fury that Beatrice has entertained against Claudio and the prince she now vents on Benedick. The spectators are given a vivid impression of her anguish and anger. Yet even now she engages in some witty paronomasia, and laughter is further provoked by the spectacle of Benedick vainly trying to dam her flood of vituperation. The text makes clear that he is literally unable to get a word in, as he pronounces only the first two syllables of her name:

> *Beat.* Sweet Hero! She is wrong'd, she is sland'red, she is undone.
> *Bene.* Beat—
> *Beat.* Princes and Counties! Surely, a princely testimony, a goodly count, Count Comfect . . . (4.1.310–12)

With Benedick's question "Think you in your soul the Count Claudio hath wrong'd Hero?" (4.1.325) comes the final modulation. The scene shifts to a quiet mode in which there is no longer laughter. Without wit or buffoonery, Benedick simply and soberly announces his intention to challenge Claudio. The actor discards his previous masks, and the audience understands him to be in profound earnest.

With Dogberry entering hard upon Benedick's exit, Shakespeare effects an immediate modulation from the somber to the hilarious. The juxtaposition of lines bespeaks a striking change of mood:

Bene. . . . Go comfort your cousin; I must say she is dead; and so, farewell.

. . . . .

Dogb. Is our whole dissembly appear'd? (4.1.327–30; 4.2.1)

Shakespeare often achieves modulations like those found in the scene from *Much Ado About Nothing.* Laughter, pain, and wonder are similarly interwoven in the scene of public trial and tortuous unravelling in *Measure for Measure.* But this scene differs from the scene of love and anguish between Beatrice and Benedick in that the playwright contrives to distance his spectators from the emotional turbulence depicted on the stage. The scene is a formal legal proceeding, and its ceremonial aspects tend to make of the audience judging observers rather than emotional participants. The text suggests that the trial is, in performance, a spectacular pageant with formal gestures and poses, repeated fanfares and gorgeous costumes. Despite this distancing, the audience is made increasingly uneasy about the trial's ultimate outcome, and the unease persists even when the spectators realize that all will be well. Like many of the play's events, the trial is stage-managed by the duke, but the spectators have throughout the play been perceiving limits in his ability to manage his theatrical power. Actors' interpretations of this character have ranged from the saintly to the smarmy, but however he is played, the playgoers will be disturbed by an apparent disparity between his words and the scene's events. Unlike most of Shakespeare's managing figures, he does not make the playgoers privy to his plans and motives. Not knowing precisely how he intends to manipulate the trial, they share Isabella's and Mariana's apprehension. Further, the duke's repeated encounters with Lucio are calculated to remind the spectators that he has not always been able to control thoroughly the people and events he has been manipulating. Their uncertainty is leavened by laughter, and the mingling of hilarity with apprehension gives the scene its peculiar quality.

The actress playing Isabella may communicate her character's unease and outrage when she is instructed to testify falsely (4.6.1–4) and when the duke insists that she is mad (5.1.63–67). Even though the spectators know the duke to be Isabella's ally against Angelo, they share her dread because they remain uncertain about his intentions and his competence.

Indeed, his ability to control events is unexpectedly challenged.

When Isabella calls on Lucio to confirm her story and her sanity, he says more than the duke wants to hear:

> *Duke.* You were not bid to speak.
> *Lucio.* No, my good lord;
>   Nor wish'd to hold my peace.
> *Duke.* I wish it now, then;
>   Pray you take note of it; and when you have
>   A business for yourself, pray heaven you then
>   Be perfect.
> *Lucio.* I warrant your honour.
> *Duke.* The warrant's for yourself; take heed to't.
> *Isab.* This gentleman told somewhat of my tale.
> *Lucio.* Right.
> *Duke.* It may be right; but you are i' the wrong
>   To speak before your time. Proceed. (5.1.78–87)

Lucio is told four times to be quiet, and the sheer repetition makes for Bergsonian laughter. As he does throughout the play, Lucio here represents the anarchic, undisciplined comic spirit that the duke, for all his magisterial seriousness, cannot control. For this reason, the comedy is most effective in performance when Lucio is played with virile energy rather than as a feckless decadent. Although the spectators are guided to abhor the profligate's morals, they cannot but laugh at his cheek. His audacious "right" usually gets a guffaw and makes it difficult for the audience to take the duke as seriously as he seems to take himself.[19]

Yet the pain that grows out of uncertainty is enriched rather than diminished by the laughter. Lucio complicates the audience's reaction to the duke by casting further doubt on his ability to control the events. If he cannot command Lucio, how will he manipulate the apparently more formidable Angelo? The laughter that Lucio elicits serves also to assure the audience that all will be well. Paradoxically, the laughter casts doubt on the duke's ability and simultaneously assures his success.

The spectators' uncertainty is enormously increased by the duke's continued harshness to Isabella. The audience knows that his apparent assaults on her veracity constitute a part of his design to bring about his version of true justice. Yet he has previously made her suffer by telling her falsely that her brother has been executed. Now, his sudden order that she be imprisoned will cause her additional anguish. The spectators may well question how much she will have to pay in personal suffering for the happy ending of which they are assured but she is not. At our production, the audience gasped in pained surprise when it heard the duke command Isabella to prison. Since the play is less well known to most audiences than *As You Like It* or *Twelfth Night,* responses in the theater to its surprises have greater freshness and spontaneity.

The surprised pain soon gives way to surprised laughter. When Friar Lodowick is named as Isabella's possible suborner, Lucio surpasses himself in audacity by accusing the absent friar of slandering the duke. Knowing that the duke and the friar are one, the spectators know that Lucio overreaches himself by ascribing his own calumnies to the friar. Nothing appeals more strongly to any group's derisive mirth than the anticipated punishment of a figure who has given the group pleasure while allowing it to enjoy a sense of moral superiority. The playgoers come to view him as the class clown. They let him make them laugh, and they are eager to turn on him with gleeful derision when he gets himself into trouble. He repeats and amplifies his accusation that the friar has slandered the duke, and every time he does he draws longer and louder laughter. But the laughter grows uncomfortable when Lucio begins to make bawdy jokes at Mariana's expense. He alienates the audience by introducing his scurrility into a sequence of genuine anguish. As the duke's puzzling intentions become clear and as the scene approaches its crisis, the laughter that has for so long been a guide and leavener becomes an annoyance.

That laughter may be taking on a moral taint is further suggested by the byplay between Escalus and Lucio after the duke's exit. In the early scenes, Escalus has been the judge whose tact, flexibility, and humor have notably distinguished him from Angelo. In this scene, the lines and action suggest that Lucio is growing manic and the benign judge is looking foolish. Losing something of his former stature, Escalus anticipates the inflexible and violent stance he will take when the duke reenters in his friar's disguise. He is the last person the audience would expect to resort to torture, yet it is he who commands the supposed friar to the rack. In one respect, the playwright is engaging in the dramatic device of plunging events to a seeming nadir before effecting the apparent miracle of the denouement. But Shakespeare is also illustrating with laughter the ease with which even the best judgment can be tainted or confused.

The shrill laughter and judicial violence intensify when the seeming friar appears. As with other Shakespearean scenes in which laughter and violence combine, the lines and action suggest a farcical staging. In our production, Lucio and the friar grappled over the properties and costume pieces the duke had used to effect his disguise. The last laugh was the duke's, and it came at Lucio's expense: "Thou art the first knave that e'er mad'st a duke" (5.1.354). As the other characters realized the friar's true identity, they froze in genuine terror. The unmasked duke allowed a second of absolute silence before he delivered his line to Lucio. Timing his delivery perfectly, the actor usually drew an ovation.

With the duke's resumption of unquestioned authority, the scene shifts into a more deeply serious mode. Events force the playgoers to examine their own feelings about both Angelo's fate and Mariana's and Isabella's reactions to it. The duke invokes the Biblical passage from which the play's title derives and pronounces the death sentence that Angelo has desired:

> The very mercy of the law cries out
> Most audible, even from his proper tongue,
> 'An Angelo for Claudio, death for death!'
> Haste still pays haste, and leisure answers leisure;
> Like doth quit like, and Measure still for Measure.
> . . . .
> We do condemn thee to the very block
> Where Claudio stoop'd to death, and with like haste.
>
> (5.1.405–9, 12–13)

The spectators know well that Claudio has stooped to death upon no block, so the duke's insistence on condemning the former judge to the same block to which that judge had condemned the young man should sound like a pardon to those who are listening to it with sufficient attention. Shakespeare is guiding the audience emotionally and imaginatively to concentrate on Isabella and Mariana—to understand and sympathize with their agony while knowing that its cause is illusory.

Mariana implores the duke to pardon Angelo and puts intolerable pressure on Isabella. That Isabella can overcome her own pain and revulsion and second Mariana's plea for mercy is one of the greatest of the many miracles that Shakespeare's comedies depict. When she kneels and speaks, the scene modulates into a new key of wonder.

In describing what his important production achieved, Peter Brook defines the climactic nature of this moment:

> When I once staged the play, I asked Isabella, before kneeling for Angelo's life, to pause each night until she felt the audience could take it no longer, and this used to lead to a two-minute stopping of the play. The device became a voodoo pole, a silence in which all the invisible elements of the evening came together: a silence in which the abstract notion of mercy became concrete for that moment to those present.[20]

With this moment, it becomes clear that the duke's design in keeping secret the preservation of Claudio's life is to ascertain whether Isabella can truly render the deeds of mercy. The miraculous transformation in Isabella may provide the best reason for playing the duke as at least well-intentioned. If he is portrayed as a manipulative hypocrite or a man racked by secret guilts and perversions, the wonder that is essential to this play's last scene may be overwhelmed by satiric malice or unrelieved bleakness. Jerry Turner's 1978 Ashland production featured a tormented duke and a bleak ending.[21] In Peter Brook's 1950 R.S.C. production, which achieved its climax with Isabella's kneeling for Angelo's life, Harry Andrews played a serious, ruminative, and benevolent duke.[22] The persisting disparity between the duke's words and his actions will insure that the spectators' sense of joy and wonder is disturbed, but that sense need not be wholly lost. The play ends in joy but it is a complex joy of which discomfort is an integral part.

In composing comedies that are imbued with a genuine sense of pain, Shakespeare always faces the problem of how to bring them to appropriate comic conclusions without sacrificing either their dramatic unity or their moral integrity. In *Measure for Measure*, a suggestion of pain persists and becomes a part of the happy ending. By contrast, *The Merchant of Venice* concludes joyously. Yet this play, like *Measure for Measure*, treats grave questions of justice and mercy, and characters with whom the audience is deeply engaged suffer and are brought close to death. Shakespeare does not combine this suffering with the laughter and wonder of the final act. Instead, he modulates from suffering to the festivity of the play's conclusion.

So powerful is the audience's memory of that suffering that the happy conclusion will perforce be tempered. Morris Carnovsky observes that the usurer's "fate sings in our minds after he's gone, his figure haunts the carefree gardens of Belmont."[23]

Yet the playwright contrives to distance the audience from that memory. Through a series of modulations, he brings the play from pain to wonder. Immediately following Shylock's departure from his trial, the playwright arouses laughter by exploring the comic possibilities inherent in the women's disguises and their husbands' ignorance of their identities. But for a scant two lines, these possibilities had been held in abeyance while the trial had gone forward. Bassanio's dilemma over the demanded ring constitutes a restatement in a comic key of one of the play's central themes—the extent to which love can be expressed or bound by material objects, whether those objects be rings, ducats, or pieces of human flesh. By raising laughter in connection with this theme, Shakespeare finds the most efficacious way of releasing the audience from the pain of the trial scene. Bassanio delights the audience by addressing his wife in the reverent tones due to the mysterious stranger who has been his friend's savior. Portia's cryptic reply combines grave and merry implications:

> He is well paid that is well satisfied,
> And I, delivering you, am satisfied,
> And therein do account myself well paid.
> My mind was never yet more mercenary.
> I pray you, know me when we meet again.
>
> (4.1.410–14)

She is daring her husband to penetrate her disguise and is reminding the audience obliquely that her wedding night had been postponed so that Bassanio could hasten to Antonio in Venice. She has now insured her husband's return and her own subsequent satisfaction. She is also expressing solemn joy that she has been able to save Antonio from peril. As is the case with the heroines in all Shakespeare's middle comedies, the actress must range with effortless swiftness between sobriety and laughter.

As the scene continues, the audience's ironic amusement grows even stronger. Loud and hearty laughter will attend Portia's attempt to take her husband's ring and Bassanio's snatching his hand away. The scene can turn into a farcical chase, with Bassanio fleeing the apparent lawyer's demands:

And for your love, I'll take this ring from you.
Do not draw back your hand: I'll take no more,
And you in love shall not deny me this.

(4.1.422–24)

This exchange can prove in performance one of the playwright's funniest duets of love and error.

By the time the scene is over, the playgoers' memories of Shylock will have been subordinated to their anticipation of the fun that Portia will have at her ringless husband's expense. The play continues in this new mode when Gratiano is shown in the act of giving Portia his master's ring and Nerissa announces her intention of getting his ring. The women laugh in anticipation of their husbands' confusion and embarrassment and the audience is invited to join the laughter. Only the briefest mention is made of Shylock, as the audience observes Portia and Nerissa bringing him the deed of gift that they plan to present to Jessica and Lorenzo. There is no gloating in his defeat, no reaction of any kind. The play simply moves on, as the life that he has threatened and interrupted proceeds through its natural course of laughter and celebration. But before the business of the rings reaches its funny climax, Shakespeare effects yet another modulation and initiates a sequence that gives weight and solemnity to the mirth dominating the play's close. This modulation occurs when the action passes from Venice, the bustling center of commerce and law, to Portia's estate at Belmont, a place that partakes not a little of fairy tale, dream, and wonder.

The spectators have not previously been allowed to enjoy uninterrupted the magic air of Belmont. At the play's opening it was disturbed by the derisive laughter that attended Portia's suitors and their foolish choices. Then, just as Bassanio and Portia were beginning to rejoice in their new marriage, a messenger with news of Antonio's danger destroyed the festive mood. With this grim news all happiness and celebration vanished for a time from the play. Now, with the trial over and the audience bent upon anticipation of laughter when the husbands' rings are demanded, Shakespeare restores a sense of wonder by allowing his audience to enjoy Belmont's magic without interruption. If the play in production employs modern scenographic resources, the contrast between Venice and Belmont can provide a primary stimulus to the imaginations of the designers. In keeping with the many interruptions, the design can be so contrived that Belmont's beauty is muted and disturbed during the early scenes. As the fifth act opens, scenery, lighting, and costumes can combine to create a spectacle of astonishing beauty.

At first, the wonder is not unmixed with pain. Jessica's and Lorenzo's invocation of night is peculiarly double-edged. To be sure, the verse takes on a lyrical, unhurried quality, such a tone as has not been heard in this play since Portia's frank gift of herself to Bassanio. But these slow, meditative rhythms, full of the spirits of harmony and love, are full also of oblique reminders of erotic tragedy. As lovers in romance are wont to do, Jessica and Lorenzo compare themselves with other lovers and liken their night of love to other amorous nights out of legend. But each love tale they recall has its dreadful associations: Cressida's name is synonymous with falsehood; Dido is a type of the abandoned lover turned to suicide; the story of Pyramus and Thisby ends with a double catastrophe; and Medea kills her children. These associations would doubtless have suggested themselves readily to an Elizabethan audience, and they will not be altogether lost on a contemporary one. Shakespeare is not, I think, suggesting that Jessica and Lorenzo are or will become a similarly tragic couple, but the joyful feelings called forth by the invocation of night and love are tempered by suggestions of potential anguish. The characters' voices might grow hushed and grave as they recall these ill-fated lovers. In writing verse that suggests pain even in the midst of such great joy, Shakespeare effects a modulation from the trial scene's anguish to the conclusion's joy without creating a sense of aesthetic disunity.

Even as the lovers are speaking their complex invocation, the playwright reminds the audience how often happy plans and happy occasions have been interrupted in this play. Jessica and Lorenzo are interrupted twice, and particular attention is called to these interruptions:

> *Jes.* I would out-night you, did no body come;
>   But, hark, I hear the footing of a man.
> *Lor.* Who comes so fast in silence of the night?
>
> (5.1.23–25)

The surprise entrance of a messenger to two lovers may call to mind Salerio's earlier entrance to Bassanio and Portia that had so thoroughly displaced the mirth. These lovers might show a similar apprehension at this interruption. But this messenger brings news of Portia's return, and his description reminds the audience that she has worked a miracle and done a genuine act of salvation. The air of sanctity is not allowed to grow oppressively solemn. Hardly do Jessica and Lorenzo hear of Portia's homecoming than Launcelot Gobbo bursts onto the stage and bawls out his tidings of Bassanio's return. The lines give Gobbo's actor scope to create the greatest possible contrast with the quiet and lyrical love duet, rushing about the stage, repeatedly colliding with Jessica and Lorenzo and shouting his speeches in their ears. His noise and bustle effectively shatter the sense of solemnity and holiness. One of Gobbo's functions throughout is to make the audience laugh at some of the play's soberest ideas. Now he insures that laughter will be a part of the playgoers' reaction to the return to Belmont of its master and mistress.

Thus, the play establishes many moods and passes through many modes once Shylock has been defeated. The audience does not forget Shylock, but the play's modulations take the spectators' primary focus away from him and encourage them to share in genuine festivity.

Only after moving through all these moods and their appropriate styles of language and action does the playwright give his audience a sequence of uninterrupted wonder. By the time the spectators reach that sequence they have been gradually distanced from the pain. The wonder is now aesthetically and morally acceptable in a way that it would not have been had Shakespeare passed to it immediately from the painful trial scene. There would have been something gloating, something mean, in moving directly from Shylock's defeat to the spectacle of his daughter listening to music. The festive conclusion might then have seemed forced and out of place. Occurring as it does by way of many modulations, it seems right and proper.

The scenes that convey most strongly the anguish caused and suffered by Shylock unfold with urgency and haste. Only after the threat has passed and the play returns to Belmont do characters have the luxury of time to enjoy and wonder at music and beauty. Yet as Lorenzo praises the power of music, he describes Shylock's profoundest lack, and his wonder mixes with sadness. The actor might grow sober as he calls Shylock to mind and recognizes the damage that a man without music can do to himself and others. In effect, Lorenzo sums up Shylock and, for the time, dismisses him.

Portia enters to the music and her initial lines continue in the mode of grave joy and reflection, but soon laughter mingles with the wonder. Her jokes create a prelude to the ring plot, and the play shifts into the merry mode of sexual comedy. The audience perceives that Portia, for all her seemingly divine powers, is a laughter-loving and thoroughly human creature. The play leaves as firm a conviction as any comedy of courtship can that her marriage will continue happy.

But this play has been far more than a comedy of courtship. Perhaps no civil audience in a century that has witnessed Babi-Yar, Birmingham, and the West Bank, as well as Auschwitz, will tolerate a fairy tale's felicity enacted by people who have been seen to display such religious and racial hatred. A playwright who contrives such a final act, however carefully modulated and lyrically expressed, may himself be implicated in the mutual hatreds that constitute his subject. Some directors under-line the play's disturbing qualities and deliberately reduce its comic and lyrical potential. In Michael Kahn's 1967 production with Morris Carnovsky at Stratford, Connecticut, the Christians' cupidity and anti-Semitism were emphasized, and their other qualities were largely ig-nored. Portia was depicted as a "teasing, bitchy heiress," while Jessica and Lorenzo were played as vulgar parvenus. They had to be made drunk in order to justify their lyric scene in the fifth act.[24] Bill Alexan-der's 1987 R.S.C. production featured Antony Sher's Shylock in conflict with a brutally anti-Semitic society. Deborah Findlay's Portia, no crea-ture of fairy tale, exhibited ostentatious wealth and ugly racism. The fifth-act duet about the night was undercut by a self-mocking Lorenzo and a staging that kept the lovers far apart.[25]

Such productions play against the text, altering the conclusion of mirth, laughter, and wonder. Directors like Kahn and Alexander may be implying that such a conclusion is morally inappropriate to so disturbing a play. Shakespeare's later dark comedies demonstrate the dramatist's growing awareness of the aesthetic and moral uses of the ironically muted comic triumph. A playwright who continues to ex-plore in comedy the causes and consequences of evil and anguish some-times finds it a problem to conform to the happy ending dictated by comic convention and tradition. In comedy after comedy, Shake-speare seeks new ways of meeting this problem.

5

ENDINGS

THE DISCUSSION IN THE PREVIOUS CHAPTER FOLLOWS from the premise that, for the audience in the theater, a play is experienced temporally. Over a finite period, which in contemporary theaters usually lasts somewhat longer than the two hours mentioned by the chorus in *Romeo and Juliet,* a story unfolds, each of whose succeeding events and moods is affected and partially shaped by what precedes it. The enacted story, with its intellectual and emotional appeals and its hold upon and manipulation of the imagination, works its magic on the playgoers by means of accumulation. As the play develops, events take on an ever richer and more urgent context. Only after the playgoer has viewed the production can the phenomena of analysis and criticism properly begin.[1]

When viewers become potential critics, they hold in their minds an idea that is possessed of definite and describable shape, structure, and meaning, which have been conferred upon it by the accumulating events and the intellectual, emotional, and imaginative reactions these elicit. Each scene, each speech—in great plays, each word and gesture— makes its necessary contribution. But the scene that does most to confer and define shape, structure, and meaning is the last scene of all, the scene that ends the strange, eventful history.

Jaques's famous comparison in *As You Like It* of the life of a man to a play seems deeply pessimistic because the play, for Jaques, ends in "second childishness and mere oblivion; / Sans teeth, sans eyes, sans taste, sans every thing" (2.7.165–66). The action on the stage contradicts this assertion since Jaques's words are juxtaposed with the entrance of Adam, a man who is near the end of his life, but who is not by a long shot the second child. If Adam is played as a vigorous old man whose fighting spirit does not succumb to the extremes of hunger and exhaustion, the contrast will be theatrically effective. What the audience hears in the speech and sees in the entrance constitute opposing arguments in a debate, and the assumption that lies behind both speech and spectacle is that the end has most to do with conferring meaning and structure. The debate implied in this scene is one manifestation of an assumption deeply embedded in our culture. That the word *end* can be used to denote both conclusion and purpose is another. Shakespeare often so uses the word, and he has Peter Quince unconsciously pun on its double meaning in his prologue to "Pyramus and Thisby": "To show our simple skill, / That is the true beginning of our end."[2]

For literary theorists and practitioners, from Aristotle to Dürrenmatt, the end contributes mightily to whatever sense of moral significance or aesthetic satisfaction a literary work can impart. The generic terms *tragedy* and *comedy* connote dominant tones and prescribed endings. Shakespeare's tragedies end in death. His comedies, even the atypical *Love's Labour's Lost,* end in marriage—either celebrated, confirmed, or at least distantly expected. No exploration of the effects of Shakespeare's comedies on the audience in the theater is complete without a discussion of endings.

Given both their importance and their generic prescription, it follows that flawed endings can do incalculable harm to the plays they conclude. That a dramatist does not take enough trouble with endings is a serious charge. That Shakespeare does not take enough trouble with endings is held by a number of critics.[3] Preeminent among these is Johnson, whose censure on this point is sweeping and severe:

> It may be observed, that in many of his plays the latter part is evidently neglected. When he found himself near the end of his work, and in view of his reward, he shortened the labour to snatch the profit. He therefore remits his efforts where he should most vigorously exert them, and his catastrophe is improbably produced or imperfectly represented.[4]

Of *All's Well That Ends Well,* a play whose title states the comic prescription, Johnson notes that Shakespeare, hastening to his conclusion, finds "matter sufficient to fill up his remaining scenes and therefore, as on other occasions, contracts his dialogue and precipitates his action."[5]

Shakespeare's problems with the prescribed comic conclusion become particularly acute in such comedies as search most deeply into the causes and consequences of evil and anguish. He rarely dissipates evil by a simple wave of the dramatist's wand. Evil characters are disposed of without being adventitiously dismissed. Common sense and dramatic custom suggest two ways for him to dispose of such characters. He either has them defeated and cast out of the happy society toward which every comedy points, or he has them embraced and included in the new, harmonious order, offering his audience the hope that they will reform, that their moral mendings have already begun. "They say best men are moulded out of faults," says Mariana of Angelo,[6] and she could just as well be speaking of all the flawed characters— Proteus, Bertram, Posthumus, Iachimo, Leontes—who are embraced and included, faults and all, in the scenes of restoration that conclude so many of Shakespeare's comedies.

The endings that most deeply vex Johnson and other critics are those in which people who have done appalling things are too quickly and extravagantly forgiven. In three of Shakespeare's comedies such people are taken in marriage by their victims. Having done most to thwart the comic aspirations of the other characters and of the audience, they suddenly become central participants in their plays' comic triumphs. Johnson objects not so much to the generosity of these actions as to their precipitancy. And Shakespeare indicates in plays written at several points in his career that he, too, is aware that a certain length of time is required to render acts of repentance and forgiveness morally satisfactory and dramatically credible. In his early play *Love's Labour's Lost,* he breaks with comic tradition by imposing a year-long penance on the young lords and pushing their nuptials into offstage futurity. In his late play *The Winter's Tale,* he brings Time onto the stage to announce that Leontes "shuts up himself" for sixteen years.[7] In both these plays he seems to be adhering to the notion that sin must bring down its just proportion of suffering upon the sinner.

He is suggesting simultaneously that the long process of repentance and the soothing of suffering by time are undramatic. Leontes' years of sorrow are talked of but not seen, and the audience at *Love's Labour's Lost* is left to hope but not to be certain that the young lords of Navarre will be taken by their ladies after their year of trial. The undramatic nature of repentance and forgiveness may enter into Shakespeare's choice to have *All's Well That Ends Well* and *Measure for Measure* end as they do. If one grants his awareness that slow time makes for credible penance, one may infer that he acts deliberately and not carelessly when he fashions the endings to the so-called problem comedies.

I will grant immediately that this hypothesis probably does not apply to the workshop comedy, *The Two Gentlemen of Verona*. It is generally agreed that the conclusion to this play is botched. The sober Bullough, who usually eschews evaluative comments, remarks on this ending's shortcomings.[8] The director Margaret Webster writes that this is the one play of Shakespeare that she would happily leave to the study and the classroom.[9] The final scene likely has much to do with her judging the play unfit for the theater.

Yet much can be learned from this ending. It reveals characteristics that grow increasingly prominent in subsequent plays. The first of these is the pastoral setting. This is the playwright's earliest use of the forest, a setting outside the normal law and custom of court and city, as a place of self-discovery and renewal. As with Shakespeare's later pastoral comedies, scenic designs for productions of this play must imaginatively suggest the forest and give visual emphasis to those qualities described in the verse:

> This shadowy desert, unfrequented woods,
> I better brook than flourishing peopled towns.
> Here can I sit alone, unseen of any,
> And to the nightingale's complaining note
> Tune my distresses and record my woes.
>
> (5.4.2–6)

These commonplaces are scarcely distinguishable from what one finds in the myriad Elizabethan pastorals, but out of such material Shakespeare makes miracles in *A Midsummer Night's Dream, As You Like It,* and *The Winter's Tale.*

The dramatist also develops in subsequent plays the device of placing in the gravest peril those characters whom the audience has come most deeply to care about, so that he may effect a complete reversal with most striking dramatic and theatrical effectiveness. The audience is assured by Valentine's watching presence that all will be well. He need only show himself to the other characters to change their terrors to joys. In comedy after comedy, Shakespeare makes an important character's presence or true identity known to the spectators but hidden from the other characters. The unexpected appearance of an undisguised Rosalind or Vincentio, a restored Marina, or a seemingly resurrected Hero or Helena, turns apparent evil into real good.

Thus far, there is nothing to blame in the ending to *The Two Gentle-men of Verona*. These devices are so successful that Shakespeare wrings changes on them throughout his career, and few critics tax him for repeating himself. The ending's flaws grow out of the playwright's exploration, for the first time in drama, of a problem of evil in a context of romance. As M. St. Clare Byrne points out in reviewing Michael Langham's 1957 R.S.C. production, "the problem with *Two Gentlemen* is that one of them isn't."[10] Having depicted Proteus as a betrayer of love and friendship, the dramatist creates the problem of how to dispose of this offender in a manner consonant with the comic prescription. In the so-called festive comedies, Shakespeare makes his chief repository of evil a misfit, an alien, an exile, someone who by nature cannot and should not be included in the harmonious new order. Shylock the Jew, Don John the bastard, Malvolio the bourgeois puritan, all are rejected, excluded, cast out. Even Egeus the heavy father is simply overborne. But Proteus, who has committed such offenses as Shakespeare invests with deepest abhorrence through-out his career, is by his nature and function central to whatever new society will emerge at his play's end. He is a young gentleman and lover. His sweetheart, who still loves him in spite of everything he has done to her, is a character with whom the audience most deeply sympathizes. If he is cast out, what will become of her? Proteus is not rejected. Valentine denounces him in sadness and rage, and he says he is sorry:

> My shame and guilt confounds me.
> Forgive me, Valentine; if hearty sorrow
> Be a sufficient ransom for offence,
> I tender't here; I do as truly suffer
> As e'er I did commit.
>
> (5.4.73–77)

These assertions constitute all the audience will hear of penance and remorse. The actor will have to make the best of them, convincing the audience that he is suffering as much for his sins as Posthumus and Leontes in later plays suffer for theirs. The anguish of his vic-tims extends over much of the play, and the audience is made to feel it deeply. Considerations of aesthetic and moral balance require that Proteus should feel such suffering as he has caused before he is forgiven. In spite of the actor's best efforts, the sole speech of contrition will probably not convince most spectators that his sorrow is a sufficient ransom, and in that may lie the most insuperable of this ending's problems in production. To stylize the repentance or play it for laughs will compound the problem of balance. Julia's scenes of anguish are too affecting to be dismissed in the play's final moments with cheap laughs. St. Clare Byrne warns that if "the actors decide to guy the conclusion and get the audience to laugh with them, they will get their curtain applause, but it will not save the play as such."[11] The only valid possibility is to strive for sincerity and conviction.

Another problem arises because Valentine's forgiveness is as extravagant as it is immediate: "And, that my love may appear plain and free, / All that was mine in Silvia I give thee" (5.4.82–83). Shakespeare gives Silvia nothing to say about being consigned to the man who has just tried to rape her. This is the first of those open-ended silences that require actors and directors to make hard choices in productions of his comedies. In a 1975 production at Stratford, Ontario, Silvia was depicted as an accomplished flirt.

> In her final interchange with Proteus . . . she managed to be provocative and challenging and then visibly excited by his advances, rather than resolute, admonitory and finally frightened. You felt that she was enjoying herself, and that the touch of chagrin in her silence following Valentine's intervention was as much the result of being prevented from dealing with Proteus in her own way as in finding herself for once not the center of attention.[12]

Valentine's questionable generosity is forestalled only by Julia's self-revelation. She accuses Proteus, and he replies with a sentiment hardly flattering to either of the women: "What is in Silvia's face but I may spy / More fresh in Julia's with a constant eye?" (5.4.114–15). And the play speeds away from further consideration of this couple. In less than two minutes of stage time, the figures who had joined with Proteus to block Valentine's marriage are disposed of, the outlaws are pardoned, and all the characters troop off to their mutual happiness. This ending is too crowded with matter. As I noted in a previous chapter, Valentine's final speech suggests that wonder may be part of the scene's intended effect.[13] However, the causes of wonder are passed in review without being communicated emotionally and imaginatively to the audience.

How can the scene be salvaged in production? I have argued that Proteus's repentance should be played with sincerity and conviction, but once that serious moment is past, perhaps the most effective directorial strategy is to exaggerate deliberately the characters' emotions. Proteus's and Valentine's couplets, like the lovers' couplets in *A Midsummer Night's Dream,* encourage the actors' stylization and the spectators' detachment. Shakespeare is probably not writing intentional parody of romance here as he may be doing in the last scene of *Cymbeline.* But the audience will be better entertained and the play in production better served if the scene is played as if he were. Michael Langham's 1957 R.S.C. production achieved such an exaggeration by adopting as its setting a milieu similar to that of *Northanger Abbey.* Langham used the essential frivolity of Regency costumes to persuade the audience to accept the play as artificial comedy, set in an age where romantic absurdity could be taken for granted.

> The preposterous ending is prepared for at the start and comes as a perfect climax, with its sensibility and its swooning and its threat of suicide with a pistol by the repentant Proteus to give a plausible period cue for Valentine's offer to surrender Silvia.[14]

Shakespeare's strongest reaction to the ending to *The Two Gentlemen of Verona* occurs in what may be his next comedy, *Love's Labour's Lost.*[15] In this play, the king of Navarre and his bookmates are neither pardoned nor taken in marriage by the queen of France and her ladies. A year-long penance is laid on the young men, a penance that bears a Dantesque relation to their peculiar faults. These faults are not to be compared with the betrayals and other crimes committed or attempted by Proteus. The four lords of Navarre are aspiring scholars, and they suffer from an infirmity common to their kind, a mixture of arrogance and insularity that unfits them to meet problems outside their chosen cloister. One cannot help but note the apparent inconsistency of a playwright who in one comedy swiftly pardons a would-be rapist, and in a subsequent comedy imposes a lingering penance on men whose only crimes are pride and folly.

This very inconsistency suggests that Shakespeare is here reacting to the ending of the earlier play. Even more suggestive is his deliberately breaking the comic prescription in order to avoid such an ending. Berowne calls attention to this radical departure:

> Our wooing doth not end like an old play:
> Jack hath not Jill. These ladies' courtesy
> Might well have made our sport a comedy.
>
> (5.2.862–64)

Further, in putting the marriages off for a year, Shakespeare places them outside the traditional temporal confines of comedy. As Berowne notes, a twelvemonth is "too long for a play" (5.2.866). Behind his phrase lies the assumption that even though comic prescription is being broken, the law of time cannot be broken. The dramatist cannot represent events that are a year apart. He refuses to slide over the year of penance and give his audience the satisfaction of seeing the nuptial.

Why he refuses deserves a moment's consideration. Elizabethan playwrights often break the law of time. But this law is broken more frequently in tragedy or history than in comedy. Until *Pericles* and *The Winter's Tale*, in which the law of time is notoriously broken, Shakespeare chooses to confine his comedies to periods that may be measured in days, weeks, or months, but never in years. In this early play, the dramatist deprives characters and audience of their fundamental comic satisfaction so as to gain a more satisfactory balance between crime and punishment. In *The Two Gentlemen of Verona*, he allows the comic prescription to overbear every other consideration in his ending. Since marriages must happen, he gives the audience a quick one-two punch of repentance and forgiveness and gets on with the business of matrimonial arrangements. In *Love's Labour's Lost*, he breaks the comic prescription and imposes a penance whose duration can be fairly measured against the wrongdoing.

For its first four acts, the play gives pleasure by fulfilling traditional comic expectations. As soon as the playgoers learn that the lords have imposed celibacy on themselves, they will expect Ferdinand, Berowne, and the rest to fall in love. Once the men have contracted to "woo these girls of France" (4.3.367), comic law dictates that the ladies should eventually relent and the audience should be treated to a nuptial feast. Yet the play's title warns that this will not be the case. Although its witty alliteration is proper to comedy, it bespeaks a situation precisely opposed to the traditional comic movement.

The play begins to move away from comedy when the ladies denounce the disguised lords' folly and perjury. "The blood of youth burns not with such excess / As gravity's revolt to wantonness" (5.2.73–74). Performers of the scene are encouraged by their lines to guide the audience to laugh with the ladies at the noble fools, but ideally the laughing audience should also be disturbed by the strength of the princess's anger. Moral passion is not out of place in Shakespeare's comedies. What makes for a departure from comedy is that the dissonant notes persist and intensify beyond the cessation of the action. The ladies' rage overwhelms their laughter when they rebuke the lords for breaking their oaths:

> Nor God, nor I, delights in perjur'd men.
> . . . .
> Now by my maiden honour, yet as pure
> As the unsullied lily, I protest,
> A world of torments though I should endure,
> I would not yield to be your house's guest;
> So much I hate a breaking cause to be
> Of heavenly oaths, vow'd with integrity.
>
> (5.2.346–56)

Such speeches have not been wholly absent from the play's earlier scenes.[16] But their marked increase in frequency and fierceness helps create in the final act a permanent shift in tone.

The quality of the play's laughter also begins to change. Although partaking of mockery and malice, the laughter in the first four acts never wholly loses its essential good humor and good nature. But in the fifth act, it grows cruel as the lords realize that they have been tricked. Having had their sport destroyed by mockery, the lords proceed to outdo the ladies in malice by generating ugly laughter at the rustics' expense.

In several respects, the lords deserve the ladies' witty malice. Moreover, and more important, they match the ladies in wit, ability, and rank, and are therefore fair targets. To exercise courtly wit upon the rustics is an offense analogous to a gentleman drawing a weapon on a social inferior. Holofernes and Don Armado have earned a scourge of wit, but the lords are not proper ministers of justice.[17]

The attacks on Holofernes and Don Armado are characterized by little genuine wit and much personal abuse. They are most effective when played with a nasty quality of one-upsmanship. Holofernes has the dramatic best of it when he reprimands his social betters. Don Armado has sufficient self-possession to command the lords to silence, and when they continue their abuse he issues a reprimand, which, although inappropriately phrased, is the most telling they have yet received. The lines must not be played for laughs: "The sweet war-man is dead and rotten; sweet chucks, beat not the bones of the buried; when he breathed, he was a man" (5.2.652–53). The baiting soon gives place to the farcical violence of a challenge and a proposed duel. The dramatist is showing that the atmosphere created by verbal abuse can foster physical abuse as well. The laughter proper to farce mixes with the pain resulting from the threat of actual harm. The mood of hilarity and violence resembles those generated by the first-act brawl in *Romeo and Juliet*, the protracted lovers' quarrel in *A Midsummer Night's Dream*, or the interrupted fight between Cesario and Sir Andrew in *Twelfth Night*. When Mercade radically and permanently alters the play's mood, he comes into a scene whose wild laughter and potential danger make for the best foil to set off his sober news. Mercade's entrance is one of the play's central moments, as important to its action as Sebastian's fifth-act entrance is to *Twelfth Night* or Isabella's kneeling for Angelo's life is to *Measure for Measure*. J. C. Trewin criticizes John Barton's otherwise exemplary R.S.C. production for its failure to call sufficient attention to the ambassador's arrival,[18] and Robert Speaight suggests that Mercade ideally should have a long, slow entrance.[19]

But why does the playwright bring news of death to darken the conclusion of a comedy? The erring lords are not betrayers and rapists, like the pardoned Proteus of his earlier comedy, but they have broken their words and abused their social inferiors. Before they can marry the ladies they have so ineptly courted, they will require pardon of a sort not usually needed by lovers in comedy. Such a pardon may, in the brief final moments of a play, smack of similar aesthetic and moral shortcomings as mar the conclusion of *The Two Gentlemen of Verona*. But Shakespeare does not repeat an earlier mistake. He brings on a messenger from the world both outside the cloister that Navarre and his bookmen have chosen, and outside the usual confines of comedy. The announcement that the king of France has died is hardly shocking; he has been described throughout as decrepit and bedridden. But it changes once for all the play's mood, and the change it brings about is used to suggest how unfit these men are for a life of marriage to these women. Mercade's news creates a situation in which the ladies can impose a penance without appearing to be self-righteous punishers.

Two equal and opposite forces exert themselves on the spectators.

The first of these is the old erotic pull of comedy: against all the odds and despite all the follies, the audience wants the lords and ladies to marry. To that end the play has been moving ever since the early exposition of the blocking law of celibacy, which the audience has always known would be broken. Countering this force is the sense that the lords are not sufficiently purged of their folly and pride. This sense is intensified by the new atmosphere that pervades the scene. Whatever has gone before, now is simply not the proper time for matrimony. The inappropriateness of marriage in this suddenly sober world was stressed in the 1979 Stratford, Ontario, production, set in the early years of the twentieth century.

A distant rumbling was heard over the horizon. The principals paused, looking at each other, puzzled. Was it thunder or gunfire? The *belle epoque* ended with the guns of the Marne on the horizon. As in the text, fame yields to death.[20]

The conflict at the play's end is succinctly expressed in the interchange between the princess and the king:

King. Now, at the latest minute of the hour,
    Grant us your loves.
Prin. A time, methinks, too short
    To make a world-without-end bargain in.

                                                    (5.2.775–77)

The comedy concludes in a manner both morally satisfactory and dramatically credible. But there is one respect in which this conclusion is not wholly satisfactory, and Shakespeare does not comparably conclude any of his other comedies. The ending of a play should give shape and definition to the whole. But the conclusion to this play runs counter not only to the general movement of comedy, but to the particular direction insisted upon by the first four acts. This play, which might have been overwhelmed by the concord proper to comedy, ends instead in uneasy discord and may leave the audience with the Johnsonian sense of a conclusion in which nothing is concluded. The real ending is a year and a penance distant. Rather than giving shape to the whole, the conclusion uneasily imposes real gravity upon artificial wit. Even the final songs continue the sense of imposed unease. To be sure, they partially restore the comic spirit, and they satirize the underside of marriage with their implications of cuckoldry and grimy domesticity. But Shakespeare reverses their natural order. Time out of mind, comedy moves from winter to spring. The songs in this play move in the opposite direction. If a second spring follows the winter of greasy Joan's discontent, the audience does not see it.[21]

Never again in comedy does Shakespeare write an ending that runs counter to the movement of his play. When he comes again after several years of comic writing to assay endings in which wrongdoers are pardoned, the unease of these conclusions follows naturally from the unease of the plays that they conclude. In *Measure for Measure,* as we have seen, the audience is uncertain about the duke's plans and his competence to carry them out, and this uncertainty becomes a part of the play's resolution. The uncertainty persists even after Isabella's plea that Angelo be spared and the seeming resurrection of her brother. After Claudio's entrance, he, Isabella, Mariana, and Angelo remain silent for the rest of the play. The reader may imagine, and almost every director stages, an embrace between brother and sister, and perhaps also an embrace between Mariana and Angelo. In such expressions of joy there is no need for words. But awkwardness mixes with the joy when the duke proposes to Isabella. His breaking off the proposal before it is properly uttered may suggest that he himself is not unaware that it is ill-timed and badly placed. His speech and its failure to elicit a verbal response from Isabella certainly create a problem for actors and directors. Margaret Webster solved the problem by having the duke address his speech as follows:

> [To Isabella] If he be like your brother, for his sake
>   Is he pardon'd; and for your lovely sake,
> [To Claudio] Give me your hand and say you will be mine,
> [To Isabella] He is my brother too. But fitter time for that.
>   (5.1.488–91)[22]

This may solve some problems but it creates others. "Give me your hand and say you will be mine" is an odd way to greet a prospective brother-in-law, even for a character who does as many odd things as the duke. Further, to initiate a proposal of marriage while brother and sister are passionately if silently greeting each other makes for an uncomfortable moment. Once again, perhaps with the best intentions, the duke seems not to account for the sensibilities of the people he is trying to help. How Isabella responds to the proposal remains a choice for the actress and director, but the play's text does not encode a reaction of unalloyed joy.

Laughter mingles with the unease when the duke turns to Lucio. Their exchange draws laughter because of Lucio's unabated audacity, and because Shakespeare has so arranged meetings between these two characters that all their encounters will seem funny to the audience and will diminish the duke's stature, even in his moments of apt remission. But before the characters leave the stage, the laughter abates and the unease increases. In his final speech, the duke for a second time expresses his intention to marry Isabella, and she for a second time makes no verbal response. Again the actress and director are faced with a difficult choice, but however the moment is staged, it will leave the audience uneasy as the play concludes. Peter Brook accepted as

> equally natural, that is to say, equally Elizabethan, [Isabella's] compliance with the duke's ardent designs and her ultimately easy abandonment of her religious calling for marriage to a man she has known for five minutes.[23]

But Estelle Kohler, in a 1969 R.S.C. production, played an Isabella whose chastity had been corrupted by pride. The play ended with her alone on stage, unresponsive to the duke's proposal.[24] In the 1975 Stratford, Ontario, production to which I have previously referred, Martha Henry's Isabella was awakened by desire,

> but in that awakening, she found only cause for an excruciating self-contempt. The prospect of marriage to the duke filled her with physical revulsion, and the theatre darkened round her face, twisted in agony.[25]

In its mixture of laughter and unease, as well as in many of its details, this ending resembles the conclusion to *All's Well That Ends Well*. Each is a public scene that needs to be staged with the pomp and ceremony appropriate to a formal, judicial proceeding. The chief business of each scene is a disentangling of apparently riddling and equivocal truth from apparently bold and forthright lies. In both scenes, a wrongdoer is forgiven and taken in marriage by the woman he has hurt. In each case, the forgiveness may appear precipitant and thus both morally and dramatically unsatisfactory. Both scenes suggest but do not develop the possibility of forgiving and reclaiming a character whom the audience finds despicable. But Angelo's forgiveness, even though it happens quickly, seems both hard won and substantially validated by Isabella's decision to beg for mercy rather than revenge. Far more disturbance is generated by the duke than by the fact of Angelo's pardon. In this respect, the two endings differ greatly. Moreover, events in *Measure for Measure* are manipulated by the duke, who is present for most of the scene, while events in *All's Well That Ends Well* are manipulated by the absent Helena. She differs radically from the duke in that the audience knows exactly what she intends to do, and it knows further that she will be gloriously able to execute her design.

Uncertainty and disapprobation grow out of the swiftness with which she and everyone else forgive Bertram. As Johnson observes:

> Decency required that Bertram's double crime of cruelty and disobedience, joined likewise with some hypocrisy, should raise more resentment; and that though his mother might easily forgive him, his king should more pertinaciously vindicate his own authority and Helen's merit: of all this Shakespeare could not be ignorant, but Shakespeare wanted to conclude his play.[26]

Yet Bertram proves forgivable for a number of reasons that the play explores. Comic resolutions are possible only when the worst consequences of evil intentions are forestalled. Death is the unchanging and unchangeable tragic fact. That Desdemona and Cordelia die has much to do with making their plays tragedies. That Helena, Claudio, Marina, Perdita, and Hermione live has much to do with making their plays comedies.[27] When life comes where death has been acknowledged and mourned, much may be forgiven. In *All's Well That Ends Well*, everyone thinks that Helena is dead and suspects that Bertram has had a hand in her death. When the great difference between what he has actually done and what they fear he has done becomes clear to them, their relief and joy lead them to join Helena in forgiving him.

But why does Helena forgive him? Her conduct in the final moments is implicit throughout the play; it constitutes the resolution toward which the action has been moving. Her love for Bertram and purpose to reclaim him constitute the character's driving force. Throughout the play, the actress must communicate the strength and persistence of Helena's passion, since that passion is one of the play's premises.

In order to understand how its ending follows naturally from its beginning and middle, the spectators must be brought to understand and accept this premise. Northrop Frye, commenting on Rymer's famous blast of *Othello*, argues that any play can seem ludicrous to one who does not accept its conventions.[28] Any play can also seem ridiculous to one who does not accept its premises. Playwrights and actors are kinds of storytellers, and every storyteller understands that a story must start somewhere. Listeners to the story are asked to accept simply as given a certain situation with certain implications. The situation out of which grow both *All's Well That Ends Well* and the story from Boccaccio on which it draws is particularly difficult to accept. Some of the discomfort caused by the play's ending derives from this difficulty of acceptance. A poor girl loves an aristocrat who scorns her, and she performs impossible tasks in her quest to win him. As Frye notes, she bears a greater resemblance to Psyche than to the man-catching heroines of any number of modern problem plays.[29] Yet in his Edwardian production, Trevor Nunn took seriously

> Shaw's famous observation that Helena was a precursor of Ibsen's new woman. By leaping to the Ibsen-Shaw time-frame, the director has brought a fresh and illuminating context to an implacably courageous heroine who will do anything and everything to get the man with whom she has a neurotic, even nymphomaniacal obsession.[30]

Although the 1959 Tyrone Guthrie production also had an Edwardian setting, Zoe Caldwell drew on her extraordinary personal charisma to depict Helena as a heroine of mythological resonance, capable of working miracles.[31]

Part of Helena's willingness to put up with so much perfidy from Bertram derives from her unquestioning recognition of the gulf between their social stations. Discussing his reasons for transplanting the play to an Edwardian milieu, Trevor Nunn argued that the audience must also be persuaded to understand and accept this gulf.

> I came to realize how important this social and class distinction was to the play, and it was something I never felt to be palpable, tangible, in Elizabethan or Jacobean settings. We are not close enough to that time, we don't know enough, we can't read the detail. But we've all seen "Upstairs, Downstairs." We all know every tiny innuendo of class distinction from the age immediately before our own.[32]

Helena's objective throughout the play is to bridge the social gulf, to catch Bertram, forgive him, and pursue her marriage with him. This is the end that she works miracles to achieve. That she knows her end will involve pain as well as joy is made clear by her words of encouragement to the Florentine women who aid her:

> But with the word the time will bring on summer,
> When briers shall have leaves as well as thorns
> And be as sweet as sharp. . . .
> All's Well That Ends Well. Still the fine's the crown.
> Whate'er the course, the end is the renown.
>
> (4.4.31–36)

Helena's end is Shakespeare's end. The play's title and much of its imagery suggest that the dramatist is giving serious thought to the problem of endings.[33] Just as "love's labour's lost" is a statement that runs counter to the comic movement, the title to this play succinctly expresses the prescription that defines comedy. Shakespeare's use of this phrase, both as title and as repeated motto or refrain throughout the play, suggests that he is deliberately exploring the properties and limitations inherent in that prescription. He dramatizes the paradox at the heart of comedy by showing briefly his laboring women in Marseilles seeking the king who has traveled to Rousillon. The scene gives a sense of struggle, inconvenience, and hope, and it can be staged so as to display the characters' exertions and exhaustion:

> *Gent.* He hence remov'd last night, and with more haste
>   Than is his use.
> *Wid.* Lord, how we lose our pains!
> *Hel.* All's Well That Ends Well yet,
>   Though time seem so adverse and means unfit.
>
> (5.1.23–26)

Time seems even more adverse as the final scene develops. The action is dominated by the king, and the actor of this complex part must communicate the character's unconquerable sorrow at Helena's seeming loss. In time, his grief mixes with fear and rage, and these feelings contribute to the scene's dominant mood. Superior in its knowledge of Helena's plans, the audience will not share the king's emotions, yet the spectacle of this mighty figure's anguish cannot but be affecting on the stage. Even more vexing to the spectators is Bertram's behavior.

The actor will be most effective if he plays the scene with aristocratic charm, revealing only in the moments immediately before Helena's final entrance the character's cold contempt for the Florentine riffraff who are accusing him. A chief source of this ending's discomfort is the juxtaposition of such forgiveness with such an exhibition of cowardice and mendacity. The growing anxieties of characters and spectators are occasionally but importantly leavened by laughter. When Lafeu, whose daughter Bertram is set to marry, hears of the young man's attempted seduction of Diana, his reaction is characteristically pungent: "I will buy me a son-in-law in a fair, and toll for this" (5.3.145–46). The laugh is welcome in so grim a context, but like the joy that it may augur, Lafeu's remark is mixed with pain in its evocation of the passing bell and its suggestion that Bertram is a figure to be mourned.

The scene of unraveling initiated by Diana also contains its moments of laughter. She defends her assailed reputation by telling the aged king, "By Jove, if ever I knew man, 'twas you" (5.3.281). Her line's incongruity may make the audience laugh, and the laughter would help bring about the transition from rage, grief, and fear to the uneasy joy and wonder of the conclusion. Tyrone Guthrie's production used laughter in this scene as a means to usher in the play's final wonder.

> When the king finally loses patience with Diana's riddling mystifications and orders her off to prison, she resists and there is an undignified struggle into which Miss Badley [the widow] launches herself like an infuriated Yorkshire terrier. . . . Guthrie prepares the most exquisitely touching moment in the whole play with one of the biggest laughs of the evening. The widow disengages herself from the scrimmage, draws herself up to her full five foot nothing of ruffled dignity, and with set face and pursed lips, the embodiment of pained affront, hobbles doggedly across the full width of the stage to fetch Helena. The mood of the audience as a whole is adjusted by that laugh, and the tone of the scene changes with it. The tension is broken, and we are swung over by the intrusion of the ridiculous from the edge of ill humour to gaiety and pleasurable anticipation.[34]

Helena's entrance imparts miracle and meaning to Diana's riddles. If she is dressed as a bride, her appearance will create the greatest possible contrast to the care-worn traveler of the previous scene. The other characters cannot at once discern the difference between appearance and reality:

Is there no exorcist
Beguiles the truer office of mine eyes?
Is't real that I see?

(5.3.298–300)

Although everyone is astonished by Helena's seeming return from
the other side of the grave, the wonder that she brings with her
is fraught with pain. Her reply to the king's amazed question communicates to both the characters and the spectators the terrible and enduring
anguish that Bertram has made her suffer:

No, my good lord,
'Tis but the shadow of a wife you see,
The name and not the thing.

(5.3.300–302)

Bertram's brief speeches after his wife's entrance give the actor an
opportunity to suggest that the character may be capable of such
feelings as render him forgivable and redeemable. Yet even the hope
created by his lines is mixed with unease engendered by the trite
neatness of his final couplet. It is revealing to compare Guthrie's staging
of this moment with Nunn's. Byrne writes of the Guthrie production:

When at the end of the play Bertram has a concluding couplet which
is perhaps the worst that any actor could be asked to speak, I did
not hear him speak it. I did not knowingly shut my ears. Actress and
producer simply persuaded me at that critical moment to be all eyes
and feeling. I saw nothing but Helena and what she did; I heard nothing
but what she had said—accepted the gesture of contrition and perhaps
of the beginnings of love with which he knelt and clung to her. It
was her moment. Her words and the stage picture had said all there
was to say. And from Dame Edith down, every single member of the
cast acted that moment. You did not watch them—you felt them feeling
its impact. There was no need for Bertram to speak, and if his words
had been adequate, they would have been out of character. (Actually,
of course, the impossible couplet was spoken simply and firmly.)[35]

In Nunn's production, Bertram expressed a mixture of compliance
and stubborn individuality in his final couplet with a pointed stress
on "if."

When [Helena] finally appeared, he went to take her hand, but did not actually do so. . . . This wary meeting between husband and wife contrasted strikingly with Helena's intensely moving reunion with the countess. . . . Left alone, Bertram and Helena walked upstage together, their hands still apart.[36]

Whether Bertram is forgivable or not, Helena's immediate aim is not to pardon him, as Isabella pardons Angelo. Her first purpose is to change the eternal not, to which he has coldly and punningly referred, into a knot eternal. What there is of forgiveness and private pain for this couple the audience does not see. Johnson argues that there is much left out of the closing scene that the spectators might have reasonably expected to witness. He notes especially the absence of a "pathetical interview" among Bertram, his mother, his wife, and the king.[37] The audience is given only the most indirect suggestion of such an interview, and the indirection is dramatically underscored by the fact that Bertram addresses his final words not to his wife but to his sovereign.

A theme implicit in the play's last scene is given explicit expression in an incisive remark of Dorothy L. Sayers, whose double occupation of mystery writer and theologian results in much speculation on crime and forgiveness:

Forgiveness is the restoration of a good relationship, but it doesn't abolish the consequences of the offense, nor is it going back to where we were before the offense was committed, it's got to be a new relationship.[38]

All's Well That Ends Well, like Shakespeare's other comedies in which wrongdoers are forgiven and included in the final rejoicing, does not directly concern itself with the difficult emergence of a new relationship. The true ends of all these comedies are the new beginnings that exist in potential when the actors leave the stage for the last time. Spectators learn perhaps more than they would like about the human cost that must be paid for these endings of qualified happiness. For those who do not like thorns in their briers, who prefer comic sweetness unmixed with sharpness, the experience may be less than satisfactory.

When Shakespeare, toward the end of his career, again takes up the problem of the comic ending in which wrongdoers are pardoned and accepted, he still chooses not to portray the working out of new relationships between those wrongdoers and their victims. The audience hears no prolonged final conversations between Posthumus and Imogen or between Hermione and Leontes. But in the two later plays, the wrongdoers frankly confess and truly repent. Each may be said to have paid as much, short of death, as it is possible to pay for their sins. The difference between the portrayed penances of Posthumus and Leontes and those of Bertram and Angelo may suggest that Shakespeare was not himself wholly satisfied with the endings to the so-called problem comedies.

Throughout his career the playwright experimented with the comic ending. Further evidence of his preoccupation may be found in the epilogue to *All's Well That Ends Well*. It resembles other Shakespearean epilogues in that its most readily apparent function is to ask the audience for applause. But most epilogues gently dispel the dramatic illusion and comfortably return the audience to the world outside the theater. In this brief, abrupt epilogue there is little that is gentle or comfortable about the return from illusion to reality. As soon as the king finishes his last speech, he announces: "The King's a beggar, now the play is done" (5.Ep.1). The actor might violently divest himself of the role, flinging his regalia to the floor and sweeping downstage to talk directly to the audience. Moreover, he makes explicit reference in his final lines in the character of the king to the fact that the story cannot be properly said to have ended: "All yet seems well; and if it end so meet, / The bitter past, more welcome is the sweet" (5.3.326–27). These lines suggest that the good ending is conditional, depending upon the long process of forgiveness and renewal of which the audience sees only the beginning. They suggest further that the good ending is only apparent. After a play so profoundly concerned with the differences between reality and appearance, the spectators will be put on their guard by the word *seems,* on which the actor might lay particular stress. But in the epilogue, appearance changes unexpectedly to reality. The good ending, now actual and not apparent, depends not on the unseen conversations among Bertram, his mother, his wife, and the king, but simply on the audience's being pleased with the play. "All is well ended if this suit be won, / That you express content" (5.Ep.2–3). The actor might stress *is* to balance the previous stress of *seems.* The juxtaposition of the story's conditional ending with the play's formal ending forces the audience to look squarely at the paradox inherent in every comic ending, and the contemplation of a paradox is never a comfortable experience.

No one likes to be made uncomfortable, especially by comedy. There may be pain aplenty during the course of the play, but the ending must promote the illusion that all pain has been dispelled:

> Jack shall have Jill;
> Nought shall go ill;
> The man shall have his mare again, and all shall be well.
> *(A Midsummer Night's Dream*, 3.2.461-63)

In the problem comedies, Shakespeare is exploring limitations in the form he has brought so close to perfection in *As You Like It* and *Twelfth Night.* Yet even these plays, which I have never heard anyone call problem comedies, explore in their conclusions paradoxes and limitations. The end of *As You Like It* may not be problematic, but the mass coupling that puts Jaques in mind of the ark is accompanied by a number of disturbing surprises. Any one of these might strain the credulity or jar the comic equilibrium of the spectators.

Perhaps the greatest single surprise is the announcement that the bad duke Frederick has been converted and is consequently no longer a threat or an obstacle. For Johnson, consistent in his objections to Shakespeare's endings, this is yet another example of the playwright's impatient foreshortening. Shakespeare loses a chance to communicate a moral in not showing the usurper's conversion by the hermit.[39] And readers of Lodge's "Rosalind," the narrative on which the play draws, may likewise raise their eyebrows at the dramatist's summary disposal of a villain that Lodge must do away with in a lengthy battle. But such objections do not really apply to a play in which quick change and surprise have become part of the order of things. The audience has been jolted frequently, and this jolt is consistent in its inconsistency with what has gone before. If Oliver can be so quickly converted, why not Frederick? If the forest can produce the god of marriage himself, why not a persuasive hermit as well? The playgoers, having taken pleasure in so many previous surprises, and already inclined to wonder and rejoice at the celebration, will simply have their joy and wonder increased at this removal of the last obstacle to perfect felicity.

In the midst of the rejoicing comes an unexpected, dissonant note. Jaques announces his voluntary exile. He has always separated himself from the lovers and the duke's happy rustics, so his decision to make this separation permanent is hardly surprising. But it keeps the other characters and the spectators from unalloyed rejoicing. There is, to be sure, a possible source of laughter in Jaques's departure. He characteristically does not like to see people too happy, and the audience is often encouraged to laugh at that characteristic. Still, his departure and the duke's reaction to it create a sober mood:

> *Jaq.* . . . So to your pleasures;
> I am for other than for dancing measures.
> *Duke S.* Stay, Jaques, stay.
> *Jaq.* To see no pastime I. What you would have
> I'll stay to know at your abandon'd cave.
> *Duke S.* Proceed, proceed. We will begin these rites,
> As we do trust they'll end, in true delights.
>
> (5.4.186–92)

Jaques's action tempers the mirth. The actor playing the duke can communicate genuine sadness and loss when he pleads with Jaques to stay, and there may be a tentative quality about the closing couplet, a pause before its final phrase, a sense that one cannot be certain of lasting joy.

Before the comedy ends the audience will be surprised yet once more by Rosalind's speaking the epilogue. This should not be surprising; Rosalind has thoroughly dominated the play. Yet Shakespeare makes his boy actor acknowledge such a reaction in the audience. "It is not the fashion to see the lady the epilogue; but it is no more unhandsome than to see the lord the prologue" (5.Ep.1–2). Some of this speech's hermaphroditic charm is lost when it is recited by a modern actress rather than an Elizabethan boy actor. Even so, the lines invite anyone who speaks them to move with Rosalind's characteristic dexterity between the personae of boy and woman.

By the time the speech is done, the graceful transition from fiction to reality is complete. But this transition does not begin with the beginning of the epilogue. It is happening after a fashion throughout the play. Time and again, the audience's engagement with the action is broken by self-conscious references to the theater. The pastoral illusion, although interrupted by sequences in what Robert Weimann calls the "non-representational mode,"[40] is never wholly dissipated. The final dispelling of the illusion, completed by the epilogue, is begun by Jaques be Boys's entrance: "Let me have audience for a word or two" (5.4.145). The use of the word *audience* cannot fail to remind the playgoers who and where they are. In production, Jaques de Boys's entrance is usually accompanied by a spectacular piece of theatrical artifice. The duke responds to the young man's news with lines whose regal assurance, dispensation of rewards, and use of couplets strongly suggest that they will constitute the last speech in the comedy. The actor should impart to them a sense of authority and closure. It is a conventional conclusion, spoken by the character who, by convention, has most right to speak it. All that is needed is a dance. In our production, music sounded and the characters began to dance as the duke finished speaking. Jaques's words cut through the music and interrupted the revels.

The three final surprises—the news of Frederick's conversion, Jaques's self-exile coming after a speech that seems to be the play's last, and the epilogue spoken by a lady—create a sense of dissolution that underlies the final merriment. Even as the play is coming to a triumphant conclusion, it is coming apart. Like Shelley's cloud, the dramatist seems to arise and unbuild his fragile creation just as it approaches completion.[41]

In what may be his happiest comedy, Shakespeare is exploring limitations and paradoxes whose examination brings about so much vexation for actors, directors, audiences, readers, and critics in his subsequent darker comedies. He continues this questioning in *Twelfth Night.* This is probably his next comedy after *As You Like It,* although it is possible that the two tragedies *Julius Caesar* and *Hamlet* intervene between the two comedies. *Twelfth Night* may be Shakespeare's most nearly perfect comedy, but its final sense of joy is far from perfect. The wondrous meeting between Sebastian and Viola is preceded by a disturbing scene between Sir Toby and Sir Andrew that conveys the violence of farce without its laughter.[42] After the mutual restoration of brother and sister and the joyful talk of a double wedding, it becomes clear that the lovers' complete happiness depends upon Malvolio. In durance at Malvolio's suit is the sea captain who is holding Viola's clothes, and without those clothes the marriage plans cannot go forward. More than the wedding depends on Viola's proper clothes. In the apparel in which she enters in the play's second scene—the only scene in which the audience sees her as herself—remains something of her true identity. By making the full restoration of this identity depend on Malvolio, Shakespeare introduces an imperfection into the lovers' joys. In the event, those joys remain imperfect, incomplete. Viola's complete resumption of herself will only happen after the play has ended. Orsino's last speech, referring to this event and the marriages that depend on it, significantly takes the future tense.

The unreconciled Malvolio blocks the wished-for consummation. Formerly an object of derisive laughter, he does not in his final scene continue to make the audience guffaw. His very appearance opposes the comic spirit. No mention is made of his garments, but it is unimaginable that he should be seen in the yellow stockings and cross-garters that were the clothes of his humiliation. Very likely he has changed back into the black garments in which he has first appeared. The presence of a black-clad figure, a reminder of death, creates dissonance at the end of a comedy in which all should point toward new and happy life. Malvolio's manner of speech creates an even harsher dissonance. For the first time in the play, the dramatist confers on the steward the dignity of blank verse. His references to those very indignities that have created so much malicious mirth cannot but make the audience smile—even laugh. But the laughter mixes with the pain of genuine humiliation. While it is possible for the actor to play the speech strictly for laughs, that playing that does not make the audience wince as it laughs will be an annoying departure from the speech's bias.

Fabian's confession, also ennobled by blank verse, and Feste's whimsical statement of the principles of poetic justice do not alter the steward. Indeed, Feste's conclusion that revenge comes with time inflames him further:

> Clo. . . . And thus the whirligig of time brings in his revenges.
> Mal. I'll be reveng'd on the whole pack of you. (5.1.362–64)

If the actor stresses *I'll* in his final line, he will demonstrate that the character is making his own use of Feste's doctrine. Malvolio's last line constitutes an unresolved discord.

As in *As You Like It*, the mirth is not displaced, although Malvolio's rage damages the comic triumph more than does Jaques's melancholy. *Twelfth Night* is importantly unlike *As You Like It* in that the number of truly rejoicing characters left on the stage at the end is small. In *As You Like It*, the audience sees a quadruple wedding, has the satisfaction of viewing Rosalind in women's clothes, hears Hymen's blessing, and observes that the duke and his courtiers are rejoicing with the central couples. In *Twelfth Night* only the two couples are happy. Sir Toby and Maria are offstage, and the audience's last sight of Sir Toby has not been pleasant. Of Malvolio's feelings there can be no doubt, and the feelings of the silent Antonio, who has lost Sebastian forever in the moment of finding him, must be mixed. Although the character has no lines, the situation encourages the actor to communicate silent wonder and pain. Antonio ought not to leave the stage at the play's end with the joyful couples. After a loving and farewell look to Sebastian, he might exit in a different direction, presumably to return to his proper element, the sea.

Twelfth Night does not offer at its conclusion the sense of a large, new society. The number of true celebrants is smaller than in any other comedy of Shakespeare. The joy and wonder are genuine and profound, but fragile and embattled. Comic joy exists only for the few and the fortunate. Somewhere unseen, Sir Toby nurses his wounds and Malvolio nurses his rage. Feste's final song, which serves some of the functions of an epilogue, augments the sense that comic joy is embattled and transitory. The fool sings about a slipping-down life and the grimy sides of such achieved maturity and matrimony as the play has celebrated:

> But when I came to man's estate,
> 'Gainst knaves and thieves men shut their gate,
> But when I came, alas! to wive,
> By swaggering could I never thrive.
>
> (5.1.379–85)

The song's repeated refrain is hyperbolical.[43] It doesn't rain every day, but it does rain occasionally, even on the brightest days. Feste's song, as well as returning the spectators to themselves and asking for applause, tempers the happiness by exploring its nature and durability.

In his most assured comic masterpieces, Shakespeare pursues the sort of questioning that makes for so much vexation in the darker comedies. Amid the final laughter and wonder there exists both in the festive comedies and the problem plays a sense of suffering and sadness, pain and evil. In the comedies in which suffering and evil are so much more pervasive, so much less easily contained or circumvented, such disturbance naturally cuts deeper and leaves the audience at the end to contemplate a more searchingly qualified comic triumph. In *The Tempest*, his last great play, Shakespeare continues to search the problems and paradoxes of the comic ending. Indeed, this play contains the most famous meditation on endings in imaginative litera-

ture. The speech and its surrounding action explore yet again the
problem of ending a comedy and finding the most appropriate disposition of evil in the new comic world.

It will be remembered that Prospero is presenting a wedding-masque
to Ferdinand and Miranda. During the dance following the blessings
that have been pronounced over the newly betrothed couple, the old
magician suddenly recalls that Caliban and his accomplices are coming
to kill him. In his agitation, he makes a sudden and unprepared end
to his entertainment:

> *Enter certain Reapers, properly habited; they join with the Nymphs in*
> *a graceful dance; towards the end whereof Prospero starts suddenly,*
> *and speaks; after which, to a strange, hollow, and confused noise,*
> *they heavily vanish.*
>
> Pro. *(Aside)* I had forgot that foul conspiracy
> Of the beast Caliban and his confederates
> Against my life; the minute of their plot
> Is almost come. *(To the Spirits)* Well done; avoid; no more!
>
> (4.1.SD, 139–42)

Prospero as maker of masques is here doing what Shakespeare as
maker of comedies would never do. He is creating a world from
which evil is wholly excluded. When evil intrudes upon him, taking
him unawares, he makes a sudden, confused and hollow end to his
show. Just how the dancers "heavily vanish" is a technical problem
that every production must solve. But there should be something grace-
less, awkward, and turbulent about the masquers' departure. Ferdinand
and Miranda, Prospero's audience, respond to his agitation with a
like agitation. In trying to explain to them the alarming departure
of the creatures who had been entertaining them, he utters his thoughts
about endings.

When Shakespeare makes the ending to his play in which Prospero
is a character, he does not startle, confuse, and agitate his audience.
He prepares carefully for his ending, and when it is accomplished,
he returns his spectators gracefully and gently to their own world.
As we have seen, Prospero achieves his greatest miracle when he chooses
virtue over vengeance. The choice involves both gain and loss. He
regains his humanity, but he breaks his staff, frees his spirits, and
loses his daughter in marriage. The magnitude of what he is gaining
and losing can be inferred from lines he speaks near the play's end:

> And in the morn
> I'll bring you to your ship, and so to Naples,
> Where I have hope to see the nuptial
> Of these our dear-belov'd solemnized,
> And thence retire me to my Milan, where
> Every third thought shall be my grave.
>
> (5.1.306–11)

His final decision, which forces him to give up so much, fits him for a retirement such as Lear envisions—an unburdened crawl toward death.

Not all that Prospero gets when he abjures his rough magic is joyous. He is obliged to forgive his criminal brother, and the moment of forgiveness is bitter. There is no suggestion that the wrongdoer will mend or that the forgiver has any trust in a new relationship:

> For you, most wicked sir, whom to call brother
> Would even infect my mouth, I do forgive
> Thy rankest fault—all of them; and require
> My dukedom of thee, which perforce I know
> Thou must restore.
>
> (5.1.130–34)

The joy of the play's concluding events is strangely tempered by bitterness and loss.

The simultaneous pain and wonder carries through to the last words the audience hears. Even as Prospero joyfully invites the Neapolitan lords to enter his cell, he gives Ariel a last task and wistfully sets the spirit free. Then, in the epilogue, he speaks lines that embrace both the magician giving up his powers and the actor giving up his role. Like the actor playing the king of France in *All's Well That Ends Well*, the actor playing Prospero should divest himself of ducal finery before he addresses the audience. In the play's last lines, he adverts to the pain and joy inherent in his ending:

> And my ending is despair
> Unless I be reliev'd by prayer,
> Which pierces so that it assaults
> Mercy itself, and frees all faults.
>
> (5.Ep.15–18)

When Paul Scofield delivered this speech in his 1975 performance as Prospero, we in the audience felt the joy and pain that come together in the play's last scene. We had seen that exterior and interior evil must be mastered, and we had seen also that joy and wonder, affirmation and comic triumph, can flourish even in a world where evil exists too.

The playwright maintains his artistry through the epilogue, the speech in which both magician and actor seem to leave their artistry behind. Indeed, the tetrameter couplets call attention to themselves after the blank verse of Prospero's other speeches. Unlike Prospero, Shakespeare does not suddenly banish his art and stop his show. Although the magician has released his spell, the dramatist does not release his until after the last word has been spoken. He knows how to create a tempered but enduring sense of comic triumph, enduring because tempered. So disturbing but not alarming his audience, he brings his revel to an end.

NOTES

Introduction

1. Bruno Walter, *Gustav Mahler* (London: Hamish Hamilton, 1958), p. 86.

2. Compare Bernard Shaw, "The Dying Tongue of Great Elizabeth," in *Shaw on Theatre*, ed. E. J. West (New York: Hill and Wang, 1958), p. 97; see also Christopher Durang, *The Marriage of Bette and Boo* (New York: Dramatist's Play Service, 1985), p. 84.

3. Anthony B. Dawson, "*Measure for Measure*, New Historicism, and Theatrical Power," *Shakespeare Quarterly* 39 (1988): 339.

4. Ibid.

5. Steven Urkowitz, "Five Women Eleven Ways: Changing Images of Shakespearean Characters in the Earliest Texts," in *Images of Shakespeare; Proceedings of the Third Congress of the International Shakespeare Association, 1986*, ed. Werner Habicht, D. J. Palmer, and Roger Pringle (Newark, Del.: University of Delaware Press, 1988), p. 304. Compare Ann Pasternack Slater, *Shakespeare the Director* (Sussex: The Harvester Press, 1982), pp. 26–27. Slater demonstrates that many "oblique imperatives" to the actors are embedded in the dialogue of Shakespeare's plays.

6. Clive Barnes, "A Magical *Midsummer Night's Dream*," *New York Times*, 21 January 1971, sec. 2, p. 27.

7. Robert Speaight, "Shakespeare in Britain," *Shakespeare Quarterly* 21 (1970): 448.

8. Roberta Krensky Cooper, *The American Shakespeare Theatre, Stratford, 1955–1985* (Washington, D.C.: The Folger Shakespeare Library, 1986), p. 242.

9. Benedict Nightingale, "Manhandling the Classics: or Director 10 Shakespeare 0," *New York Times*, 29 January 1984, sec. 2, p. 1.

10. Henri Bergson, *Laughter*, in *Comedy*, ed. Wylie Sypher (Garden City, N.Y.: Doubleday, 1956), pp. 66–67.

11. Maynard Mack, "Engagement and Detachment in Shakespeare's Plays," in *Essays on Shakespeare and Elizabethan Drama in Honor of Hardin Craig*, ed. Richard Hosley (Columbia: University of Missouri Press, 1962), pp. 275–96; E. A. J. Honigmann, *Shakespeare: Seven Tragedies, The Dramatist's Manipulation of Response* (London: Macmillan, 1976); Jean Howard, *Shakespeare's Art of Orchestration: Stage Technique and Audience Response* (Champaign: University of Illinois Press, 1984).

12. Sir Philip Sidney, *An Apology for Poetry*, in *Elizabethan Critical Essays*, ed. G. Gregory Smith (Oxford: Oxford University Press, 1904), p. 199.

13. Sidney, *Apology*, pp. 151–52.

14. M. C. Bradbrook, *The Growth and Structure of Elizabethan Comedy* (1955; reprint, London: Chatto and Windus, 1973), pp. 31–32. The 1973 reprint includes a useful commentary on Peter Brook's production of *A Midsummer Night's Dream*, pp. 210–12.

15. Sidney, *Apology*, pp. 199–200.

Chapter 1. Laughter

1. *The Two Gentlemen of Verona*, 3.1.372. All citations to Shakespeare refer to *William Shakespeare, The Complete Works*, ed. Peter Alexander (London: Collins, 1971).

2. Harley Granville-Barker, *Prefaces to Shakespeare*, vol. 2 (Princeton: Princeton University Press, 1946), p. 143. Granville-Barker's invaluable prefaces appeared serially from 1927 to 1935. The 1946 reissue contains commentary by Muriel St. Clare Byrne.

3. This is a commonplace among theorists of laughter, whose most authoritative exponents are Thomas Hobbes, Henri Bergson, and Sigmund Freud, as well as Sidney.

4. Compare Joan Hartwig, "Cloten, Autolycus and Caliban: Bearers of Parodic Burdens," in *Shakespeare's Romances Reconsidered*, ed. Carol McGinnis Kay and Henry E. Jacobs (Lincoln: University of Nebraska Press, 1978), pp. 94–96.

5. Robert Speaight, "Shakespeare in Britain," *Shakespeare Quarterly* 20 (1969): 437–38. Compare M. St. Clare Byrne, who describes the Olivia in a 1957 Peter Hall production as a "kittenish typist on holiday" ("The Shakespeare Season at the Old Vic, 1957–58 and Stratford-upon-Avon, 1958," *Shakespeare Quarterly* 9 [1958]: 403–4).

6. Berners W. Jackson, "Shakespeare at Stratford, Ontario, 1975," *Shakespeare Quarterly* 27 (1976): 27–28.

7. Stanley Wells, "Shakespeare Performances in London and Stratford-upon-Avon, 1986–7," *Shakespeare Survey* 41 (1988): 166.

8. St. Clare Byrne, "The Shakespeare Season at the Old Vic," *Shakespeare Quarterly* 9 (1958): 403–4.

9. This scene is perhaps based on an actual rebuke that was given to a party of primero players, including Shakespeare's friend and patron, the Earl of Southampton, whose noise may have disturbed the queen. See Geoffrey Bullough, ed. *Narrative and Dramatic Sources of Shakespeare* (New York: Columbia University Press, 1958–1975), 2:284.

10. C. L. Barber, *Shakespeare's Festive Comedy: A Study of Dramatic Form and Its Relation to Social Custom* (Princeton: Princeton University Press, 1972), p. 6.

11. Speaight, "Shakespeare in Britain," *Shakespeare Quarterly* 20 (1969): 438 and Arnold Edinborough, "Canada's Permanent Elizabethan Theatre," *Shakespeare Quarterly* 8 (1957): 555.

12. Roberta Krensky Cooper, *The American Shakespeare Theatre*, p. 225.

13. Jackson, "Stratford, Ontario, 1975," *Shakespeare Quarterly* 27 (1976): 28.

14. Ralph Berry, "Stratford Festival Canada," *Shakespeare Quarterly* 32 (1981): 180.

15. Eric Bentley, *The Life of the Drama* (New York: Atheneum, 1964), p. 312.

16. Wells, "Shakespeare Performances," p. 167. Compare Ralph Berry, "*Twelfth Night:* The Experience of the Audience," *Shakespeare Survey* 34 (1981): 118.

17. See J. L. Styan, *Shakespeare's Stagecraft* (Cambridge: Cambridge University Press, 1967), pp. 1–3. Compare Ann Pasternak Slater, *Shakespeare the Director*, pp. 26–27.

18. C. Walter Hodges, *The Globe Restored* (London: Ernest Benn, 1953), p. 32.

19. Jonson plays with a similar idea and bit of staging in the last act of *The Devil Is An Ass*.

20. See below, pp. 169–71.

21. See Bergson, *Laughter*, pp. 170–71. The work on laughter by psychologists and their disciples from Freud to Norman Holland may lead some to dismiss any discussion of Bergson's essay as engagement in an ancient controversy. Although I acknowledge Bergson's limitations, my intention is to suggest his real usefulness as a guide to the kinds of laughter in Shakespeare's comedies.

22. Bergson, *Laughter*, pp. 67–68. 102–5.

23. Ibid., p. 63.

24. Ibid., p. 188.

25. Ibid.

26. Ibid., pp. 188–89.

27. L. C. Knights, "Notes on Comedy," in *Comedy, Meaning and Form*, ed. Robert W. Corrigan (San Francisco: Chandler, 1965), pp. 181–82. First published in *The Importance of Scrutiny*, ed. Eric Bentley (New York: New York University Press, 1964).

28. Bergson, *Laughter*, pp. 159, 166.

29. George Meredith, "An Essay on Comedy," in Sypher, p. 43, and Suzanne Langer, "The Comic Rhythm," in Corrigan, pp. 133–34. The essay is taken from Langer's *Feeling and Form* (New York: Scribner, 1953), pp. 326–59.

30. Bergson, *Laughter*, p. 63.

31. Ibid., pp. 93–94.

32. Robert Weimann, *Shakespeare and the Popular Tradition in the Theater: Studies in the Social Dimension of Dramatic Form and Function* (Baltimore: Johns Hopkins University Press, 1978), p. 258.

33. Bentley, *The Life of the Drama*, pp. 241–42.

34. Shakespeare seems to have been taken by these images. See *As You Like It*, 2.7.148, and *The Tempest*, 5.1.102.

35. John Russell Brown, "The Presentation of Comedy: The First Ten Plays," in *Shakespearian Comedy*, ed. John Russell Brown and Bernard Harris, Stratford-upon-Avon Studies, vol. 14 (London: Edward Arnold, 1972), p. 10.

36. Aldous Huxley, "Tragedy and the Whole Truth," in *Collected Essays* (New York: Harper and Brothers, 1958), pp. 96–97.

37. Compare the New Arden Edition, ed. Clifford Leech (London: Methuen, 1969), p. xxxv. See also Bullough, *Narrative and Dramatic Sources*, 1:203.

38. Robert Y. Turner, *Shakespeare's Apprenticeship* (Chicago: University of Chicago Press, 1974), pp. 181–83.

39. Joseph H. Summers, *Dreams of Love and Power: Essays on Shakespeare* (Oxford: Oxford University Press, 1985), p. 110.

40. Compare Roger Warren, "Shakespeare in Stratford and London, 1982," *Shakespeare Quarterly* 34 (1983): 85.

41. Northrop Frye, *Anatomy of Criticism* (Princeton: Princeton University Press, 1957), p. 179.

42. Bullough, *Narrative and Dramatic Sources*, 1:13–14, 39.

43. David Knight, "*The Comedy of Errors*—Not Just a Silly Play," *On-Stage Studies* 8 (1984): 27–28.

44. Richard David, "Stratford 1954," *Shakespeare Quarterly* 5 (1954): 386.

45. Bullough, *Narrative and Dramatic Sources*, 1:57.

46. Ibid., 1:63.

47. Ibid., 1:88.

48. Mack, "Engagement and Detachment," p. 293.

49. Bernard Beckerman, *Dynamics of Drama: Theory and Method of Analysis* (New York: Knopf, 1970), p. 14.

50. J. C. Trewin, *Shakespeare on the English Stage: 1900–1964* (London: Barrie and Rockliff, 1964), pp. 15–16. Trewin notes that a piece of hackwork like *The Merry Wives of Windsor* remained popular in the theater while plays like *Troilus and Cressida* and *The Winter's Tale* were seldom performed. Since 1964 the balance has shifted somewhat. Compare Jeanne Addison Roberts, *Shakespeare's English Comedy:* The Merry Wives of Windsor *in Context* (Lincoln: University of Nebraska Press, 1979), p. xi; pp. 84–118.

51. Allardyce Nicoll, *The World of Harlequin: A Critical Study of the Comedia del'Arte* (Cambridge: Cambridge University Press, 1963), pp. 19–23.

52. Langer, "The Comic Rhythm," p. 133.

53. Francis Toye, *Giuseppe Verdi: His Life and Works* (New York: Vintage Books, 1959), p. 203. First published by Knopf, 1931.

Chapter 2. Pain

1. Robert Speaight, "Shakespeare in Britain," *Shakespeare Quarterly* 19 (1968): 372.

2. The Oxford English Dictionary illustrates with Shakespearean usages the following definitions: "agreement, accord, harmony, consonance, concord; agreement in qualities, likeness, conformity, correspondence" and "conformity of feelings, inclinations, or temperament, which makes persons agreeable to each other; community of feeling; harmony of disposition."

3. Una Ellis-Fermor, *Shakespeare the Dramatist and Other Papers* (London: Methuen, 1961), p. 37.

4. R. S. Crane, *The Languages of Criticism and the Structure of Poetry* (Toronto: University of Toronto Press, 1953), p. 171.

5. The betrayal of love and friendship is a recurring theme in the plays and sonnets. Compare J. B. Leishman, *Themes and Variations in Shakespeare's Sonnets* (Oxford: Hutchinson and Co. 1963), pp. 50–52, 103–7.

6. Bullough, *Narrative and Dramatic Sources,* 1:206.

7. Ibid., 8:14.

8. Roberta Krensky Cooper, *The American Shakespeare Theatre,* p. 159.

9. Swinburne remarks, "I could never reconcile my instincts to Helena." See Algernon Charles Swinburne, *A Study of Shakespeare* (London: Chatto and Windus, 1909), p. 147. But compare G. Wilson Knight, *The Sovereign Flower* (London: Methuen, 1958), p. 95.

10. A. P. Riemer, *Antic Fables: Patterns of Evasion in Shakespeare's Comedies* (New York: St. Martin's Press, 1980), pp. 44–45.

11. Cooper, *The American Shakespeare Theatre,* p. 159.

12. Irving Wardle, "Mingled Yarn, Good and Bad," *Times* (London), 18 November 1981, p. 13.

13. See below, pp. 159–66.

14. Cressida is his only other false lover, but her peculiar combination of weakness, calculation, and sensuality does not come suddenly into being; it is revealed in various ways through all her scenes.

15. See Harold Jenkins, "Shakespeare's *Twelfth Night,*" in *Shakespeare: The Comedies,* ed. Kenneth Muir, Twentieth Century Views (Englewood Cliffs, N.J.: Prentice-Hall, 1964), pp. 73–75. First published as Rice Institute Pamphlet 45, 1959.

16. Bullough, *Narrative and Dramatic Sources,* 2:272.

17. A. C. Sprague, *Shakespeare and the Actors, The Stage Business in His Plays: 1660–1905* Cambridge: Harvard University Press, 1944), pp. 22–23.

18. Elmer Edgar Stoll, *Shakespeare Studies: Historical and Comparative in Method* (New York: Frederick Ungar, 1960), pp. 263–68. Often reprinted, this seminal study was first published by Macmillan in 1927. See also Anthony Hecht, *Obbligati: Essays in Criticism* (New York: Atheneum, 1986), pp. 147–54; and Norman Rabkin, *Shakespeare and the Problem of Meaning* (Chicago: University of Chicago Press, 1981), pp. 5–9. Rabkin describes the interpretive controversies that the play engenders and develops his argument that simultaneous, seemingly contradictory responses may be evoked in audiences and readers.

19. Berners W. Jackson, "Stratford Festival Canada," *Shakespeare Quarterly* 28 (1977): 202.

20. T. S. Eliot, *Essays on Elizabethan Drama* (New York: Harcourt Brace and Co., 1932), p. 62.

21. A. P. Rossiter, *Angel with Horns and Other Shakespeare Lectures* (Plymouth, England: Longmans, 1962), p. 13.

22. Ann Jennalie Cook, "*The Merchant of Venice* at the Other Place," *Shakespeare Quarterly* 30 (1979): 159.

23. Derek Cohen, *Shakespearean Motives* (New York: St. Martin's Press, 1988), p. 118. But compare Northrop Frye, *A Natural Perspective: The Development of Shakespearean Comedy and Romance* (New York: Columbia University Press, 1965), pp. 131–32, and Bentley, *The Life of the Drama*, pp. 242–43.

24. Margaret Webster, *Shakespeare Without Tears* (New York: McGraw Hill, 1942), pp. 70–72.

25. Alan C. Dessen, "Oregon Shakespearean Festival," *Shakespeare Quarterly* 29 (1978): 280.

26. Arnold Edinborough, "Shakespeare Confirmed: At Canadian Stratford," *Shakespeare Quarterly* 6 (1955): 435.

27. Alice Griffin, "New York Season: 1961–1962," *Shakespeare Quarterly* 13 (1962): 552.

28. Cooper, *The American Shakespeare Theatre*, p. 133.

29. Cook, "*The Merchant of Venice*," p. 159.

30. Jackson, "Stratford Festival Canada," *Shakespeare Quarterly* 28 (1977): 202–3.

31. Cooper, *The American Shakespeare Theatre*, p. 47.

32. Wells, "Shakespeare Performances," p. 163. Compare John Russell Brown, "The Realization of Shylock: A Theatrical Criticism," in *Early Shakespeare*, ed. John Russell Brown and Bernard Harris, Stratford-upon-Avon Studies, vol. 3 (London: Edward Arnold, 1961), p. 188. See also Sprague, *Shakespeare and the Actors*, pp. 21–22.

33. Compare Hecht, *Obbligati*, p. 190–92.

34. Kenneth Tynan, *Tynan on Theatre* (London: Penguin, 1964), p. 11.

35. L. G. Salingar, *Shakespeare and the Traditions of Comedy* (Cambridge: Cambridge University Press, 1974), pp. 299–300, 322.

36. The multiplicity of sources makes this distinction less cut and dried than it might appear. George Whetstone is concerned in the birth of *Measure for Measure*, and Painter's version of Boccaccio's tale claims an interest in *All's Well That Ends Well*. See Bullough, *Narrative and Dramatic Sources*, 2:389, 442.

37. Bernard Weinberg, *A History of Literary Criticism in the Italian Renaissance*, vol. 2 (Chicago: University of Chicago Press, 1961), 1074–1105.

38. Richard P. Wheeler, *Shakespeare's Development and the Problem Comedies:*

Turn and Counterturn (Berkeley: University of California Press, 1981), pp. 1–16, 32–34; Harriet Hawkins, *Likenesses of Truth in Elizabethan and Restoration Drama* (Oxford: Oxford University Press, 1972), pp. 52–53.

39. Rossiter, *Angel with Horns*, p. 75.

40. Paul Scofield, who played Don Pedro in a production in which John Gielgud played Benedick and Margaret Leighton played Beatrice, is a notable exception. See Trewin, *Shakespeare on the English Stage*, p. 220.

41. Walter Kerr, "A *Much Ado* with a Bit More Ado Than It Needs," *New York Times*, 21 October 1984, sec. 2, p. 3.

42. Sprague, *Shakespeare and the Actors*, pp. 55–56.

43. 1.1.138–251; 2.1.162–232; 2.3.33–200; 3.2.1–66; 5.1.110–85.

44. 1.1.1–78; 2.1.1–70; 3.1.24–106; 3.4.34–88.

45. Roger Warren, "Shakespeare in Stratford and London, 1982," *Shakespeare Quarterly* 34 (1983): 83.

46. Frank Rich, "The Royal Shakespeare's *Much Ado*," *New York Times*, 15 October 1984, sec. 3, p. 12.

47. Kerr, "A *Much Ado*," sec. 2, p. 3.

48. Robert Speaight, "Shakespeare in Britain," *Shakespeare Quarterly* 22 (1971): 442.

49. Trewin, *Shakespeare on the English Stage*, p. 220, and St. Clare Byrne, "The Shakespeare Season at the Old Vic," p. 409.

50. David Richman, "Dramatic Symbiosis in *Much Ado About Nothing*," *On-Stage Studies* 8 (1984): 49–50.

51. Alan S. Downer, "A Comparison of Two Stagings: Avon and London," *Shakespeare Quarterly* 6 (1955): 429.

52. Mel Gussow, "*Much Ado* by the Yale Rep," *New York Times*, 20 March 1983, sec. 1, p. 54.

53. Warren, "Shakespeare in Stratford and London," p. 83.

54. See below, pp. 134–37.

55. Cooper, *The American Shakespeare Theatre*, p. 48.

56. Robert Speaight, "Shakespeare in Britain," *Shakespeare Quarterly* 28 (1977): 186.

57. St. Clare Byrne, "The Shakespeare Season at the Old Vic, 1957–58," *Shakespeare Quarterly* 9 (1958): 409.

58. Robert Speaight, "Shakespeare in Britain," *Shakespeare Quarterly* 16 (1965): 313.

59. Salingar, *Shakespeare and the Traditions of Comedy*, p. 307.

60. Compare the New Arden Edition, ed. J. W. Lever (London: Methuen, 1965), pp. lvi–lix.

61. Anthony B. Dawson, "Much Ado about Signifying," *Studies in English Literature* 22 (1982): 211–21.

62. Riemer, *Antic Fables*, p. 40.

63. Dessen, "Oregon Shakespearean Festival," p. 279.

64. Arnold Edinborough, "The Director's Role at Canada's Stratford," *Shakespeare Quarterly* 20 (1969): 444.

65. Dessen, "Oregon Shakespearean Festival," p. 279.

66. Edinborough, "The Director's Role at Canada's Stratford," pp. 444–45, and Lewis Funk, "Strange Comedy Done Uncertainly in Canada," *New York Times*, 13 June 1969, p. 41.

67. Berners W. Jackson, "Shakespeare at Stratford, Ontario, 1975," *Shakespeare Quarterly* 27 (1976): 30.

68. J. C. Trewin, "Shakespeare in Britain," *Shakespeare Quarterly* 29 (1978): 219.

69. Dawson, "*Measure for Measure*," p. 339.

70. See Robert Ornstein, "Historical Criticism and the Interpretation of Shakespeare," *Shakespeare Quarterly* 10 (1959): 3–9; and Clifford Leech, "The Meaning of *Measure for Measure*," *Shakespeare Survey* 3 (1950): 66–73, and Wheeler, *Shakespeare's Development*, pp. 13–16, 134–42.

71. Joseph H. Summers, "The Masks of *Twelfth Night*," in *Shakespeare, Modern Essays in Criticism*, ed. Leonard F. Dean (New York: Oxford University Press, 1967), pp. 134–35. (Originally appeared in *The University Review* 22 [Autumn 1955]: 25–32.)

72. Bentley, *The Life of the Drama*, pp. 250–51.

Chapter 3. Wonder

1. *Much Ado About Nothing*, 1.1.18–19.

2. J. V. Cunningham, *Woe or Wonder: The Emotional Effect of Shakespearean Tragedy* (Chicago: The Swallow Press, 1964), p. 77.

3. Eric Bentley, Introduction to *Naked Masks, Five Plays by Luigi Pirandello*, ed. Bentley (New York: E. P. Dutton, 1952), p. ix.

4. Berners W. Jackson, "Shakespeare at Stratford, Ontario, 1975," *Shakespeare Quarterly* 27 (1976): 28.

5. 3.4.363–67.

6. T. W. Baldwin, *William Shakespeare's Small Latin and Lesse Greeke*, vol. 2 (Urbana: University of Illinois Press, 1944), 69–238; Virgil K. Whitaker, *Shakespeare's Use of Learning: An Inquiry Into the Growth of His Mind and Art* (San Marino, Calif.: Huntington Library, 1953), pp. 14–44.

7. Cunningham, *Woe or Wonder*, pp. 62–64.

8. Sidney, *Apology*, p. 199.

9. Ben Jonson, "To The Memory Of My Beloved Master William Shakespeare," in *Ben Jonson*, ed. C. H. Herford and Percy and Evelyn Simpson (Oxford: Clarendon Press, 1925–1952), vol. 8, lines 17–18.

10. John Milton, "On Shakespeare, 1630," in *John Milton: Complete Poems and Major Prose*, ed. Merritt Y. Hughes (New York: Odyssey Press, 1957), lines 7–8.

11. The criticisms of Hawkins and Wheeler to which I have referred in the previous chapter are in the tradition of censures by Jonson, Rymer, and even Dryden, in his preface to *Troilus and Cressida*. Milton, whose praise of Shakespeare I have quoted, implicitly censures him in the note prefixed to *Samson Agonistes*, referring to "the poet's error of intermixing comic stuff with tragic sadness and gravity; or by introducing trivial and vulgar persons which by all judicious hath been counted absurd; and brought in without discretion, corruptly to gratify the people" (in the Hughes edition, p. 550).

12. Samuel Johnson, "Preface to Shakespeare," in *The Yale Edition of the Works of Samuel Johnson*, vol. 7, ed. Arthur Sherbo (New Haven: Yale University Press, 1968), pp. 66–67.

13. F. M. Cornford, *The Origins of Attic Comedy* (Cambridge: Cambridge University Press, 1934), pp. 15–16. The book was first published in 1914. Cornford also discusses romantic comedy's debt to Euripides.

14. Bullough, *Narrative and Dramatic Sources*, 1:8–10, 40, 50.

182   LAUGHTER, PAIN, AND WONDER

15. In addition to the sources for *The Comedy of Errors,* one can cite Montemayor's romance and Scala's comedia scenario, which are both sources to *The Two Gentlemen of Verona,* the farce *Gl'Ingannati* and Riche's romantic treatment of similar events, both sources for *Twelfth Night,* and Greene's *Pandosto* and his jests of cony-catching, which contribute to *The Winter's Tale.* See Bullough, *Narrative and Dramatic Sources,* 1:225, 256; 2:286, 344; 8:156, 214.

16. Harold Brooks, "Themes and Structure in *The Comedy of Errors,*" in Brown and Harris, eds., *Early Shakespeare,* p. 64.

17. Bullough, *Narrative and Dramatic Sources,* 2:269.

18. C. S. Lewis, *Surprised by Joy: The Shape of My Early Life* (New York: Harcourt Brace and Co., 1955), p. 15.

19. Bullough, *Narrative and Dramatic Sources,* 1:203.

20. See W. Robertson Davies, *Shakespeare's Boy Actors* (London: J. M. Dent, 1939), pp. 168–70, and Gary Jay Williams, "A Dance for Our Disbeliefs: The Current *A Midsummer Night's Dream* of the RSC," *Theatre* 13, no. 3 (Summer/Fall 1982): 61. Compare Bradbrook, *The Growth and Structure of Elizabethan Comedy,* pp. 210–12; Sprague, *Shakespeare and the Actors,* pp. 50–55; and Trewin, *Shakespeare on the English Stage,* pp. 56–59.

21. Peter Brook, *The Empty Space* (London: McGibbon and Kee, 1968), p. 89.

22. Ibid.

23. Margaret Croyden, "A Hidden Dream of Sex and Love," *New York Times,* 17 January 1971, sec. 2, p. 15.

24. Robert Speaight, "Shakespeare in Britain," *Shakespeare Quarterly* 21 (1970): 448.

24. Frye, *A Natural Perspective,* pp. 105–6. The passage Bottom departs from is: "Eye hath not seen, nor ear heard: neither hath entered into the heart of Man the things which God hath prepared."

26. Cunningham, *Woe or Wonder,* pp. 77–78.

27. R. W. Dent, "Imagination in *A Midsummer Night's Dream,*" in *Shakespeare: 400,* ed. J. B. McManaway (New York: Holt, Rinehart and Winston, 1964); Norman Rabkin, *Shakespeare and the Common Understanding* (New York: The Free Press, 1967), pp. 203–4.

28. John Russell Brown, *Shakespeare's Dramatic Style* (London: Heineman, 1970), pp. 96–103.

29. Irving Wardle, "The Answer Lies in the Soil," *Times* (London), 23 July 1981, p. 13.

30. St. Clare Byrne, "The Shakespeare Season at the Old Vic, 1956–57 and Stratford-upon-Avon, 1957," *Shakespeare Quarterly* 8 (1957): 467.

31. Jack J. Jorgens, "New York Shakespeare Festival, 1973," *Shakespeare Quarterly* 24 (1973): 424.

32. E. M. Nuttall, "Jaques and Caliban: Two Unassimilable Men," in Brown and Harris, eds., *Shakespearian Comedy,* pp. 234–35.

33. Wardle, "The Answer Lies in the Soil," p. 13.

34. Frye, *Anatomy of Criticism,* p. 171.

35. The scenes are powerful enough to have inspired the finest of T. S. Eliot's "Ariel Poems."

36. John Barber, "Simplicity Works in Realistic *Pericles,*" *Times* (London), 5 April 1979, p. 15.

37. Compare Rabkin, *Shakespeare and the Common Understanding,* pp. 194–200, 211-16.

38. No stage direction is given to this effect, but the action is referred to in

a subsequent speech. See 5.1.99. George Wilkins's narrative, which may be based on the play, describes in some detail the old man's assault on his daughter. See Bullough, *Narrative and Dramatic Sources*, 6:543–44.

39. Robert Speaight, "Shakespeare in Britain," *Shakespeare Quarterly* 20 (1969): 435.

40. *King Lear*, 5.3.198.

41. Speaight, "Shakespeare in Britain," p. 435.

42. Berners W. Jackson, "Shakespeare at Stratford Ontario," *Shakespeare Quarterly* 24 (1973): 408.

43. Granville-Barker, *Prefaces to Shakespeare*, vol. 2, pp. 77–83. Compare Rabkin, *Shakespeare and the Common Understanding*, p. 210–13. Rabkin extends Granville-Barker's line of thought and argues that the play, like *A Midsummer Night's Dream*, is about the act of imagination, the acts of play making and play watching.

44. Summers, *Dreams of Love and Power*, pp. 39–42.

45. Christopher Murray, "Shakespeare at the Abbey," *Shakespeare Quarterly* 32 (1981): 175.

46. These propositions were given a suggestive treatment in "Shakespeare's Notebook," an unpublished lecture delivered by Virgil K. Whitaker at Stanford University in 1972.

47. Ralph Berry, "Stratford Festival Canada," *Shakespeare Quarterly* 30 (1979): 169.

48. Speaight, "Shakespeare in Britain," *Shakespeare Quarterly* 20 (1969): 436.

49. Berry, "Stratford Festival Canada," *Shakespeare Quarterly* 30 (1979): 169.

50. Robert Speaight, "Shakespeare in Britain, 1975," *Shakespeare Quarterly* 27 (1976): 15.

51. Summers, "The Masks of *Twelfth Night*," pp. 189–90. My views on Prospero and on *The Tempest* in general were also influenced by a production in which I acted at Stanford University, directed by Michael Hackett, May 1975.

52. Compare Barbara A. Mowat, *The Dramaturgy of Shakespeare's Romances* (Athens: University of Georgia Press, 1976), pp. 106–8. See also Gerald M. Berkowitz, "Shakespeare at the 1988 Edinburgh Festival," *Shakespeare Quarterly* 40 (1989): 77.

53. St. Clare Byrne, "The Shakespeare Season at the Old Vic, 1956–57," *Shakespeare Quarterly* 8 (1957): 488.

54. Robert Smallwood, "Stratford-upon-Avon, 1988," *Shakespeare Quarterly* 40 (1989): 87.

55. Eric Walter White, *Benjamin Britten: His Life and Operas* (Berkeley: University of California Press, 1970), p. 85. Reprinted by permission.

Chapter 4. Moods

1. Johnson, "Preface to Shakespeare," vol. 7, p. 68.

2. Shakespeare collaborated with Fletcher on this play, so he may not himself have written the prologue. Yet he almost certainly gave it his consent and approbation. See Cyrus Hoy, "The Shares of Fletcher and His Collaborators in the Beaumont and Fletcher Canon, VII," *Studies in Bibliography* 15 (1962): 79–80.

3. Madeleine Doran, *Endeavors of Art: A Study of Form in Elizabethan Drama* (Madison: University of Wisconsin Press, 1963), pp. 102–8.

4. Many prologues and inductions of this period propose bargains. The most

elaborate contract is put forth by Ben Jonson in the induction to *Bartholomew Fair*.

5. T. S. Eliot, "East Coker," in *The Complete Poems and Plays, 1909–1950* (New York: Harcourt Brace and Co., 1952), p. 128.

6. W. B. Yeats, *Essays and Introductions* (New York: Macmillan, 1961), p. 195; Richard Ellman, *The Identity of Yeats* (London: Macmillan, 1954), p. 57.

7. Susan Snyder, *The Comic Matrix in Shakespeare's Tragedies* (Princeton: Princeton University Press, 1979), p. 59.

8. See Frank Kermode, *The Sense of an Ending: Studies in the Theory of Fiction* (New York: Oxford University Press, 1966), p. 52; and Frye, *A Natural Perspective*, pp. 11–12.

9. H. C. Colles, ed., *Grove's Dictionary of Music and Musicians*, 3rd ed. (London: Macmillan, 1927).

10. See the note on this line in the New Arden Edition, ed. A. R. Humphreys (London: Methuen, 1966).

11. Colles, ed., *Grove's Dictionary*.

12. St. Clare Byrne, "The Shakespeare Season at the Old Vic, 1957–58 and Stratford-upon-Avon, 1958," *Shakespeare Quarterly* 9 (1958): 404.

13. Joseph Verner Reed, Letter to "Drama Mailbag," *New York Times*, 28 February 1971, sec. 2, p. 7.

14. In the opera, the fairy queen's name is spelled Tytania.

15. 3.4.1–41.

16. Ralph Berry, "Stratford Festival Canada," *Shakespeare Quarterly* 29 (1978): 226.

17. Compare John Russell Brown, "Theatrical Research and the Criticism of Shakespeare and His Contemporaries," *Shakespeare Quarterly* 13 (1962): pp. 451–53. See also Trewin, *Shakespeare on the English Stage*, pp. 130, 220.

18. St. Clare Byrne, "The Shakespeare Season at the Old Vic, 1957–58," *Shakespeare Quarterly* 9 (1958): 409.

19. Summers, *Dreams of Love and Power*, p. 42. Like Paulina, Lucio "comically desacrilizes the language of royal power and civil judgment by refusing to take it seriously."

20. Brook, *The Empty Space*, p. 89.

21. Dessen, "Oregon Shakespearean Festival," p. 280.

22. Alice Venezky, "The 1950 Season at Stratford-upon-Avon," *Shakespeare Quarterly* 2 (1951): 75.

23. Cooper, *The American Shakespeare Theatre*, p. 47.

24. Ibid., p. 132.

25. Stanley Wells, "Shakespeare Performances," p. 163.

Chapter 5. Endings

1. See Kermode, *The Sense of an Ending*, p. 52 and Frye, *A Natural Perspective*, pp. 11–12.

2. *A Midsummer Night's Dream*, 5.1.110–11.

3. For an amusing survey of critical disapprobation, see Riemer, *Antic Fables*, pp. 4–7, 23–24.

4. Johnson, "Preface to Shakespeare," vol. 7, pp. 71–72. Although I allude to a number of writings on Shakespeare's endings produced during recent years, I maintain that Johnson's are still the most important strictures. It is with his ghost that anyone who writes on this subject must wrestle.

5. Johnson, "Preface to Shakespeare," vol. 7, p. 400.

6. *Measure for Measure*, 5.1.437.

7. *The Winter's Tale*, 4.1.19.

8. Bullough, *Narrative and Dramatic Sources*, 1:203. He compares himself to the swooning Julia in thinking Valentine's generosity quixotic.

9. Webster, *Shakespeare Without Tears*, pp. 143–44.

10. St. Clare Byrne, "The Shakespeare Season at the Old Vic, 1956–57 and Stratford-upon-Avon, 1957," *Shakespeare Quarterly* 8 (1957): 466.

11. Ibid.

12. Jackson, "Shakespeare at Stratford, Ontario, 1975," *Shakespeare Quarterly* 27 (1976): 26.

13. See above, pp. 96–97.

14. St. Clare Byrne, "The Shakespeare Season at the Old Vic, 1956–57," *Shakespeare Quarterly* 8 (1957): 466.

15. The dating of the early comedies is so uncertain that no argument can be securely based on it. See the New Arden Edition of *Love's Labour's Lost*, ed. Richard David (London: Methuen, 1960), pp. xxvi–xxxii, and Alfred Harbage, *Shakespeare Without Words and Other Essays* (Cambridge: Harvard University Press, 1972), pp. 118–21.

16. See 2.1.91–93 and 4.1.21–35.

17. Compare Harley Granville-Barker, *Prefaces to Shakespeare*, First Series (London: Sidgwick and Jackson, 1927), p. 45. Granville-Barker argues that the laughter at the nine worthies probably seemed less caddish to its original audience. Even so, the lords' conduct is censured both by the ladies and by the course of the play's events. In the comparable sequence in *A Midsummer Night's Dream*, the audience does not perceive such plain malice or feel such genuine discomfort.

18. J. C. Trewin, "Shakespeare in Britain," *Shakespeare Quarterly* 30 (1979): 153.

19. Robert Speaight, "Shakespeare in Britain," *Shakespeare Quarterly* 19 (1968): 372.

20. Ralph Berry, "Stratford Festival Canada," *Shakespeare Quarterly* 31 (1980): 174.

21. Frye, *A Natural Perspective*, pp. 117–18. Compare Cyrus Hoy, *The Hyacinth Room: An Investigation Into the Nature of Comedy, Tragedy, and Tragicomedy* (New York: Knopf, 1964), pp. 37–38, and Rabkin, *Shakespeare and the Common Understanding*, pp. 255–56. For an alternate view, see Riemer, *Antic Fables*, pp. 23–24.

22. See the description of this production in Summers, *Dreams of Love and Power*, p. 119.

23. Unsigned review, *Times* (London), 10 March 1950, p. 10.

24. Robert Speaight, "Shakespeare in Britain," *Shakespeare Quarterly* 21 (1970): 444.

25. Jackson, "Shakespeare at Stratford, Ontario, 1975," *Shakespeare Quarterly* 27 (1976): 29.

26. Johnson, "Preface to Shakespeare," vol. 7, p. 400.

27. So powerful are the hope, restoration, and renewal springing from the continuing lives of Perdita and Hermione that the audience is willing to rejoice even though Mamillius and Antigonus are unreclaimable victims of Leontes' destructive passion.

28. Frye, *A Natural Perspective*, p. 12.

29. Ibid., pp. 42–44.

30. Frank Rich, "The Royal Shakespeare *All's Well That Ends Well*," *New York Times*, 14 April 1983, sec. 3, p. 15.

31. St. Clare Byrne, "The Shakespeare Season at the Old Vic, 1958–59 and Stratford-upon-Avon, 1959," *Shakespeare Quarterly* 10 (1959): 555.

32. Benedict Nightingale, "Has *All's Well* Escaped Its Past?" *New York Times*, 10 April 1983, sec. 2, p. 1.

33. Ian Donaldson, "*All's Well That Ends Well:* Shakespeare's Play of Endings," *Essays in Criticism* 27 (1977): 34–55.

34. St. Clare Byrne, "The Shakespeare Season at the Old Vic, 1958–59," *Shakespeare Quarterly* 10 (1959): 556–57.

35. Ibid., p. 555.

36. Roger Warren, "Shakespeare at Stratford and London, 1982," *Shakespeare Quarterly* 34 (1983): 79–80.

37. Johnson, "Preface to Shakespeare," vol. 7, p. 403.

38. Janet Hitchman, *Such a Strange Lady, A Biography of Dorothy L. Sayers* (New York: Harper and Row, 1975), p. 145.

39. Johnson, "Preface to Shakespeare," vol. 7, p. 265.

40. Weimann, *Shakespeare and the Popular Tradition in the Theater*, pp. 75–76, 235.

41. Compare Ann Barton, "*As You Like It* and *Twelfth Night:* Shakespeare's Sense of an Ending," in Brown and Harris, eds., *Shakespearian Comedy*, pp. 163–69, 173–79.

42. See above, pp. 87–88.

43. Summers, "The Masks of *Twelfth Night*," p. 142.

BIBLIOGRAPHY

Baldwin, T. W. *William Shakespeare's Small Latin and Lesse Greeke*. Urbana: University of Illinois Press, 1944.

Barber, C. L. *Shakespeare's Festive Comedy: A Study of Dramatic Form and Its Relation to Social Custom*. Princeton: Princeton University Press, 1972.

Barber, John. "Simplicity Works in Realistic *Pericles*." *Times* (London), 5 April 1979, p. 15.

Barnes, Clive. "A Magical *Midsummer Night's Dream*." *New York Times*, 21 January 1971, sec. 2, p. 27.

Barton, John. *Playing Shakespeare*. London: Methuen, 1984.

Beckerman, Bernard. *Dynamics of Drama: Theory and Method of Analysis*. New York: Knopf, 1970.

Bentley, Eric. *The Life of the Drama*. New York: Atheneum, 1964.

——————, ed. *Naked Masks, Five Plays by Luigi Pirandello*. New York: E. P. Dutton, 1952.

Bergson, Henri. "Laughter." In *Comedy*, edited by Wylie Sypher, 61–192. Garden City, N.Y.: Doubleday, 1956.

Berkowitz, Gerald M. "Shakespeare at the 1988 Edinburgh Festival." *Shakespeare Quarterly* 40 (1989): 75–83.

Berry, Ralph. "Stratford Festival Canada." *Shakespeare Quarterly* 29 (1978): 222–25.

——————. "Stratford Festival Canada." *Shakespeare Quarterly* 30 (1979): 167–76.

——————. "Stratford Festival Canada." *Shakespeare Quarterly* 31 (1980): 167–76.

——————. "Stratford Festival Canada." *Shakespeare Quarterly* 32 (1981): 176–80.

——————. "*Twelfth Night:* The Experience of the Audience." *Shakespeare Survey* 34 (1981): 111–19.

Bradbrook, M. C. *The Growth and Structure of Elizabethan Comedy*. London: Chatto and Windus, 1973.

Brook, Peter. *The Empty Space*. London: McGibbon and Kee, 1968.

Brown, John Russell. *Shakespeare in Performance*. London: Edward Arnold, 1966.

——————. *Shakespeare's Dramatic Style*. London: Heinemann, 1970.

——————. "Theatrical Research and the Criticism of Shakespeare and His Contemporaries." *Shakespeare Quarterly* 13 (1962): 451–61.

Brown, John Russell, and Bernard Harris, eds. *Early Shakespeare*, Stratford-upon-Avon Studies, vol. 3, London: Edward Arnold, 1961.

——————, eds. *Shakespearian Comedy*, Stratford-upon-Avon Studies, vol. 4. London: Edward Arnold, 1972.

Bullough, Geoffrey, ed. *Narrative and Dramatic Sources of Shakespeare*. New York: Columbia University Press, 1958–75.

Byrne, M. St. Clare. "The Shakespeare Season at the Old Vic, 1956–57 and Stratford-upon-Avon, 1957. *Shakespeare Quarterly* 8 (1957): 461–93.

—————. "The Shakespeare Season at the Old Vic, 1957–58 and Stratford-upon-Avon, 1958." *Shakespeare Quarterly* 9 (1958): 507–31.

—————. "The Shakespeare Season at the Old Vic, 1958–59 and Stratford-upon-Avon, 1959." *Shakespeare Quarterly* 10 (1959): 545–69.

Cohen, Derek. *Shakespearean Motives*. New York: St. Martin's Press, 1988.

Colles, H. C., ed. *Grove's Dictionary of Music and Musicians*. 3d ed. London: Macmillan, 1927.

Cook, Ann Jennalie. "*The Merchant of Venice* at the Other Place." *Shakespeare Quarterly* 30 (1979): 158–60.

Cooper, Roberta Krensky. *The American Shakespeare Theatre, Stratford, 1955–1985*. Washington: The Folger Shakespeare Library, 1986.

Cornford, F. M. *The Origins of Attic Comedy*. Cambridge: Cambridge University Press, 1934.

Crane, R. S. *The Languages of Criticism and the Structure of Poetry*. Toronto: University of Toronto Press, 1953.

Croyden, Margaret. "A Hidden Dream of Sex and Love." *New York Times*, 17 January 1971, sec. 2, p. 15.

Cunningham, J. V. *Woe or Wonder: The Emotional Effect of Shakespearean Tragedy*. Chicago: The Swallow Press, 1964.

David, Richard. "Stratford 1954." *Shakespeare Quarterly* 5 (1954): 385–95.

Davies, W. Robertson. *Shakespeare's Boy Actors*. London: J. M. Dent, 1939.

Dawson, Anthony B. "*Measure for Measure*, New Historicism, and Theatrical Power." *Shakespeare Quarterly* 39 (1988): 328–41.

—————. "Much Ado about Signifying." *Studies in English Literature* 22 (1982): 211–21.

Dessen, Alan C. "Oregon Shakespearean Festival." *Shakespeare Quarterly* 29 (1978): 278–86.

Donaldson, Ian. "*All's Well That Ends Well:* Shakespeare's Play of Endings." *Essays in Criticism* 27 (1977): 34–55.

Doran, Madeleine. *Endeavors of Art: A Study of Form in Elizabethan Drama*. Madison: University of Wisconsin Press, 1963.

Downer, Alan S. "A Comparison of Two Stagings: Avon and London." *Shakespeare Quarterly* 6 (1955): 429–35.

Durang, Christopher. *The Marriage of Bette and Boo*. New York: Dramatist's Play Service, 1985.

Edinborough, Arnold. "Shakespeare Confirmed: At Canadian Stratford." *Shakespeare Quarterly* 6 (1955): 435–41.

—————. "Canada's Permanent Elizabethan Theatre." *Shakespeare Quarterly* 8 (1957): 511–15.

—————. "The Director's Role at Canada's Stratford." *Shakespeare Quarterly* 20 (1969): 443–47.

Eliot, T. S. *Essays on Elizabethan Drama.* New York: Harcourt Brace and Co., 1932.

Ellis-Fermor, Una. *Shakespeare the Dramatist and Other Papers.* London: Methuen, 1961.

Ellman, Richard. *The Identity of Yeats.* London: Macmillan, 1954.

Frye, Northrop. *A Natural Perspective: The Development of Shakespearean Comedy and Romance.* New York: Columbia University Press, 1965.

————. *Anatomy of Criticism.* Princeton: Princeton University Press, 1957.

Funk, Lewis. "Strange Comedy Done Uncertainly in Canada." *New York Times,* 13 June 1969, p. 41.

Granville-Barker, Harley. *Prefaces to Shakespeare,* First Series. London: Sidgwick and Jackson, 1927.

————. *Prefaces to Shakespeare.* Princeton: Princeton University Press, 1946.

Griffin, Alice. "New York Season: 1961–62." *Shakespeare Quarterly* 13 (1962): 553–59.

Gussow, Mel. *"Much Ado* by the Yale Rep." *New York Times,* 20 March 1983, sec. 1, p. 54.

Harbage, Alfred. *Shakespeare Without Words and Other Essays.* Cambridge: Harvard University Press, 1972.

Hartwig, Joan. "Cloten, Autolycus and Caliban: Bearers of Parodic Burdens." In *Shakespeare's Romances Reconsidered,* edited by Carol McGinnis Kay and Henry E. Jacobs, 91–103. Lincoln: University of Nebraska Press, 1978.

Hawkins, Harriet. *Likenesses of Truth in Elizabethan and Restoration Drama.* Oxford: Oxford University Press, 1972.

Hecht, Anthony. *Obbligati: Essays in Criticism.* New York: Atheneum, 1986.

Hitchman, Janet. *Such a Strange Lady, A Biography of Dorothy L. Sayers.* New York: Harper and Row, 1975.

Hodges, C. Walter. *The Globe Restored.* London: Ernest Benn, 1953.

Honigmann, E. A. J. *Shakespeare: Seven Tragedies, The Dramatist's Manipulation of Response.* London: Macmillan, 1976.

Howard, Jean E. *Shakespeare's Art of Orchestration: Stage Technique and Audience Response.* Champaign: University of Illinois Press, 1984.

Hoy, Cyrus. *The Hyacinth Room: An Investigation Into the Nature of Comedy, Tragedy, and Tragicomedy.* New York: Knopf, 1964.

————. "The Shares of Fletcher and His Collaborators in the Beaumont and Fletcher Canon, VII." *Studies in Bibliography* 15 (1962): 71–90.

Huxley, Aldous. *Collected Essays.* New York: Harper and Brothers, 1958.

Jackson, Berners W. "Shakespeare at Stratford, Ontario, 1973." *Shakespeare Quarterly* 24 (1973): 405–11.

————. "Shakespeare at Stratford, Ontario, 1975." *Shakespeare Quarterly* 27 (1976): 24–33.

————. "Stratford Festival Canada." *Shakespeare Quarterly* 28 (1977): 197–206.

Jenkins, Harold. "Shakespeare's *Twelfth Night.*" Rice Institute Pamphlet, 45, 1959.

Johnson, Samuel. *The Yale Edition of the Works of Samuel Johnson,* vol. 7, edited by Arthur Sherbo. New Haven: Yale University Press, 1968.

Jorgens, Jack J. "New York Shakespeare Festival, 1973." *Shakespeare Quarterly* 24 (1973): 423–28.

Kermode, Frank. *The Sense of an Ending: Studies in the Theory of Fiction.* New York: Oxford University Press, 1966.

Kerr, Walter. "A *Much Ado* with a Bit More Ado Than It Needs." *New York Times,* 21 October 1984, sec. 2, p. 3.

Knight, David. "*The Comedy of Errors*—Not Just a Silly Play." *On-Stage Studies* 8 (1984): 27–32.

Knight, G. Wilson. *The Sovereign Flower.* London: Methuen, 1958.

Knights, L. C. "Notes on Comedy." In *Comedy, Meaning and Form,* edited by Robert W. Corrigan, 181–92. San Francisco: Chandler, 1965.

Langer, Suzanne. "The Comic Rhythm." In *Feeling and Form,* 326–50. New York: Charles Scribner's Sons, 1953.

Leech, Clifford. "The Meaning of *Measure for Measure.*" *Shakespeare Survey* 3 (1950): 66–73.

Leishman, J. B. *Themes and Variations in Shakespeare's Sonnets.* Oxford: Hutchinson and Co., 1963.

Lewis, C. S. *Surprised by Joy: The Shape of My Early Life.* New York: Harcourt Brace and Co., 1955.

Mack, Maynard. "Engagement and Detachment in Shakespeare's Plays." In *Essays on Shakespeare and Elizabethan Drama in Honor of Hardin Craig,* edited by Richard Hosley, 275–96. Columbia: University of Missouri Press, 1962.

McGuire, Philip C. *Speechless Dialect.* Berkeley: University of California Press, 1985.

McManaway, J. B., ed. *Shakespeare: 400.* New York: Holt, Rinehart and Winston, 1964.

Meredith, George. "An Essay on Comedy." In *Comedy,* edited by Wylie Sypher, 3–60. Garden City, N.Y.: Doubleday, 1956.

Mowat, Barbara A. *The Dramaturgy of Shakespeare's Romances.* Athens: University of Georgia Press, 1976.

Muir, Kenneth, ed. *Shakespeare: The Comedies.* Twentieth Century Views. Englewood Cliffs, N.J.: Prentice-Hall, 1964.

Murray, Christopher. "Shakespeare at the Abbey." *Shakespeare Quarterly* 32 (1981): 173–76.

Nicoll, Allardyce. *The World of Harlequin: A Critical Study of the Comedia del'Arte.* Cambridge: Cambridge University Press, 1963.

Nightingale, Benedict. "Has *All's Well* Escaped Its Past?" *New York Times,* 10 April 1983, sec. 2, p. 1.

————. "Manhandling the Classics: or Director 10 Shakespeare 0." *New York Times,* 29 January 1984, sec. 2, p. 1.

Ornstein, Robert. "Historical Criticism and the Interpretation of Shakespeare." *Shakespeare Quarterly* 10 (1959): 3–9.

Rabkin, Norman. *Shakespeare and the Common Understanding.* New York: The Free Press, 1967.

————. *Shakespeare and the Problem of Meaning.* Chicago: University of Chicago Press, 1981.

Reed, Joseph Verner. Letter to "Drama Mailbag." *New York Times*, 28 February 1971, sec. 2, p. 7.

Rich, Frank. "The Royal Shakespeare *All's Well That Ends Well*." *New York Times*, 14 April 1983, sec. 3, p. 15.

——————. "The Royal Shakespeare's *Much Ado*." *New York Times*, 15 October 1984, sec. 3, p. 12.

Richman, David. "Dramatic Symbiosis in *Much Ado About Nothing*." *On-Stage Studies* 8 (1984): 43–59.

Riemer, A. P. *Antic Fables: Patterns of Evasion in Shakespeare's Comedies*. New York: St. Martin's Press, 1980.

Roberts, Jeanne Addison. *Shakespeare's English Comedy: The Merry Wives of Windsor in Context*. Lincoln: University of Nebraska Press, 1979.

Rossiter, A. P. *Angel With Horns and Other Shakespeare Lectures*. Plymouth, England: Longmans, 1962.

Salingar, L. G. *Shakespeare and the Traditions of Comedy*. Cambridge: Cambridge University Press, 1974.

Shakespeare, William. *William Shakespeare, The Complete Works*, edited by Peter Alexander. London: Collins, 1971.

Sidney, Sir Philip. *An Apology for Poetry*. In *Elizabethan Critical Essays*, edited by G. Gregory Smith, 148–207. Oxford: Oxford University Press, 1904.

Slater, Ann Pasternak. *Shakespeare the Director*. Sussex: The Harvester Press, 1982.

Smallwood, Robert. "Stratford-upon-Avon, 1988." *Shakespeare Quarterly* 40 (1989): 83–94.

Snyder, Susan. *The Comic Matrix in Shakespeare's Tragedies*. Princeton: Princeton University Press, 1979.

Speaight, Robert. "Shakespeare in Britain." *Shakespeare Quarterly* 16 (1965): 313–24.

——————. "Shakespeare in Britain." *Shakespeare Quarterly* 19 (1968): 367–77.

——————. "Shakespeare in Britain." *Shakespeare Quarterly* 20 (1969): 435–43.

——————. "Shakespeare in Britain." *Shakespeare Quarterly* 21 (1970): 439–51.

——————. "Shakespeare in Britain." *Shakespeare Quarterly* 22 (1971): 359–65.

——————. "Shakespeare in Britain." *Shakespeare Quarterly* 27 (1976): 15–24.

——————. "Shakespeare in Britain." *Shakespeare Quarterly* 28 (1977): 184–90.

Sprague, A. C. *Shakespeare and the Actors, The Stage Business in His Plays: 1660–1905*. Cambridge: Harvard University Press, 1944.

Stoll, Elmer Edgar. *Shakespeare Studies: Historical and Comparative in Method*. New York: Macmillan, 1927.

Styan, J. L. *Shakespeare's Stagecraft*. Cambridge: Cambridge University Press, 1967.

Summers, Joseph H. *Dreams of Love and Power: Essays on Shakespeare*. Oxford: Oxford University Press, 1985.

——————. "The Masks of *Twelfth Night*." In *Shakespeare, Modern Essays in Criticism*, edited by Leonard F. Dean, 134–42. New York: Oxford University Press, 1967.

Swinburne, Algernon Charles. *A Study of Shakespeare*. London: Chatto and Windus, 1909.

Toye, Francis. *Giuseppe Verdi: His Life and Works.* New York: Vintage Books, 1959.

Trewin, J. C. "Shakespeare in Britain." *Shakespeare Quarterly* 29 (1978): 212–21.

—————. "Shakespeare in Britain." *Shakespeare Quarterly* 30 (1979): 151–58.

—————. *Shakespeare on the English Stage: 1900–1964.* London: Barrie and Rockliff, 1964.

Turner, Robert Y. *Shakespeare's Apprenticeship.* Chicago: University of Chicago Press, 1974.

Tynan, Kenneth. *Tynan on Theatre.* London: Penguin, 1964.

Unsigned review. *Times* (London), 10 March 1950, p. 10.

Urkowitz, Steven. "Five Women Eleven Ways: Changing Images of Shakespearean Characters in the Earliest Texts." In *Images of Shakespeare; Proceedings of the Third Congress of the International Shakespeare Association, 1986,* edited by Werner Habicht, D. J. Palmer, and Roger Pringle, 292–304. Newark: University of Delaware Press, 1988.

Venezky, Alice. "The 1950 Season at Stratford-upon-Avon." *Shakespeare Quarterly* 2 (1951): 73–79.

Walter, Bruno. *Gustav Mahler.* London: Hamish Hamilton, 1958.

Wardle, Irving. "The Answer Lies in the Soil." *Times* (London), 23 July 1981, p. 13.

—————. "Mingled Yarn, Good and Bad." *Times* (London), 18 November 1981, p. 13.

Warren Roger. "Shakespeare in Stratford and London, 1982." *Shakespeare Quarterly* 34 (1983): 79–88.

Webster, Margaret. *Shakespeare Without Tears.* New York: McGraw Hill, 1942.

Weimann, Robert. *Shakespeare and the Popular Tradition in the Theater: Studies in the Social Dimension of Dramatic Form and Function.* Baltimore: Johns Hopkins University Press, 1978.

Weinberg, Bernard. *A History of Literary Criticism in the Italian Renaissance.* Chicago: University of Chicago Press, 1961.

Wells, Stanley. "Shakespeare Performances in London and Stratford-upon-Avon, 1986–7." *Shakespeare Survey* 41 (1988): 159–82.

West, E. J., ed. *Shaw on Theatre.* New York: Hill and Wang, 1958.

Wheeler, Richard P. *Shakespeare's Development and the Problem Comedies: Turn and Counterturn.* Berkeley: University of California Press, 1981.

Whitaker, Virgil K. *Shakespeare's Use of Learning: An Inquiry Into the Growth of His Mind and Art.* San Marino, Calif.: Huntington Library, 1953.

White, Eric Walter. *Benjamin Britten: His Life and Operas.* Berkeley: University of California Press, 1970.

Yeats, W. B. *Essays and Introductions.* London: Macmillan, 1961.

INDEX